Off-Road

with
CLARKSON,
HAMMOND AND MAY

BEHIND THE SCENES OF THEIR
"ROCK AND ROLL" WORLD TOUR

For Alfie

Off-Road

with
CLARKSON,
HAMMOND AND MAY

BEHIND THE SCENES OF THEIR
"ROCK AND ROLL" WORLD TOUR

Phillipa Sage

AD LIB

First published in 2021 by Ad Lib Publishers Ltd
15 Church Road
London, SW13 9HE

www.adlibpublishers.com

Text © 2021 Phillipa Sage

Paperback ISBN 978-1-913543-72-3
eBook ISBN 978-1-913543-29-7

A CIP catalogue record for this book is available from the
British Library.

Every reasonable effort has been made to trace copy-
right-holders of material reproduced in this book, but if any
have been inadvertently overlooked the publishers would be
glad to hear from them.

Printed in the UK
10 9 8 7 6 5 4 3 2 1

Contents

Preface   7

Intro – How did I end up with the best job in the world?   11

The Cast – The usual suspects and more   18

Our Routine – How we rocked and rolled   20

My Essential Kit – Everything you need for three middle-aged men on tour   25

Pre-World Tour – McDonald's, not oysters   27

Just Call Me Horse   40

The World Tour Begins – Johannesburg and Dublin (well, it's a start)   49

Johannesburg, Sydney, Auckland, Hong Kong – Proper international touring   70

Back to Reality – London, Birmingham and Dublin again   95

Meet Beau Vas Deferens   105

CONTENTS

Richard, You're Fired!   115

Anyone for Cricket?   124

Jeremy Gets Married Again   131

Rabbits – NO ENTRY   141

No, In Your Backside   155

Richard Pulls a Moose   166

Get Me a Range Rover and Some Bear Stew   176

Is That James May or Arnold Schwarzenegger? 181

Paparazzi   186

Police Escort   195

Bigger than the Beatles?   204

Is That Brian May?   208

Vodka and Caviar   212

Not Interrailing   224

That Punch   240

Time to Sober Up   250

To Quote Wham! (the greatest pop band
in the world – in my fourteen-year-old brain),
'THE FINAL'   260

After the Bubble Burst   267

Thank Yous...   270

Preface

For over ten years I was honoured and privileged to tour the world with arguably the most famous trio in the world; Clarkson, Hammond and May. Just like the Bee Gees. (Maybe not just like them? Then again, they have all had hair like them at some point.)

Anyway, I started out in 1997 working with *Top Gear* on their live events at London and Birmingham's International Motor Show, and at the very beginnings of *Top Gear Live*, at Silverstone.

Top Gear Live evolved from entertaining a few families and petrolheads in a small arena, trackside at Silverstone, into a worldwide stadium tour entertaining crowds as big as 50,000 odd. The shows started out with a motorised sofa being driven by Tiff Needell (an original *Top Gear* presenter), whilst Jeremy Clarkson argued with Quentin Willson (another original *Top Gear* presenter) about which Ferrari was best.

As the crowds grew, so did the shows. Incredible stunts, such as 'Car Bungee' and the Stig in a Rage Buggy doing a Hot Wheels style 360° loop the loop, were performed along with motoring acts from around the world, including a team of French motorcyclists who performed in a giant metal sphere, sometimes with Richard Hammond standing inside as they whizzed just above his head or past the tips of his toes. But for all this drama and spectacle, the highlights of the shows were the uncut banter from Clarkson, Hammond and

May. Banter that would ordinarily be cut from the TV shows wasn't edited on tour; performing live in arenas around the world, they were off-road!

From the humble beginnings of Silverstone and Earls Court Exhibition Centre, complete with crap coffee served in polystyrene cups, we went on to take over race circuits with huge motoring festivals, including F1 cars and the likes of Lewis Hamilton playing car football. The show became the Cirque du Soleil of the motoring world, well almost, just a bit shabby around the edges. Especially the leading men.

And so the coffee became fresher, most of which I served. Helicopters and superyachts were added and I was very lucky to join the circus and tour with the three most famous middle-aged, very 'stupid', clever and funny men who knew a bit about cars. I became part of the show's family, a 'sister', a 'mother', and girlfriend to one of them – the most controversial one. The three of them were affectionately known to me as 'my boys'. I was also privileged to work on the TV show on a few occasions and then, finally, Amazon's *The Grand Tour*.

In the beginning, over twenty years ago, I was making tea in the green room (the room where celebrities rest and prepare backstage, apparently painted green in the olden days). I went on to become PA to all three presenters whilst on tour. As the tour rolled on, I was given more responsibility, and was involved in the logistics and pre-tour planning, working alongside the whole production team and management. I was given many titles from 'Horse' to 'Green Room Director'.

Amazingly, even though the boys toured for over twelve years with *Top Gear Live* and, laterally, *Clarkson, Hammond and May Live*, many of you fans out there will not have known this incredible motoring theatre was going on. Big as they were across the globe, I was often very frustrated that our live audiences weren't even bigger, because I know a lot of you would have loved to have seen the boys live and uncut, producing brilliant and funny shows every time. I should know – I've sat through hundreds of them, including all the rehearsals, and have laughed at the same gags again and again. I loved it.

This book is a celebration of what Clarkson, Hammond and May created, achieved and survived (!) whilst also producing one of the most successful and most watched TV programmes – at the last count, 350 million viewers in the world. Which reminds me that I must also pay tribute to, and dedicate this book to, the long-suffering crew and production team who made huge contributions to make all of it possible. Big up to the 'Bubble' (our tour family nickname) and *all* who 'sailed' with her.

And of course I must add that none of this would have happened if it wasn't for Chris Hughes, our Tour Manager, who masterminded the whole thing, along with his hard-working dedicated team and the backing of BBC Worldwide.

Clarkson, incredibly, performed in every single show around the world, in every city, in every country, and this alongside presenting every single *Top Gear* episode, writing three newspaper columns and producing an annual DVD. He was amazing at it.

I loved every minute of touring, and from the beginning took photos of all the madness that went on backstage, of the incredible shows, of our crazy nights out and of our adventures around the globe. These were just for me, initially, to complement my own personal memories, but the team encouraged me to take more and more, with the intention of one day creating a book of all our behind-the-scenes antics, for all the millions of fans out there to enjoy. We wanted to share the laughs that we had as a crazy 'dysfunctional family' on tour.

It's only since it all stopped that I've had time to put it all together. I've had great fun reminiscing and feel very lucky to have been part of an extraordinary, ridiculous but incredible journey.

There have been tears, tantrums, dramas, plus exhaustion, and the obligatory sex-and-drugs-and-rock-and-roll. It was like touring with rock stars, complete with private jets, supercars, superyachts, champagne and monumental hangovers.

I've also had a few surreal moments. Playing beach cricket with AC/DC in Sydney, lunching with giraffes in South Africa, taking a helicopter to have fish and chips on the beach in New Zealand, having a police escort in a Range Rover, just for me, in Durban, being so proud of and overwhelmed by my boys performing to a stadium crowd of over 50,000 in Poland, eating a caviar picnic on a train going from Moscow to St Petersburg, and so on and so on... I'll stop now. It's all here, in this book you are about to read. My very special 'touring diary'.

Intro

How did I end up
with the best job in the world?

I have always been a bit of a tomboy. Not a very good one as I was such a wimp, but I lived in trousers or jodhpurs (mad about horses as well as cars) most of the time. I wasn't a dress sort of girl. I was happier in mud rather than make-up; I still am. I have always had an interest in cars, possibly inspired by the fact that my dad had a new company one every year.

Dad was a design engineer and always had an eye for design and detail. I clearly remember each car we had right down to the number plates, from about the age of seven. These included: a Fiat 124, which was sporty but looked like a very boxy, toy car; a turquoise Sunbeam Rapier Fastback – VERY sporty; a silver/blue metallic Citroën BX19 with the famous hydraulic suspension – so cool and fun when you are ten years old; and a Ford Granada Coupé in bronze, complete with brown vinyl roof and velour interior – it was like something out of *The Sweeney*. We then went very 'family and sensible' with several Volvo estates, which were like camper vans to us kids. In those days before the compulsory 'Clunk click before every trip' (compulsory seatbelts for those too young to remember), we would take it in turns to sleep on sleeping bags and duvets on top of the luggage, in the

11

boot, all the way to Cornwall or the South of France, for our family holidays.

Doesn't everyone get excited about new cars?

When I reached driving age, I couldn't wait to get my independence and be able to set off on adventures. I had already pinched the keys of my mum's old VW Beetle and driven around the garden with my best friend as a passenger and my younger brother on the bonnet pretending to be a monkey, as if we were on safari – happy days.

It was important to me at the time to have the right look and spec of car. I loved the Mark 1 Ford Escorts. All the best boys had one, although the VW Golf GTI was the highest accolade in those days for us youngsters. My older brother had a Mark 1 with its raunchy exhaust and engine tune. Disappointedly, I ended up with my first purchase being a beige Ford Fiesta, coincidentally the same first car as Jeremy Clarkson.

The boring and very sensible nature of the beige Fiesta drove me to work harder so I could graduate to a navy VW Golf. My decision was highly influenced by the stylish and beautiful Paula Hamilton (the model used by VW at the time), but unfortunately, all I could afford was one that was about eight years old. So to make me feel better, I just pretended I'd had it from new. It's weird what matters when you are eighteen. I thought I was some way towards looking as classy as Paula and it might help attract the man of my dreams. It didn't – note to all you teenage dreamers out there.

To improve my street cred further, I would borrow my mum's Suzuki jeep convertible. So much fun, especially when I spontaneously left the road to demonstrate its 4x4 capabilities across a field, much to the hilarity of my unsuspecting friends. Much fun was had in that car (and a great deal of posing) until I was banned from borrowing it, after leaving it outside the pub with the roof down during a

Hertfordshire 'tropical' storm. Despite me driving around till 1am with the heaters on full blast – plus baling out buckets of water from the foot wells – I could not hide from my mother the fact that I had ruined the interior and accelerated the mould factory in the roof – oops!

My next car showed a more sensible side of me. It was a three-year-old, very exciting, closest-I-got-to-new Vauxhall Astra, with dog-tooth cloth interior. Unfortunately, I crashed it twice, once totally not seeing the 10-ton low-loader parked in our driveway – well it wasn't usually there – it was a shock and surprise as I reversed at speed on my usual exit for work. I'm never good first thing in the morning. Luckily, not long after, in morning rush hour, an equally blind driver hit me in exactly the same place. She literally drove through and along the side of my car as I was innocently waiting in the junction, then drove off! Luckily this was all played out in front of many witnesses, so she was tracked down, insurance details were exchanged, and my car was put back together as if nothing had happened.

However, it was then stolen from outside a friend's house during a big night out which had left me a little worse for wear. I was confused to wake up and see a space where I had left my car. It left me wondering just how much I had drunk, as I was sure I'd left my car there, in the now empty space.

I had. It had been joyridden and left for dead in a river. I had to pay hundreds of pounds for its recovery and release from the police. Oh, the injustice!

Making good out of a bad situation after the Astra was written off, I splashed out and treated myself to a black Golf GTD with much-cooler black-and-red check seat fabric. My real low point in car ownership was a Mini Metro, the most awful car I've ever not had the joy to drive. On the upside I didn't have it for long as its suspension collapsed over a speed bump and I left it to Rest in Peace.

Cars: I love them and loathe them. They are just money pits. I still think every time I buy one, 'Ahh, now, this won't lose its value.' I've recently taken a hit on my latest 'investment', having to downgrade from the excellent Range Rover Evoque, as a result of losing most of my work. I thought I'd compensate for the downgrade by having fun with one of my favourite cars ever − my friend, my oh-so-cute, rare metallic blue Land Rover Defender 90, named Ranulf.

What a special club to belong to. I remember so well getting my first nod and wave from a fellow, all-suffering Defender driver. I love its simplicity. When bits fall off, which happens regularly due to its Meccano-like build quality, it makes me smile. The nuts and bolts just can't hold on forever as you bounce along. I regularly have the sun visor land in my lap. The all-essential snorkel rattles against the windscreen and, if too many bolts go missing, it whistles at high speed. However, if you lose one of your wing mirrors, it only costs £7.50, a snip compared to the £500 and a week in the garage if you lose one of your Evoque 'ears'. Defenders; I love them and can't wait to have another one. As you can probably tell, the interest and passion for cars and adventure was there, so when I got asked to work at the Birmingham Motor Show I jumped at the chance.

I was working for Renault and I had spent several days at their headquarters, in Swindon (coincidently where Richard and Mindy Hammond were working in those days), learning everything there was to know about the Renault Laguna, from its top speed to its boot capacity, in preparation for any questions that I might be asked whilst on the exhibition stand.

The Motor Show was epic. Two weeks of hard work, but a lot of fun. It started with Press Day, which was very exciting with cameras, celebrities, models, racing drivers and champagne everywhere. From then on, I never had what I call a proper job, and my only ambition was to never have one!

It was at this first Motor Show that I was approached (I'd like to say headhunted, but I think it was more 'fancied the look of') by an events company, Drive and Survive. They had most of their work in the motor industry, employing racing drivers, professional drivers and attractive women to run car launches and product training. I was asked to go to their base in Berkshire at the Transport Research Laboratory for an interview, with a view to becoming one of their bank of staff.

That was an experience in itself. The office was on a secure site where a whole road system, including a motorway, was set up for testing vehicles or motoring gadgets, like traffic cameras and the safety of cars. It was fascinating. There was a Test shed that had a huge winch in it to which a car would be fastened. The cars would then be released, fired off at different speeds to crash into barriers, testing both barrier and car for safety. The whole set-up was like a life-size, 3D children's play mat. It was set amongst dense forest, complete with herds of red deer to provide a real 'elk test' – that's a test all car manufacturers use to measure the stability of a car if it has to swerve at speed (as if an elk had just run out in front of you). The test track was used by many manufacturers to secretly test their latest models and was also used for film and TV to create car chases, roadblocks, etc. There was an air of mystery and excitement about the place.

My interview was in a small, cobbled-together office in a very unexciting prefab building, set at the side of the test track, all within earshot of tyre squealing and the crashing of metal on metal. It was all very relaxed and, after a fun and humorous interview, I was signed up and soon working on car launches and corporate events for various car manufacturers around the UK and the rest of Europe.

One fateful day I was asked to attend an interview/casting at the BBC Worldwide offices, where they produced *Top Gear* magazine. The job was to be part of the team on the *Top Gear* stand at the London Motor Show.

There must have been about twenty of us 'gorgeous girls' and 'handsome boys' who were paraded through the *Top Gear* magazine offices and led to a meeting room with the standard help-yourself tea and coffee flasks, a plate of substandard biscuits and curled-up sandwiches. At the time it made me feel really special – I had made it, to even be considered to work with these guys at THE BBC. We were interviewed by Adam Waddell, of BBC Worldwide and in charge of *Top Gear* magazine. I remember being cheeky and not afraid to ask questions, which I think helped my case. We were questioned about our sales experience, because as part of our job we would be selling *Top Gear* magazine and merchandise. They needed an enthusiastic team who could be trusted, as we would be handling a lot of cash. We were sent on our way, to be informed in a few days whether we had made the team or not.

I did. I was chosen to look after the presenters and other corporate VIP guests, management and staff from BBC Worldwide backstage. The set up at Earls Court was a couple of booths selling the magazine and merchandise leading to an exclusive exhibition area with a stage displaying a few special cars and an area for the boys to perform a Q&A. There was standing room only for spectators and a few boys toys like *Sega Rally* along with another circular merchandise booth where, after the boys performed, they signed autographs, which was a real bunfight of incredibly eager fans.

This was back in 1997, when James and Richard hadn't been 'born'. It was the start of my extraordinary twenty-year journey working in the company of Jeremy Clarkson and Andy Wilman, and all their genius. I looked after Jeremy,

Tiff Needell and Quentin Willson (the then presenters of *Top Gear*) and Andy Wilman, the producer and long-time friend of Jeremy, backstage in the first green room I'd ever seen. It was not green.

Green rooms are often dark dingy places in what little space there is left behind the stage, studio or stadium. Sometimes they are ridiculously luxurious, complete with massage chairs, fully stocked bars, five-star catering, top-spec entertainment systems and staff at your beck and call. Here, where I started, there were polystyrene cups, instant coffee, Family Circle biscuits and any old chair that was available. The 'must have', and biggest demand from the talent in those days, was ash trays, which were legal indoors then.

Those first two weeks at the London Motor Show, in what was Earls Court Exhibition Centre – now demolished – were hard work coupled with hard partying. Jeremy was already loud, shouty and always right. Tiff was Tiff, still the same, dependable simple man, and super-talented at throwing cars around at speed. (He came along on the journey with us on the World Tour, standing in for Richard Hammond, when he nearly killed himself, and joining some of the shows as they got bigger and bigger.) Quentin was charming and funny and went off to do car dealing. Now and again you see his grinning little face advertising something car related. Or popping up on the news as a 'motoring expert'.

I got on well with all of them, especially Clarkson and Wilman, I think largely because I didn't mind the constant volley of insults that I was also brilliant at serving right back. But on a professional level I would work until the bitter end and would always find a solution to any problem. I continued to be asked to work on all of *Top Gear Live*'s events which gradually evolved into the incredible *Top Gear Live* World Tour which I was so lucky to be a part of.

And here's how it went…

The Cast

The usual suspects and more

Jeremy Clarkson – Big Presenter
Sometimes Richard Hammond – Small Presenter
Sometimes James May – Medium Presenter
Local Presenter – Stand-in for James May or Richard Hammond
Cameo appearances from Andy Wilman – Andy Wilman
Chris Hughes, AKA The Piggy-Eyed Businessman – Tour Manager
James Cooke-Priest, AKA James Cock-Priest, AKA Johnny Boden, AKA JCP – Tour Legal Advisor, General Manager, Negotiator, I don't know
Rowland French, AKA Rowly, AKA Our Moon-Faced Producer – Our Moon-Faced Producer
Bas Bungish, AKA "BasIcanfindanycar.com" – Head of Commercial Partners
Gemma Courtenay, AKA The Boy, AKA Publicity Mouse – Marketing, Communications, and most other things
Me, Phillipa Sage, AKA Horse, AKA First Lady – General Dogsbody, Gofer, Fixer, Diplomat, Medicine Woman, Green Room Director, Talent Management – I tried
Collectively known as **THE BUBBLE**

Supported by:

Naomi Lynch – Flame Thrower and Swallower (of flames, I mean!!), **AKA The Girl with Petrol Pumps for Arms**, **AKA Rowly's (Our Moon-Faced Producer's) Girlfriend**

Neeshat Wadud – Ticketing

THE STIG – Whoever he was, **AKA Ben Collins**, and other fast drivers

Gav, AKA Gav – Bodyguard, ex-SBS

Denzel and Clinton, AKA Clenzel and Clenzel – South African Security

Olag, AKA Olag (you would not dare call him anything else) – Russian Security, ex-KGB

A Man or Woman from the BBC sent to keep us 'under control'. Our favourite – **Duncan Gray, AKA Schoolboy**

There was also an incredible Tour Crew of lighting, sound, production, choreographers, professional drivers, mechanics, dancers and backstage crew who were a hugely dedicated and hard-working team who never got thanked enough.

NB: Not too many people were harmed in the making of this Tour. The Tour was not funded by BBC licence fee payers' money.

Our Routine

How we rocked and rolled

We had a routine for each time we were away touring which essentially stayed the same but varied depending on where we were travelling to and how many shows were to be performed. Unbelievably, at the beginning, over the course of a long weekend, the boys would perform a gruelling ten shows. Saturdays involved a late-morning show, an early-afternoon show, then early-evening and late-evening shows. There was a lot of Red Bull and coffee consumed in those days.

Towards the end, as the boys grew older and more tired, the schedule became lighter on shows and heavier on leisure time. Jimmy Carr once said, 'Jeremy has gone from 0–70 in 50 years.' Amongst other unhealthy lifestyle choices, touring definitely contributed to that acceleration in ageing.

I should also explain that in the early days James hated touring so didn't come on every tour, and Richard hated being away from home too much, on top of their already gruelling filming schedule for the TV show. They took it in turns to join Jeremy. The role of the missing third presenter was given to a local celebrity. Despite it being odd not to have the original line-up, the local talent would help to get the local audience onside and add some colloquial language.

As time went on, James relaxed into touring like a rock star and became the queen of pantomime, performing and partying, and Richard became jealous and fed up with being text-bombed from a different time zone about what an amazing time we were having. So in more recent years we ended up with the perfect blend of the original trio.

Here is how a typical tour schedule would run:

Day 1

Each tour would begin with expensive black cars picking each of us up, and the 'Bubble' would assemble at an airport. Or sometimes an airport would assemble near us, with a helicopter or private plane.

'Chris Hughes's cashless holiday' (named by the boys as they never had to part with any cash) would begin. Food, drink, entertainment, clothing, transport and just about anything else they needed or wanted was paid for by the tour, or as the boys liked to think, Chris Hughes personally. Eating and drinking as much as we could endure would begin while relaxing in the airport lounge. As everyone knows, it is never the wrong time to have a glass of champagne when at an airport or on a plane.

Laughter, piss-taking and annoying practical jokes began too, such as kicking your wheely bag off its wheels, normally carried out by Chris Hughes, and goaded by Richard Hammond. This was most annoying when you were enduring the endless walk to board the plane.

Gemma, one of the tour's managers, and I would hand out scripts and schedules, ready to be ignored and lost. We would also be running around airport shops for forgotten necessities, calling ahead to our destinations to make sure hotel rooms were adequately stocked with our talent's favourite things, and permission to smoke had been granted.

Checks were made that the right spec and number of Range Rovers with suitable competent and discreet drivers were ready to meet us. Often we were still searching for said Range Rovers as we were leaving the UK – a constant issue throughout our touring days – that, and sourcing a decent, working coffee machine and a TV which actually had sound, for the green room. And every time these things were wrong we would not hear the end of it from Lord Clarkson.

Upon arrival at the airport of our destination, general panic and confusion set in trying to escort, or, rather, herd, the three well-known TV presenters through the airport (one very agitated, desperate for a fag. It was like travelling with an unexploded bomb!). Once we had located our convoy of Range Rovers the priority was loading the presenters and myself in the forward Range Rover, to set off to our luxury hotel or house. The others and the luggage would follow.

At our 'home' for the next few days, refreshments were arranged, and the boys went straight into scripting. JC would moan that the printer was too slow and shout at Rowly, the producer. There was then usually a visit to check out the show venue and any new gadgets and vehicles, followed by a run-through of the script in situ, accompanied with more moaning and shouting from JC (in his defence this was mainly justified in order to produce the best show possible).

After a long and stressful day, a low-key dinner would be arranged and a relatively early night was had by all – the presenters anyway. Often the management and producers were up all night troubleshooting or preparing for another leg of the tour in another time zone.

Day 2

After a leisurely breakfast, there was more scripting and rehearsals, PR, photo calls, interviews and lots of moaning, often resulting in JC refusing to take part in anything other than scripting or rehearsals. JM and RH would just get on with whatever was asked of them. JC always claimed he had never had to promote the TV show and would give Chris and Gemma a verbal battering every time, suggesting any local newspaper, regional TV or radio interviews were a complete waste of time.

After a long and stressful day getting through the usual 'teething troubles' of the first show, we would have dinner in a ridiculously expensive restaurant, often in our own private dining room, drinking and enjoying general stupidity and frivolity, followed by bed at some point.

Day 3

Leisure activity, often involving helicopters, yachts, 5* lunch (no drinking – the boys would recite over and over, 'show not ACE, show not ACE'; Eight Ace is an alcoholic character from the *Viz* comic, who finds it hard to focus on what he should be doing, rather than drinking ACE, his preferred tipple and pastime). And so back to work to prepare and perform the second and third shows. In the early days, there was no leisure; it was straight to work after breakfast in order to fit four shows in.

After the last show of the day, with adrenalin running high, we would have a rushed late dinner followed by our big night out at the Crew Party, lots of drinking and often a 'messy' and very late night.

Day 4

Usually started with a massive hangover, moaning, and an essential McDonald's brunch. Subsequently, the next show could be slightly subdued. This was the boys' toughest performance, pushing through a hangover, trying to enthuse an equally lacklustre Sunday lunchtime crowd. After that, a snooze was a must and a good movie in the green room, then on to the final show with a spring in their step. On the homeward straight the boys would often mess about, changing their now very familiar lines, in order to throw the next person and watch them stumble through their next line. The finale of the show was more often than not a game of car football, and on the last day there was no holding back, resulting in the almost total destruction of cars for the sake of that all-important goal. Over the years this had to be tamed in order to preserve the life of drivers and presenters, and to avoid losing the deal with the manufacturer who had supplied the cars.

And so to one of my favourite times, which I was always very involved in; 'Chris Hughes's Ridiculous Closing Ceremony'. Chris and I would shop for presents to commemorate each leg of the tour. The presents would usually relate to the place we were in or a particular incident that had occurred during our stay. Chris, Gemma, myself and some poor unsuspecting girl from the local team would dress up for the occasion and act out a ceremony or sketch in order to present the three presenters with their gifts. These ceremonies were hilarious, always great fun, and spirits were high. We would then hurry to jump into the Range Rover convoy and head to the airport.

Once back on home turf the expensive black cars reappeared, the 'Bubble' dispersed, and all would head for home until the next time.

My Essential Kit

Everything you need for
three middle-aged men on tour

Marlboro Lights for JC

Camel (blue pack) for JM

E-cigs, chargers and refills – RH

Nicotine gum – A JC must-have; he chewed it like a masticating cow on speed from the moment we stepped into the airport.

Lighters

Beef Hula Hoops

Mini Cheddars

Jelly Babies

Minstrels

Liquorice Allsorts

Berocca

Nurofen

Paracetamol

Lemsip – for man flu

Strepsils

Human spit in a can, yes for real, Glandosane, very expensive, commonly used by performers in the event of a lost voice/ dry mouth

Phone chargers

Adapters

Bottle opener/corkscrew – always, always, always (I still have one in my handbag now), along with lighters and nicotine gum. Note to self: must clear out handbag – relax.

Optrex

Lip balm

Face wipes

Deodorant

Senokot – for when you've got to go…

Imodium – for when you just can't stop…

Favourite DVDs – *Ted*, *The Wolf of Wall Street*, *Rush*, *Local Hero*, etc.

Antihistamines – JC reacts badly to stings and lots of things!

Vitamin B12 injections – the ultimate hangover cure

Black Sharpie pen – for autographs

And always not far away from me, and a must for any private plane or tour bus: water, Red Bull, Diet Coke, ginger beer, rosé wine, Sauvignon blanc, gin and tonic

AND TICKETS FOR BARBADOS! Not really, that was something Gemma and I joked about as we were always expected to have anything and everything at any time. Little did we know the tour would end up going there.

The Brownie Guides taught me one of the biggest life lessons – BE PREPARED.

Pre-World Tour

McDonald's, not oysters

Having worked with the original *Top Gear* team back in the nineties, and continuing to work on live events in the motor industry, I was approached by Adam Waddell of BBC Worldwide (the commercial arm of the BBC) and *Top Gear* magazine, to help out at the launch of the very first MPH Show in 2003 (this was the beginning of *Top Gear*'s new motoring theatre shows that evolved into the *Top Gear Live* Tour).

It was created and produced in collaboration by Brand Events (run by Chris Hughes, our Tour Manager), Clarion, another events company based at Earls Court, and the BBC's *Top Gear*. Adam Waddell asked me to help create awareness and PR for the show by sourcing and inviting celebrities, sports personalities and notable and influential people from the motor industry.

It's an exciting but stressful job, as anyone who works in PR and or with celebrities will know. You spend a lot of time trying to get hold of people, then trying to persuade them that they really want to come to said event you're promoting, and with even more persuasion and grovelling, get them to commit to performing in something they've never heard of. In this case it was to get them to take part in a go-kart race in the arena as part of the show.

The upside in this scenario was that the popularity of *Top Gear* and its presenters was so huge that with careful targeting of car enthusiasts it wasn't that difficult to sweet-talk them into coming. However, they were not obliged to or contracted to turn up, and if their Aunty Mabel were to suddenly invite them to tea and they thought they should go, they could, even if it meant letting me know half an hour before they were due to arrive.

It makes me stressed just thinking about it, as it felt like living on the edge of a cliff in strong winds. I would report to the client, Adam Waddell, that I'd booked a whole list of great names who were up for anything, then my phone would ring and whoever I'd just been boasting about would tell me they couldn't make it.

Worse still, was on the morning of the big event, after confirming your final line-up to the crew, including the much-feared Andy Wilman (executive producer of *Top Gear* and incredible perfectionist, not tolerant of imperfection), to not receive any cancellation phone calls but for several of your line-up to just not turn up.

Discussions were had at speed, of when and where said celebrities would be and what was expected of them, which included familiarising themselves with the go-karts and having a short test drive. I also ran around acres of Earls Court, acquainting myself with where things were – loos, VIP enclosures, backstage area, etc., etc., which were often still being built. I'd also be tracking down offices where people of power held all the VIP and backstage passes, one of my bugbears, as I often lost or forgot my pass. However, I became a master blagger (an essential skill for working in this environment, not just for passes but for times such as when you need cigarettes for nicotine-starved presenters and you haven't got any cash).

So after all this last-minute planning and preparation while I was standing at the entrance of Earls Court buzzing with excitement and fear of no-shows, some relief came over me as I spotted the giant that is Simon Shaw, a member of the winning Rugby World Cup squad, who had helped to persuade Kyran Bracken and Will Greenwood to join him. But as he got closer I could see that instead of Kyran and Will, there were squad members who weren't quite as recognisable at that time, Josh Lewsey, Stuart Abbott and Iain Balshaw. With absolutely no disrespect to any of them, but when you are tasked with trying to create PR you aim for the biggest, most high-profile names and that is what I'd promised Adam.

Of course, I didn't show my disappointment or fear of how Andy Wilman and Adam Waddell might react. Personally, I was delighted to meet and escort three incredibly fit and good-looking men backstage to prepare them for their go-karting performance.

Problem one, of having perhaps not the most notable members of the squad, was quickly overlooked. Problem two was a little more tricky – our sporting giants were literally too giant to fit in the go-karts!

And so to plan B (another major skill required to work in this environment of show production and talent management – be able to come up with a plan B on the spot). It was quickly decided that our sporting heroes would arrive in the arena, in true style in a blacked-out Rolls Royce Phantom, to be greeted and interviewed by Clarkson. We would then replace them with other, smaller (in stature only), willing and able celebs to take part in the go-kart race. No problem.

No problem, except someone forgot to inform Clarkson of what would happen. He was aware that rugby stars were to join him as surprise special guests at some point, but he wasn't told who, when and how. When the big moment came and the stunning Phantom swept into the arena, Clarkson couldn't see who the hell they were until our victorious World

Cup squad members were right in front of him. Forever the professional and in his true *Top Gear* style, as they climbed out of the car and walked the ten or so yards across the arena towards him, he announced, 'Here to surprise you and me, are some very fit men who have just helped to win the Rugby World Cup.' (NB: not a direct quote but words along those lines – forgive me, there have been a lot of shows and a lot of alcohol consumed so my memory isn't tip-top this far back in the proceedings!)

The audience went mad, completely regardless of how high profile these boys were and what their names were, just madly celebrating and jumping on the World Cup Win bandwagon. A great way to warm up your premiere audience. And so began the first of many, many shows that just got bigger, better, faster, louder, funnier and more spectacular as they grew, literally around the world.

After the success of this first weekend of shows, MPH '04 was booked for London, Earls Court again. I was not involved this time as I was working on other projects but I went as a guest and met Richard Hammond for the first time at the after-show party, whereupon I asked him to sit on my knee for a photo, goaded by the general excitement of the occasion and by my old friends Jeremy and Tiff who enjoyed the fact that I was way taller than Richard. I only later learnt that back then Richard absolutely hated being made a fool of in relation to his height. Feelings that he really had to suppress, which was so ironic given that ridiculing him for his height became a regular feature on *Top Gear*, and his short stature is so much part of his TV persona. Little did I know that I would become part of his personal journey in accepting what he had long felt was an inadequacy. How wrong could he be?

At this point in my life, I thought I was skipping off into the sunset to enjoy family life with my new partner and our son. Unfortunately, this wasn't to be, so when my personal life went tits up in 2006 I distinctly remember jumping at the chance to work at the London show again, leaving my boy for the first time so I could stay in London and then Birmingham as the show rolled on.

Andy Wilman had kindly given me a small supporting role looking after the presenters and the running of the green room just as I'd done back in the nineties. My tasks were menial, which was a good thing as I was a little raw from splitting up with my boy's dad, suffering from low self-esteem and general first-time mother exhaustion. I was so glad to be back at work though, with intelligent, fun and creative people including some really good old friends.

Chris Hughes was very much in charge overall. Despite the whole show being a collaborative project, he seemed to be at the head of the pile of management and didn't really like the fact that I had seemingly slipped in the side door and had got a great bond with whom he perceived were 'his talent'. I felt he was quite possessive over them and was clearly not too keen on my familiarity with them. What eventually became apparent was that he was desperate to keep the presenters happy at all times as they were his huge 'cash cow' and obviously essential to the popularity and success of the show.

The original plan was to build the profile of the unique motoring theatre show, with the *Top Gear* boys headlining, and to then roll it out and sell the concept to different venues, with the car exhibition alongside it and perhaps one or two of the boys having a cameo role now and again. I don't think anyone had anticipated it would grow all over the world and run for over twelve years with Jeremy and the boys on board all the way.

Back in 2003 the presenters were given an old caravan backstage in the dark and exhaust fume filled depths of Earls Court. Now the green room was starting its slow climb to more and more comfort and luxury as instructed by Chris, desperate to keep the boys onside. Especially Jeremy, who was very aware of his power and exerted it on numerous occasions, starting with moaning about the coffee and insisting on a Nespresso machine, eventually escalating his demands to extra helicopters!

I, naively unaware of this, was so shocked when, on my first day in the newly upgraded green room (an actual first-floor room, quite glamorous in fact, with glass frontage overlooking the inner workings of the show backstage which had now grown to include more stunt vehicles and a parade of supercars), I was snapped at by Chris for presenting a coffee to Jeremy in a polystyrene cup instead of a VIP china one. I just didn't get it, having experienced the Motor Show with Jeremy before and the glory of the *Top Gear* office, on sight, at Dunsfold, which was littered with polystyrene cups which doubled for ashtrays, amongst piles of half-eaten food and empty crisp packets scattered amongst old script papers, beer bottles, Diet Coke cans, dirty boots, clothes and random props, all framed by a tired old portacabin complete with filthy sticky floor. What was Chris worried about??

I soon learnt what was going on, but due to my long-established friendship with Jeremy and Andy it was unnatural for me to treat them as VIPs. To me they were overgrown naughty schoolboys (which is exactly what they were and was how this all began – for those who don't know, Jeremy and Andy were away at boarding school together from the age of about twelve). The whole *Top Gear* culture was to take the piss and seemingly have no respect for anyone, although the reality was, generally, there was a gentle undercurrent of fondness and actual respect amongst our trio and the crew at large. I dutifully served coffee in china mugs but it was often served with humorous contempt.

I distinctly remember the aftermath of one of the rehearsals at Earls Court which was quite long and drawn out with technical issues, car breakdowns and disputes over presenter lines. I had enjoyed watching some of the rehearsal, fulfilled my duty of supplying cold drinks and cigarettes backstage and then casually tidied and restocked the green room ready for their return. Three weary presenters ambled back into the comfort of the green room, slumping into the luxury leather sofas. There was an air of exhaustion and all were unusually quiet. Jeremy asked me quite politely for a coffee, and I broke the calm by snappily replying, 'Oh for God's sake!' – in jest of course but totally unexpected by James and Richard, who did not know me well. They roared with laughter as did Jeremy and the tone was set. That's how I continued to treat them all, as Jeremy explained to James and Richard at the time, 'Oh, she's brilliant at keeping you grounded.' However, I knew exactly when to use my humour and faux reluctant and useless catering skills (although useless did sometimes genuinely occur and that's when I had to rely on humour), and when to just keep quiet and deliver the perfect beverage at the perfect time.

As the tour progressed I became known and respected for reading the room perfectly and became a sort of diplomatic go-between, helping Chris Hughes, our Tour Manager, Rowly, our Moon-Faced Producer, and other management and production staff get the best out of our three celebrities.

In these early days the budgets weren't huge. The shows' 'stage' was a semi-circular area with huge floor-to-ceiling black cloth drapes creating giant curtains that were manned by crew who opened and closed them on cue allowing cars, presenters and performers to appear dramatically from the darkness of backstage. In the middle of the black backdrop was a huge screen that was suspended from the gantry above.

The early shows began with adverts, a bit like when you go to the cinema. About three or four ads would play on the big screen, or quite uniquely a live ad was performed like the one for Shell V-Power, one of our big sponsors: a choreographed scene of fast cars with stunt drivers pulling up to petrol pumps then roaring off having refuelled with supercharged Shell V-power, whilst a dramatic voice-over bellowed out into the arena about this amazing product.

Then our three amigos would appear in their own choice of supercar, typically James and Richard from each side of the stage and Jeremy blasting in, centre stage. He would then lead the intro and introduce his colleagues and their cars. There would be a bit of banter between them and then one of them would introduce the first act. As they disappeared offstage, a stunt driving display team would enter, accompanied by loud music and dramatic lighting. They would perform a mesmerising kind of car ballet on steroids. The stunt team was headed up by Paul Swift, son of Russ Swift who is best known for his handbrake turn and parallel-parking stunt, used in an old Montego 1.6 advert. (Google it, it's pretty impressive.) To be honest, I think Russ started the team then Paul took over. I apologise now to those reading and the people whose names I mention if I get some detail wrong. As I said before, all those years ago are a bit blurry, especially as I have worked with everyone I mention at other motoring events over the twenty-five years of working in this mad business.

The show would then continue with some ridiculous antics performed by the boys, like shopping trolley skittles. James May climbed into a shopping trolley and was told by Richard, or sometimes Tiff Needell (Tiff stood in for Richard after he famously nearly took his head off in that rocket car crash), that he would be shunted by Jeremy in a ridiculously small G-Wiz electric car, like a Smart car but a bit more shit. Jeremy would drive out in said small car and gently nudge James as a bit of a test then drive offstage to reset for the real thing. At the other side of the arena were five or more huge inflatable but quite firm rubber skittles about 8 ft tall. Richard (or Tiff) would then gee up the crowd and James, then cue Jeremy to drive back in, at which point Jeremy roared out from behind the curtain in a 480 bhp Ford Shelby Mustang shunting James and shopping trolley with quite a force and sending him hurtling towards the skittles.

This stunt began with James in just a helmet until in one performance Jeremy may have been a little over-exuberant and James crashed badly, flipping the trolley on its side and badly spraining his wrist. Someone was then sent out to buy a full set of protective knee, wrist and elbow pads – the show must go on – and Richard took James's place as 'bowling ball' in a trolley. (Oh and James was attended to at A&E.)

Other highlights of the shows back then included magicians performing huge stunts such as synchronised plate spinning on very tall wobbly poles – yes, this was actually quite a spectacle. Other stunt driving scenes were performed accompanied by glamorous girls and boys such as the acrobats who famously performed on New Year's Eve 1999 at the Millennium Dome unravelling themselves from great heights in oversized ribbon then performing a breathtaking aerial display above supercars whizzing around underneath them.

An old favourite, for all, was a life-size replica Ford Focus that flew above the arena and over the audience – it was incredibly lifelike even to our notorious motoring journalists – the audience loved it, and it had quite a hypnotic effect as you tried to work out how the hell a Ford Focus was flying – I could tell you but I'll let you wonder…

At the end of each show there was a high-octane finale involving the Stig driving at high speed competing against some kind of baddie, like a mob of street racers. The Stig always won.

Each year there was a huge amount of work put in by all the production team to develop a new show. This was totally unappreciated by Jeremy as you could never really work hard enough to satisfy his need for perfection. Rowly, AKA our Moon-Faced Producer (Rowly had a completely shaved head which graced the top of a beautifully round face), and Andy Wilman (Andy in the early days only) would scout for new and extraordinary acts to thrill and excite the audience. These included stunt motorcyclists performing in a giant colander-like globe, and champion trial bike stunt riders, such as Jason Finn, using Richard Hammond in their act, whizzing past his head by a hair's breadth or driving right between his legs as he lay on the floor praying for the brakes to work with manhood-saving precision.

Bas, AKA BasIcanfindanycar.com (a lovely, lovely most genuine, always there in a crisis kind of guy) was in charge of sourcing supercars, and he would somehow beg, steal or borrow at least ten, to adorn the show and create a very popular section of the show, 'Car Porn'. The supercars, such as the very latest Lamborghinis, Ferraris, Porsches and Rolls Royces, would parade out to a carefully choreographed routine, created by the wonderful Colin Sangster (another key crew member), Paul Swift and Rowly. The motoring supermodels glided out to a dramatic backdrop of iconic music such as Supertramp's 'Crime of the Century', dry ice and incredible lighting. Clarkson, Hammond and May would then come out, review and argue over which car was best out of the stunning collection. Bas also helped to fill the exhibition halls with static displays from various motor manufacturers.

Rowly would liaise with Andy Wilman, Jeremy and scriptwriters to create and write the whole show. I think in about 2006 'Swampy' was born. Rowly was hugely proud of it and it was quite a formidable sight.

'Swampy' was a huge old petrol tanker that had been 'pimped up', painted a dingy dark green and draped in camouflage netting. The cab had all its windows blacked out and all in all it looked very menacing. It was to go into battle along with two equally menacing comrades in the form of black, 'pimped-up' Rage Buggies, whose drivers could fire out bullets from machine guns (not real ones) mounted on board.

I can't remember if there was a storyline for this epic finale. If there was one, it was about as good as a low-budget bad porn film. Anyhow, a battle ensued between Swampy, and his sinister Rage Buggies, against our hero the Stig, who used to get a huge welcome from the audience as he roared out in his own shining white Rage Buggy.

There were flashing lights, loud bangs, pyros firing off, dry ice, smoke everywhere. It became apparent there was a monster contained in the tanker and he must be stopped. With Rage Buggies roaring around the arena and the Stig clearly winning, dodging bullets and fire with his incredibly swift and adept driving skills, the battle came to a dramatic end. The evil dark Rage Buggies were defeated, one on fire, the other limping off backstage. Another of their comrades was a pimped up, blacked out, camouflaged Saab that dramatically split in two leaving a comedic half a Saab to be driven off back stage while 'Swampy' was disabled by a lethal bullet from our hero the Stig. Flames surrounded the huge tanker in its dying moments. The huge arms of the now-exposed, once tanker-contained, monster were seen flailing about, and hilariously so were the arms of the crew member holding broom sticks supporting said monster's arms. It was a classic school play kind of moment that Rowly was NEVER going to live down.

Back in the green room there were tears of laughter from our trio mixed with despair, and as was often to be repeated as the years and shows went rolling on, poor old Rowly got a right dressing-down from Jeremy before the, let's face it, comical moment became a well-loved tour joke. It was a hard line to walk, although in this instance the 'strings' that held the show together should not have been seen and Jeremy was justified in blowing his top for lack of professionalism, largely, *Top Gear* and the boys' brand was based on their ideas and inventions not going terribly well.

Anyhow, however the shows ended, once any problems were discussed, reported and demanded to be resolved the mood was lifted by a swift beer or two before everyone was whisked off in Range Rovers for dinner, more drinking and easing of any tensions.

One of Chris Hughes's other ventures was food events such as Taste, a huge food festival involving celebrity chefs and their incredible dishes and other cottage industry food and beverages, so Chris was very well connected and able to get us the best tables at the best restaurants.

Our evenings out were often as big a production as the show itself and it was one of my jobs, along with Gemma from Brand Events, to recce restaurants, check out if we had a suitably private area with escape routes for celebrity smoking intervals, a decent wine list, a menu to cater for each of the presenters' desires, and the right amount and standard of cars to get us all there. Unless we knew the restaurant we would always have a backup booked.

In the early days things were relatively simple, although there was never a dull moment. I loved the last show of the day, when energy was high, and I often got to sit in the audience with Chris, Gemma, Bas and James Cooke-Priest (I haven't mentioned much about JCP – he was on the business side of things, a former forces man and very good looking, hence the nickname of Johnny Boden as he looked like he'd just walked out of one of his catalogues).

We were the show's biggest fans. I was the first one backstage to greet and congratulate the boys and provide them with a much-needed drink. It became a ritual that I would greet them with 'You're very brave, very clever and very funny.' I repeated this same mantra for many shows until I decided their egos were big enough and I surprised them by changing the last adjective to stupid. This was met with laughter and I was then challenged by Jeremy to come up with something new each time. It often proved a useful tool to raise the mood if something had gone wrong in the show or the audience had been a bit subdued, which could happen, especially in England with good old English reserve.

Anyhow, I've gone off at a tangent; back to our crazy nights out, such as in London, going to one of Gordon Ramsay's restaurants where we had a private dining room, which became a preference as it meant the presenters could really let their hair down and we weren't in danger of upsetting any other diners. Once wine had been selected by Chris and JCP, approved for quality and cost – a constant balancing act – Chris went off to the loo, announced to us all, in his usual uncouth way.

I don't know who instigated it but we all ended up hiding under the table including the giant that is Jeremy Clarkson. Chris was often the instigator of practical jokes, a constant and somewhat annoying clown. It was brilliant to hear him come back into a seemingly empty room and be lost for words, a rare moment indeed. As you can imagine, the silence didn't last long. It's quite difficult to keep a bunch of fully grown drunkard idiots hidden and quiet under a table. A hilarious evening followed, accompanied by delicious food and plenty of alcohol to wash it down. As was so often the case we were the last to leave.

Just Call Me Horse

Around 2006 the show expanded out to Birmingham and the enormous space of the NEC. This was scheduled just a week after London. All the cars, props, support vehicles, stunt drivers and crew had to be relocated up to Birmingham, all managed by the eternally calm Simon Aldridge and his wife, Sharon.

There were a handful of crew recruited locally and cars provided, where necessary, but around forty of us core crew travelled with the circus and were put up in hotels. In Birmingham it was the Metropole, which was hated by the presenters as it was a vast hotel right next door to the NEC. It was swarming with businessmen who were desperate to meet, or have a selfie with, our presenters – or, worse still, to ask them for specific advice on their next car purchase. Although we arranged for a cordoned-off area for our crew and our celebrity friends, it wouldn't stop drunk, over-exuberant fans finding their way in at times which could result in a little heated exchange with our big man, and sometimes our little man, who would then be hustled out of the area by Chris or JCP, while the drunkard fan was removed by hotel security. These were tense times for Chris, JCP, Gemma and myself, and as time went on and the fame grew we had to make changes to protect our heroes, the *Top Gear* brand and our ever-expanding travelling circus.

Before we upgraded from the Metropole, and simple stunts like Tiff Needell driving a 3 series BMW up a small ramp and through, yes, through a caravan, before narrowly missing the concrete perimeter of the arena, we would all head back to the hotel, and the talent and myself would be whisked from backstage and piled into VIP cars like Mercedes S-Classes – a small demand from JC. Despite it being only a short walk, it was impossible for them to do it as they would be mobbed by their overexcited audience who were piling out of the NEC.

It was then up to our rooms for a quick freshen-up and change of clothes then down to the lobby to head out. Chris had arranged for us to eat in an award-winning Indian Restaurant, Lasan, which became a firm favourite and hosted some of our most hilarious evenings. The after-dinner games of 'Girl on Girl Arm-Wrestling' began, as did 'Celebrity Loo Roll Challenge'.

I don't know how it started but I am quite competitive and I was challenged by one of the boys, probably Chris actually, as he was the overall 'Ring Master', to take on Abby. Abby was our star gymnast from the ribbon twirling opening performance and was clearly very strong. I think I must have boasted that I too was strong as I had ridden and looked after horses since I was eight and you don't hold back half a ton of real horsepower, and carry hay bales and water buckets, without building up strong biceps.

Challenge accepted, I squared up to Abby. She quite quickly got the better of me, but all the boys loved it, as did I, and I wanted to go for best of three. Chris however had grander ideas, and with eating over and drinking in full swing, he persuaded the dear staff to clear the table and provide clean white tablecloths for us to stage our arm-wrestling spectacle.

There was always a smattering of girls at dinner. Chris insisted on it, as it was a pretty male-dominated group, our little core bubble, that became known as 'The Bubble'. At this time there was Gemma, Abby the Gymnast, some random glamorous women that were involved in the exhibition and I think Lou, who was a much-loved member of the Brand Events team and a great laugh (another essential qualification needed if you were to be included in the Bubble). So once Chris had devised a tournament schedule and pairings, he became the *Gladiators* (as in the TV show) style referee standing up to count down for the test of strength to begin.

I was fortuitously sitting next to Ben Collins (the Stig) who started coaching me, pointing out that I'd lost to Abby earlier because my arms were longer and I had to counteract the negative forces of physics. He taught me to be really square on to the table with my feet, hip distance apart, and firmly rooted to the floor. With his expert coaching, and of course my strength, I swept the board and became the reigning champion – until the next time…

During this first tournament I got the nickname of 'Horse'. Chris decided that I was actually raised by horses and had become this extraordinary strong girl, slightly feral in nature. Not far from the truth!

The arm-wrestling became a favourite after-dinner game and it went international as the show started to develop its global tour. One year, back in Lasan for more delicious Indian cuisine, our Dutch guest Fascal, who was visiting to negotiate the show going to Amsterdam, was invited to join the arm-wrestling championship and she bloody took the title! Somewhere along the line, to add a bit of interest to the sport, Richard Hammond started to feature as the 'table' for the arm-wrestling to take place on. God knows how we got to this but Chris had encouraged him to lie on the dining table, ceremoniously covered him in a white tablecloth, and sponged him down in preparation with wet napkins. Richard had to prove his strength by tightening his abs whilst us girls wrestled over him! Oh my God I'm laughing now recalling it. I hope you are. Or did you have to be there?

Our behaviour became ever more ridiculous, I have to say mostly played out in empty restaurants as we were always so late to dinner and had often paid a premium to keep late-night drinking going, effectively, in our own private restaurant, although 'Celebrity Loo Roll Challenge' actually had to be played out in a full restaurant, otherwise it wasn't deemed worthy. This challenge involved James, Richard or Jeremy coming back from the loo with loo roll stuck down the back of their trousers but still attached to the roll back in the cubicle. To complete the challenge, they had to get back to the table trailing the toilet roll all the way without tearing it. This was particularly tricky in Lasan as you had to negotiate a set of stairs and a sharp turn through 'normal' diners' tables, then down another short flight of steps to our secluded corner. The big man was the champion at this, and went on to play in many tournaments including on planes and most memorably in Moscow's snow covered Red Square where all participants were nearly arrested, having actually taken loo roll from the Ritz to create a historical and unique tournament using one member of the Bubble as a human spool. Thankfully the Moscow officers recognised the big man and liked him, so they were issued with a warning and asked to dispose of all the loo roll in an appropriate way.

These crazy nights plus the hard-worked days and nights started building the most extraordinary relationships within the Bubble, our incredibly special dysfunctional family, Chris Hughes being at the head of it. There was a kind of love/ hate relationship between him and the presenters (classic sibling rivalry). Chris was always pushing them a bit further, or as Jeremy would say 'milking' them by selling them to a sponsor to perform a Q and A session at a Gala Dinner after the shows. Or signing books and merchandise to keep sponsors happy. In these early days I have to say they were pushed to the limit, doing effectively ten shows over a weekend including the dress rehearsal.

At the end of the day they were all making money, but I think the contract was loose. Or the boys didn't realise what they had signed up for. Their lives were being lived at such breakneck speed, I don't think they did. But if anyone was going to get away with 'milking' them it was Chris Hughes. Even the boys described him as the funniest man they knew. He was incredibly quick-witted and had endless energy which didn't really match his pot-bellied, bald-headed appearance. He was the life and soul of any party to the bitter end, often performing, quite well, on the piano, and singing, not quite so well, all the time conscious of keeping happy both his high-profile talent and the rest of the crew.

Talking of which, we started going out in the evenings with quite a few of the senior crew, but as time went on it became more and more difficult to manage the numbers and not upset Jeremy by sitting him next to someone boring at dinner or Richard with someone who wanted him to sit on their lap (that did actually happen, after all he's so cute, but RH is not very tactile – he's the dog equivalent of a Jack Russell, not a lapdog). So the majority of the crew would always be allocated beer money. Chris would often join them for an early drink and/or possibly a late one. He was a true copper top with his orange hair (what was left of it) just like a Duracell battery.

Our Bubble became more and more exclusive, which I found awkward sometimes as I worked alongside all the crew, but at the end of the day I think all were happy with their lot.

Along with the exclusivity of the Bubble came creativity, which was something Gemma, Chris and I led in a never-ending attempt to make our evening entertainment both original and as entertaining, if not more so, than the last mad night out.

As the shows were continually growing and becoming more spectacular and more demanding, so did the boys. A last-minute demand was made as tolerance reached an end, where, in Birmingham especially, you could not escape the noise and fumes of rehearsals and set building. Luxurious film star type Winnebagos were bought in overnight that could sit outside the arena in some relative peace. We had two of them, one for food and drink and generally hanging out, and the other an uber-quiet space where Jeremy could script-write or any of the trio could write their columns or simply rest in peace. This also doubled as a secret place for the Stig to emerge from. His identity was closely guarded at all times. (A simple strategy but even I got caught out, asking the man in the white suit, whom I knew to be Terry Grant, our stunt driver, to deal with something urgently backstage. The man in the white suite spoke and said, 'It's Paul.' I was completely confused as I'd seen Terry go in the Winnebago. I didn't know we had two Stigs.)

To spice things up for the last evening at the Metropole, Chris had decided we needed a limo instead of the usual Mercedes or Range Rovers, and he tasked me with persuading one of the exhibitors to lend or hire us one of their exhibits. With a lot of chatting up I arranged for exhibitors to juggle their exhibits, and NEC officials and security to let out one of the limos from a stand, prior to the end of the final show, in order for it to surprise our talent and rock up outside the Metropole to take us for dinner and on for further evening entertainment.

So there she was, a fully extended limo big enough to carry at least ten of us. It was decked out with full nightclub interior, lights, leather, leopard print and a fully stocked champagne bar. The boys loved it. En route to dinner, we went down the main drag in Birmingham city centre and James May, the usually quiet one, had become overcome with excitement, and maybe a little alcohol, and stood on a small table to poke his head out of the sunroof shouting abuse at the people of Birmingham. He was duly hauled in to prevent a small riot kicking off.

As a distraction an arm-wrestling contest was suggested with the new accessory of Richard Hammond, the table, laid out on the floor of the limo whilst us champagne fuelled girls battled it out on him. Nothing out of the ordinary here.

After dinner at our old favourite Lasan, not only was the food fantastic but the staff were so tolerant of our late-night arrivals and crazy behaviour. In fact I've just remembered one occasion, it must have been as plans were being made to go global because Bas wasn't with us and was abroad somewhere negotiating the next stage of the tour. It was his birthday and Chris and Gemma had arranged that we have a Skype call. The restaurant manager had let us all into his office, including JC, RH and JM. We all sang 'Happy Birthday' to Bas, before we had dinner. I don't think any restaurant could be more accommodating than that. Obviously, having three very popular TV personalities and spending lots of cash did help.

After dinner, we climbed, stumbled and fell back into our limo. This was always a dangerous point in any evening and reminds me of a quote from one of Jeremy's friends, 'One drink is never enough, two drinks are just right, three drinks are never enough!!??' We ended up at a strip club. I was squirming and not in a good way. I am not a fan of such establishments, and Jeremy was not happy but went along with it at first. James and Richard were a bit like kids in a sweet shop, for the first time, excited but unsure of what to do. It soon all got a bit uncomfortable and Jeremy insisted that we left. I don't think he wasn't enjoying it, he was more worried about stories and photos getting out.

Chris, however, had handed out a lot of cash to a few of the club's girls. His alter ego, the Piggy-Eyed Businessman, reared his ugly head, a sweaty head at that, and red-faced, from running around a strip club making sure our celebrities were happy. One of the funniest scenes, probably never seen before, started to play out. As we were all trying to bundle back into the limo and get away as quickly and discreetly as possible, Chris was begging the girls for his money back as he hadn't got anything for it, not just for him I might add (Mrs Hughes, I can assure you nothing untoward happened, there wasn't time!). I think he had planned to 'treat' a lot of us and simply keep the drinks flowing.

Jeremy went from feeling quite anxious to hysterical laughter along with the rest of us as Chris was hassling three girls in the foyer. JCP had gone back to extract him, in true military style, from the situation but gave up as Chris was now negotiating a deal with the girls to at least come and say goodbye to our celebs and then they could keep some of the money – a scene worthy of another *Hangover* movie. The girls escorted Chris back to the limo and said a most expensive goodbye to our celebs. I mean literally said, 'Goodbye'. And Chris stuffed his recouped cash back in his pockets.

On arrival back at the hotel, spirits were still high, and someone dared me to exit via the sunroof, so I did. I finished my rock and roll exit by sliding along the roof and down the windscreen. Not quite sure how I got away with that but I did; no harm done and the Bubble moved on to carry on partying in Chris Hughes and Richard Hammond's rooms, which were opposite each other. Minibars were emptied; room service was kept busy with drink orders; and general frivolity carried on. I don't remember how and when the night ended; I just remember after not enough sleep and whilst battling a hangover I was called to the hotel manager's office.

I had stumbled down the corridors from my room desperately talking to myself, 'not going to be sick, not going to be sick'. I had to negotiate a whole load of furniture in the corridor and excuse myself past several hotel staff who were bustling about whispering. All a bit strange. The strangeness was explained in quite a stern manner by the hotel manager, once I reached the privacy of his office. The furniture was the full contents of Richard Hammond's room and it had been blocking Chris Hughes's door!

I diplomatically negotiated my way out of any huge amounts being added to our room bills and any exaggerated stories getting out to the press. Apparently, there had been quite a lot of disturbance in the wee small hours.!?!? I am so missing the use of emojis whilst writing all this.

The worst outcome was the huge sum added to Chris Hughes's room bill for empty minibars, of which he had two, and a rather large porn movie bill. Someone had ordered rather a lot, on one of the TVs, without him knowing. That's what Chris said anyway.

And then there were two more shows to perform! This was a talent I was always in awe of; Jeremy, James and Richard were just incredible at going on with the show, whatever condition they were in. All I had to do was dispense more coffee at speed, mix up Berocca, hand out Nurofen and paracetamol, and make sure McDonald's was delivered as soon as they left the stage of their first performance. Ashamedly, I have to report that after doing all that, I had to take to the darkened bedroom of the Winnebago where I slept between bouts of sickness and texts, to make sure my dutiful helpers had all in place for my legends of stage and screen. I was such a lightweight, not really made for rock and roll. I could rock alright but not too good at rolling on.

The World Tour Begins

Johannesburg and Dublin (well, it's a start)

The shows evolved year on year: Chris Hughes and James Cooke-Priest attended many business meetings, and Rowly endlessly presented new ideas for the show to Jeremy, only to be told to go away and start again. To get Jeremy's approval it had to be funny and/or clever and perfect, which is obviously a huge reason behind his success.

In early 2007, the show was taken to Johannesburg. This was the beginning of what became *Top Gear*'s World Tour, although nobody knew it at the time. Chris and James had met a lovely man, Paul Edmunds, who sadly passed away this year. He ran an events company out in Jo'burg. Paul and Chris set up a company together, Brand Events South Africa, in order to host the show out there.

I wasn't considered a core member of the crew back then and Chris, AKA Piggy-Eyed Businessman, was certainly not going to waste money on a flight for me to go and pour coffee for three middle-aged men. He hadn't realised my value or how much I actually did, apart from the fact that, most importantly, I knew what kept the boys happy and that they really valued having me around as a trusted confidante.

The show was a huge hit in South Africa and plans were made to go back and hit Cape Town too. In the meantime shows went on annually in London and Birmingham. The show got bigger, as did the crew, my role and more importantly the audiences.

I became more involved with the logistics for what was now officially 'The Bubble', which meant helping out with sourcing Range Rovers for both London and Birmingham, for moving celebs from hotel to venue, going out for dinner, and emergency errands for any of the Bubble.

I was consulted on how to best set up a green room with all the personal creature comforts that Jeremy, James and Richard required, from Liquorice Allsorts for James, Minstrels for Jeremy and Berocca for Richard, to the medication they preferred. In the early days we had product placement deals; that is, for example, Red Bull and Diet Coke were provided for free by their respective marketing departments. Deals were made for meat pies, beers, massage chairs, Fatboy bean bags and coffee machines.

The day before rehearsals began, and right up to the last minute, all these things were delivered to the venue and needed assembling and displaying along with plants, furniture and big boys' toys to create a space where the boys could work, rest and play! The intention was to set up a home from home, living room, with added extras so they didn't get bored.

Gemma, Bas and I would come up with new and ingenious ways to keep the boys happy and comfortable. We had football tables, pool tables, *Pac-Man* and *Space Invaders* (seventies and eighties arcade games), coffee tables, juke boxes, fruit machines, remote-control cars, PlayStations, TVs and a pile of DVDs. One year in Earls Court an oxygen bar was set up, which was probably the most popular novelty item we ever sourced as it was awesome for hangovers.

For those of you who have never experienced one, you sit at a bar, much like any other bar, except you are given a set of tubes, like those given in hospital to provide pure oxygen, (now an all-too-familiar sight with treating Covid-19). You put them up each nostril, and those two tubes merge into one, which is then attached to a bubbling bottle of brightly coloured, scented (a scent/flavour of your choice) oxygen from the bar.

Unfortunately, all our other endeavours to provide novelty entertainment were often wasted as after the initial enthusiasm and a quick blast on a Sega Rally or a fruit machine, it was a bit like kids at Christmas – the initial excitement wore off or there would literally be arguments about someone making too much noise. Often it was Jeremy moaning about James and Richard as they were battling it out with remote-control tanks or helicopters while he was trying to script-write.

The boys would often ask me, 'What do you do all day?' They were convinced I was just putting my feet up in a massage chair whilst they were onstage. The reality was there was rarely a dull moment. Over the three or four days of preparation and live shows, things were constantly evolving, with more deliveries of things that may or may not entertain them; a constant refreshing of supplies of food, drink and cigarettes; liaising with hotels or restaurants for food and entertainment including planning pop-up crew parties and finding bands at the last minute; and the meeting and greeting of VIP guests, who may have been friends and family of the presenters or potential sponsors/business partners to take the show forward.

There were also last-minute requests for props for the show, and over the years I have had to source some very random items such as dozens of pizza bases to make pizza pants, a Rolls Royce Phantom Convertible and a selection of sex toys and women's underwear.

The pizza pants were for Jeremy to wear (over his jeans, to be clear) to prove that they were fireproof and could actually be used to cover the outside of a Space Shuttle to re-enter the earth's atmosphere; a ridiculous fact he had delighted in sharing in a discussion the boys were having, that then became part of the show. Later, Richard and James challenged him to prove his knowledge and presented him with the pizza pants. They then took a blowtorch to them, directing it right at Jeremy's 'vegetable patch', as James called it. I can confirm pizza bases are fireproof and Jeremy is ALWAYS right.

The Rolls Royce was to replace a last-minute dropout from the Car Porn line up, and the sex toys and underwear were planted in James May's suitcase, which he converted into a motorised vehicle. All in a day's/night's work!

Talking of meeting and greeting guests, there was one VIP guest meet I will never forget. I think it was at Earls Court, there or Birmingham; either way, Richard had asked me to go and meet a friend of his and his family. I set off to the front of the venue, which felt like a mile away. I was to escort them backstage to the green room to meet Richard before the start of whichever performance they were coming to see. To set the scene it's important for you to know that I am 5 ft 11 and ¾, so wearing any form of shoes I become over 6 ft, and I usually wear a heel of some kind, so I would have been standing at least 6 ft 2 in on this occasion.

I had to go to an office on site to collect their guest passes, made out in the name of a Mr Davis and family. Passes at the ready, I waited in the foyer. Richard had given a description of me to Mr Davis; tall blond, wearing black, etc., etc. I didn't have to wait long before I had to stifle my reaction to the arrival of Warwick Davis and his very small family (and I say this without any disrespect at all). For those of you who don't know, Warwick is a very successful actor, comedian and presenter who has a rare condition causing dwarfism. Warwick is only 3 ft 6 and his wife and children, also affected by dwarfism, are even smaller.

Once I had got over my initial surprise of meeting Warwick, star of many an epic movie such as many of the *Star Wars* and *Harry Potter* films, I then had to get over my awkwardness of standing over six feet tall and leading a troop of very small people through miles of exhibition centre to meet my favourite, small *Top Gear* presenter.

Oh my God, it felt like a long way; however, I am never short of small talk. (I seriously just came out with that!!) I am never fazed by anyone, be they a Hollywood movie star, the Queen or a dustman. I love making friends with all and finding out how life is for them. I have also never felt uncomfortable around disability (a good job as my son is disabled).

We all chatted along the way, and I had soon broken any barriers, with Warwick showing his self-deprecating sense of humour. Even though we talked about disability, I was still conscious to be tactful about offering help to any of them to climb what all of sudden seemed like very steep stairs.

On arrival at the green room, Jeremy was laid out on a bean bag and James was reading in one of the leather wingback chairs. Both were unaware of who was coming. Richard leapt up to greet Warwick and his family quietly, so as not to disturb his resting colleagues. I got on with providing refreshments. On hearing the coffee machine, Jeremy stirred and slowly got to his feet, pulling himself together out of his slumber, including pulling his shirt back down over his exposed belly. 'Oh God, so sorry I didn't see you,' he said to the Davis family. And so the laughter began and all the usual long and short of it gags. The comedy meeting was finished off perfectly with a commemorative photo. James sat on the sofa and Jeremy kneeled down to fit in with everyone else.

After Warwick and his family left, Jeremy ripped into Richard about the fact that he hadn't got any friends or family that were taller than him. Obviously, according to

Jeremy, so he felt superior at all times around his nearest and dearest. (Richard has got a very petite wife, Mindy, and his mum and dad are short too.) We had also met Richard's mechanic friend, shorter than him, and even his helicopter pilot, also shorter than him. He was not allowed to forget that.

As I became more established and more needed within the Bubble, it was decided to take me to Dublin, the next small step towards global touring. After my induction to rock and roll touring in London and Birmingham, I was about to take a giant leap into touring like a rock star and was booked on the private plane. (Not jet – something I learnt to do was identify aircraft, and a twin-prop private plane is a poor man's private jet. Chris, the Piggy-Eyed Businessman, got a load of grief for not booking jets but there is a HUGE price difference.)

Despite the grief the boys gave Chris for being a cheapskate, they were as excited as any of us and were secretly quite happy with the small plane. So often in the early days the boys couldn't believe how successful they had become and genuinely enjoyed moments like this. However, having trips in private planes is not as luxurious as you might think. To start with, you can hardly stand up in them unless you are Richard Hammond. You can only take a very limited amount of luggage in a soft bag, so it can be squashed into the back of the plane, often around what is offered as a toilet but which in fact is more like a bucket behind a curtain or at best a concertina plastic door. And if you think you struggle to eat on a regular plane, it is almost impossible on one of these. It's best to stick to drinking, and even that can be tricky as the ride is often very bumpy in such a small plane that can be tossed around in any wind like a leaf.

What was great about a private plane was there was no security and the enormous convenience it provided. The plane met us at Dunsfold (the track where they film *Top Gear*, which is in fact an airfield). It sat on the runway waiting until the boys had finished filming that week's show in the infamous hanger. And this was how crazy the boys' schedule could be. They literally walked off set and had one drink and a sausage roll whilst their luggage was loaded into Discoveries that were standing by to drive us the couple of hundred yards to the plane.

I loaded up a bag with a few of their favourite snacks and booze and felt very excited as I bent myself in half to board our very own flying tube. Once I had squeezed into my seat, Jeremy presented me with a replica Ming vase. In true *Top Gear* style, he said it was a special gift. Of course, following *Top Gear* protocol, I had to carry my special gift all the way to Dublin on my lap and then ensure that I got it home safely too. It is now very proudly displayed on my mantelpiece.

On arrival in Dublin we were escorted by airport cars and whisked through the private arrivals straight out to a Rolls Royce Phantom that was for the boys. Myself, Chris and JCP followed in a plain old brand new Range Rover. To add to the rock and roll arrival, Chris had arranged for a police escort. He wanted to demonstrate to the boys that he took their celebrity status seriously. Unfortunately JC, in his contrary way, didn't stop moaning, exclaiming, 'Why the bloody hell have we got a police escort?' He claimed he caused more of a problem by attracting more unwanted attention.

I was greeted by a smiley, very hospitable hospitality lady and this was the moment I knew things were stepping up all round. There was a huge Winnebago, much bigger and more luxurious than those we had had in Birmingham and London. It was full of luxury hampers from a famous Dublin deli, Donnybrook Fair. We had all been given a hamper each, myself included, containing delicious artisan, gourmet, sweet and savoury snacks. There were bowls of fresh fruit and a fridge full of chilled drinks. Even a Nespresso machine had been added especially for the big man. I learnt on this trip that anyone who partnered and hosted the show anywhere in the world was very strictly briefed about the standard expected to keep our talent comfortable and happy. However, it became apparent that this was never to be taken for granted, and it always needed to be checked, double-checked and hammered home to whoever was in charge. This was part of my responsibility, and never was the phrase 'Assumption is the mother of all fuck-ups' so true as when working in this world.

Alongside the Winnebago were two portacabins including one that was carpeted and had been decked out with a pool table and massage chairs. It had a small kitchen complete with oven, a far cry from the early days when I would wash up mugs in the ladies' loos. (The sinks I mean!) I had come equipped with my ever-growing bag of medicines and the boys' favourite sweets. One thing I'm sure most of you will have experienced if you've been travelling is you can't always get the exact chocolate or sweets that you are used to at home. And of course I always had a supply of each presenter's preferred cigarettes.

We had now in fact got a rider, which was a constant working document that was sent out to Jo'burg and now to Dublin, making sure the fridges were stocked with Diet Coke for JC, Red Bull and water for RH, and Tango and ginger beer for JM. Of course, for straight after the last show of the day, there was also Peroni beer, Sauvignon blanc (for JM), gin and tonic (for RH) and rosé (or lady petrol, as we called it; for JC). Along with their favourite drinks and snacks there was also the small, daily demand of *The Sun*, *The Mirror*, *The Telegraph* and *The Times*, as well as some local newspapers, so the presenters could look for anything interesting and current to add to the show's script. The hospitality in Dublin was amazing, so we were overflowing with everything and more.

I was also assigned local runners who were at my disposal to fetch anything at any time which was lucky as again I had overdone the alcohol on the first night – very poor form. Unfortunately, with a combination of overexcitement and stress (I'd just got a diagnosis of fragile X syndrome for my son, who was three and a half), alcohol doesn't work very well for me.

On this first morning in Dublin, one of the kind runners had asked if I was OK as I was looking a little green. I felt awful but battled through setting everything up as the boys liked: checking a printer and laptop were set up ready for scripting; coffee machine on, working and ready; newspapers laid out; ash trays and lighters at the ready. The boys could not function without nicotine. We had our own laws when it came to smoking in public spaces. Sometimes we had to pay extra to hotels or venues to create smoking rooms or incur extra cleaning costs for hotel rooms. Gemma and I have been known to run around like lunatics, emptying and hiding ashtrays and frantically trying to air green rooms before a venue or hotel official appeared.

Once I'd checked every detail, like making sure the fridges were loaded in such a way that any one of our precious celebs could find their favourite beverage in literally the blink of a man-searching eye, I made my excuses and went for a lie-down to try to prepare myself for the rest of the day.

Luckily, I had proved myself over the dozens of shows and nights out that I had endured in London and Birmingham so far. Chris had realised I had a very strong work ethic and wouldn't stop till a Rolls Royce, a pizza base supply or three fish tanks and fish had been bought, at a discounted rate; all this, while keeping three middle-aged, slightly precious TV presenters happy. So when I did get sick there was a little bit of sympathy for at least a short while, but then I was expected to be back on form ASAP. After much-needed rest and recovery time, I reappeared, to make sure lunch was to the boys' satisfaction, and I continued to support them through rehearsals and their first show in Dublin.

Meanwhile, as the boys left the hotel and headed to the venue in their luxury car with Chris, they hit a wall of Dublin's heaviest traffic at which point Jeremy demanded, 'Why the bloody hell haven't we got a police escort?!' Chris had of course cancelled it after JC's moaning the night before. A new running gag entered Chris's repertoire as we continued touring the World trying to cater to JC's every whim and ensure the smooth running of all our journeys – 'Why the bloody hell have we/haven't we?'

In order to save myself for the rest of the weekend, I opted out of going out that evening, which was frowned upon as, although it was fun, it was still work and I supported Gemma with logistics of transport to restaurants and further entertainment, which could get messy after a few drinks, when one of our stars decided he'd had enough. Chris would get into a panic and over-manage, creating a safe exit out of a crowded restaurant, bar or club and making sure the Rolls Royce was poised outside the door at just the right time.

To be fair, a tired, drunk and slightly stressed celeb making their way through equally drunk, over-exuberant fans can be quite scary, especially if there are paparazzi kicking around as well.

Well what a night I missed. The Bubble had made their way to Lillie's, a well-known and prestigious nightclub in Dublin. I think the last to bed were Jeremy and Chris at around 4am. They had joined members of U2 in the VIP lounge where all were jamming until the wee small hours.

If you didn't know, Jeremy plays drums, Richard plays guitar and James plays piano. James actually studied at music college and Jeremy became known as the Rock-a-saurus because of his huge knowledge of great tracks. He has had a lot of influence over the soundtrack to the soundtrack to the shows and the TV show.

You may have seen the 'Top Gear Band' perform on a *Top Gear* Special as part of *Children in Need*, when they performed Billy Ocean's 'Red Light Spells Danger'. On tour we discovered Chris could play piano, really quite well, and sing, not quite so well. He generally loved performing so became an honorary member of the Top Gear Band.

So, the next day in Dublin, I was the only bright-eyed one to be seen within the Bubble. Although gutted, really gutted to have missed such an epic night, I was glad to redeem myself and be on top form to 'nurse' everyone through the day. As always the boys performed regardless, which as I've said before was admirable. Not only did they have to go out and remember their lines, but the shows were really quite physical, driving at high speed in a small space throwing cars around, and not least when they came to the end of their hour or so performance, participating in what had now become the show's regular finale – Car Football.

James and Richard would make up teams with Paul Swift and some of his stunt driving team, to play a three-a-side match. These games were seriously competitive and really quite aggressive at times. The game was usually played out in small hatchbacks unless we weren't able to persuade a motor manufacturer to give over six of their finest small hatchbacks to be smashed to smithereens for the honour of performing to our audience of thousands.

In the absence of a generous car sponsor, saved from the crusher, Reliant Robin and Bedford Rascals were used. The Reliants were forever rolling over and the Bedford Rascals would tip dramatically forward flipping their back ends up. It was quite a spectacle. Extra comedy was added by naming the teams Titans and When Saturday Comes, therefore branding the cars with graffiti style team names, so when the drivers' doors were opened and RH and JM were standing behind them, RH would have TIT (from the beginning of TITANS) spelt out in front of him and JM, TURD (from the middle of SATURDAY).

The strategic painting of cars was used on several occasions, such as in one of the opening sequences when Richard arrived first, stage left, got out and purposefully closed his door, to show the branding of Morrisons down the side of his car. Meanwhile, James and Jeremy got out leaving their doors open, to break up the words that had been scribed on their cars, to create the special message of 'Morrisons are shit.' This particular slogan was to wind Richard up as he had signed up for a series of Morrisons supermarket ads. He reportedly lost a lot of money after this stunt was pulled. If he did, he took it with very good grace…

Jeremy was the referee who stood on the wall at the audience end of the arena whilst the cars hurtled about between two giant goals on wheels with a giant inflatable football. He loved being ref, making up his own rules, bombastically commentating on the game and blowing his whistle.

These games were genuinely exciting, though, and always different. Spectators often asked if they were choreographed but they certainly weren't – you really couldn't as there was no real precision in hitting ('kicking') the ball. Sometimes balls burst if they got caught between two cars in a head-on collision, so a replacement was always ready for the throw-in.

The players never held back, not even Captain Slow, James May. There were high-speed runs down the outside and handbrake turns in the goals. There was a lot of contact;

hence, it was hard to persuade manufacturers to donate cars. At least three substitutes were required for when terminal damage occurred. If damage wasn't terminal, they were literally taped up and sprayed to cover their wounds, but all were left with many, many dents. Helmets were a must as side-on collisions often resulted in the driver's head banging the door pillar. Actually, thinking about it, I've just come up with a great solution to playing socially distanced, coronavirus-safe football! It is a brilliant game. Think life-size bumper cars with a purpose.

In between all the excitement of the shows and crazy nights out, there was a little bit of relaxing done in the comfort of the green room. In fact there was nothing all three of the boys liked better than a nice cup of tea and a movie in the break between the afternoon and evening performance.

It was my responsibility to make sure they were not disturbed and had everything they needed. That sometimes even included sending the hyperactive, constantly chattering Chris Hughes away! Richard coined the phrase 'He's stuck on idling' (ticking over) as he would sometimes just ramble on, mostly humorously, but annoyingly. If I didn't get him away quickly enough in these precious quiet moments, JC would bellow at him like a very annoyed older brother and he would scamper off.

The dynamics between us, in the Bubble, were quite bizarre. Having been approved and recognised as useful, by Chris, I was now ordered never to leave the talent alone and to send out runners to fetch anything or run errands.

In the beginning I would run the entire length of the NEC, or in London, Lillie Road, collecting bacon rolls or fags and then was moaned at by Chris because I wasn't in the green room on stand-by for any need of the presenters. The celebs were never left alone on tour. It's a weird thing being a celebrity despite having the confidence, obviously, to have been able to become one in the first place. Going out on your own in the normal world, as a celebrity, can be a very daunting and intimidating experience as you are more than likely going to be recognised.

For Clarkson especially, being as outspoken as he is, there are many people who don't like him or his opinions, and they are quite prepared to shout across a street at him. Those who love him come right up to him and are desperate for a selfie and a chat. Whatever mood said celebrities are in, or whatever they are doing, they feel a pressure to be polite even to those who shout abuse or may even intrude on them waiting for a Viagra prescription. This can bring on an attack of what I call 'celebrity claustrophobia' and a slight 'toddler tantrum'.

Overexcited fans drop any form of manners and spatial awareness. So whilst on tour the non-celebrity Bubble members took on the role of security and companion for all three of them. Gemma and I were often assigned to accompany Jeremy on shopping trips or for lunch. James Cooke-Priest may accompany Richard to the gym and Chris might take James to a museum, for example.

Another thing I observed is celebrities attract celebrities. I was once shopping with Jeremy in Dublin and we bumped into Ronan Keating. The fascinating thing is that celebrities have this innate understanding and recognition of one another whether they have met or not. An example of this occurred in Moscow one evening when we were having dinner at the Ritz, where we were staying.

We were actually having quite a low-key evening enjoying a simple supper in the hotel's more casual rooftop bar when along came Sting! I, having grown up with the soundtrack of the Police, as my older brother was a massive fan, and subsequently becoming a fan myself, when Sting went solo, was more than a little star-struck.

Straight away there was mutual recognition by Jeremy and Sting – Jeremy got up to shake hands and said, 'Hello Mr Gordon Sting' (much to our amusement), and a conversation was struck up. As often happened, James and Richard were slightly overlooked, I guess partly because JC is physically so huge as well as hugely recognisable. James and Richard were usually more than happy to take a step back and let the big man take the limelight, something he was constantly battling with in a love-hate relationship.

As Sting and his crew moved off to the bar, I asked JC if he knew him or was that just a one celeb to another kind of chat. The latter was the answer. Quite bizarre but fascinating to observe.

Obviously, celebrities do tend to hang out in the same haunts, like award ceremonies, large fundraising events and expensive restaurants. They are all basically members of a very eclectic club. Chat shows are another common meeting place and in Dublin on this trip, as a PR exercise, the boys had to attend the famous Irish *Late Late Show*, hosted by a Des O'Connor type character, Pat Kenny. And I say HAD to attend, as all three presenters hated this kind of thing, and to make it worse it was filmed at about 11 o'clock in the evening and this was after performing two shows on a day that had started with a hangover.

However, the boys soldiered on, not without moaning though. Chris, JCP, Gemma and I accompanied them trying to keep their spirits up, which got harder upon arrival at the studio when they were told that it was a special edition of *The Late Late Show* and was in fact the Christmas Special, *The Late Late Toy Show*.

Imagine their delight when they learnt they had to review toys as part of their interview and that the audience was filled with loads of innocent, good old Catholic Irish kids.

We fuelled them with coffee and repeated the mantra 'Don't swear, don't swear, don't swear…'

To add to the bizarre situation we were then joined by the Duchess of York, Sarah Ferguson, who was there to promote one of her children's books, about *Budgie the Little Helicopter*. We all squeezed in a very small green room; Jeremy had met the Duchess before, as I had too (I'd taken part in one of her charity car rallies to Monte Carlo). We were all soon having a good chat together and made a plan to hit a nightclub when we had all escaped RTE's studios.

We had one of our Irish hosts arrange to get us into another exclusive nightclub in the centre of Dublin. It was like someone's house, a Georgian town house, where we were greeted by smartly dressed staff and our coats were taken in the hallway. We were then escorted upstairs to a packed 'living room' where it all got a bit overwhelming and I quickly arranged for a quieter area to be made available to us. A corner with a couple of tables was quickly cleared and our strange eclectic party set up camp there.

I was still a little fragile from my first night and I was desperate for a cup of tea, so I asked a member of staff if it was at all possible. (I'm so wild!) Shortly after, a pot of tea was delivered on a silver tray complete with cups and saucers! The Duchess was most impressed and declared to Jeremy, who she was chatting to, 'I want a Phillipa, she's amazing!' Her assistant took my mobile number. I was extremely flattered. It's amazing how far you can get just by making tea! She never called.

We didn't last too long, in what, I'm sure, was a very hip and trendy place to be. It was lovely but a bit too cramped and noisy for us all. An exit strategy was planned, and cars called to be ready and waiting outside the door. It was snowing and a small snowball fight was inevitable, started by Chris (I think perhaps the biggest kid of us all). That particular part of

Dublin was very picturesque; it was quite a lovely Christmas scene (oops, I've gone all romantic but it was a lovely moment in our weird dysfunctional Bubble family life). The Duchess went her own way, I think flying out early the next morning. We headed back to the luxury and comfort of our hotel. We had access to our very own living room for the duration of our stay. We carried on there with a nightcap or two in front of a roaring fire. All in all quite a gentle evening.

Having been assigned my own runners, I sometimes felt quite awkward basically doing nothing, hanging around in the background of the green room, acting as security and ready for action if a tea mug became empty and needed refilling or clearing away. Chris wanted me to be just like a personal butler, seen and not heard but seeing and hearing everything.

During a quiet period in Dublin I decided I could make use of the kitchen within the green room and quietly got on and made some brownies. A great success, the boys loved the home baking touch and so did Chris, not only because he's greedy (both for money and food) but because he liked me to come up with original ideas to comfort and pamper the boys when they could be feeling homesick and tired of life on the road.

These gentle and quiet times never lasted long. In Dublin one morning, James was quietly reading a newspaper, reclining in one of the massage chairs (massage chairs were now on the rider). Richard, feeling bored, decided to set fire to the bottom of James's paper. Another hilarious moment, as James didn't realise at first. I think he was totally engrossed in what he was reading at the top of his broadsheet and/or the room was filled with smoke anyway as there was constant smoking going on, especially from JC who could be a sixty a day man when bored and/or under stress.

James eventually leapt up, not really amused, which made it all the more amusing. Oh well, that passed away a few minutes until the first show was about to start and the poor sound guy arrived with the boys' sound packs and earpieces. I call him the 'poor' sound guy as he was always greeted by the boys with an 'Oh no, not you', as his arrival meant the boys had to go through the painful process of putting their earpieces in, which they described as 'fucking their ears'. They expressed sympathy for girls and questioned why we put up with it. Oh God, they were vile at times.

And so off they would go to psych themselves up for another performance, and after I had made sure they had all they needed backstage, Chris joined me to help jolly them up before they made their exuberant and often dramatic entrance for the start of the show. Chris then commandeered me, as usual, for me to help plan for our evening's entertainment and what had now become a firm fixture in our schedules, 'The Closing Ceremony'.

This ceremony had started out life at the beginning of the first shows in London, when Gemma and I and another poor backstage girl would be directed by Chris to ceremoniously deliver presents to each of the presenters. In the early days they were quite generic, maybe just a bottle of champagne for each or a large remote-control vehicle bought from a stall in the exhibition adjoining the show. Chris would then thank the presenters for all their hard work. This was combined with having a quick beer with all the incredibly hard-working crew.

As more shows were successfully completed, and Chris was keen to keep the boys onside to be able to market the show around the world, he wanted to think of more novel gifts. In Birmingham one year I had spotted, slightly out of place, a fish tank stand in the exhibition, complete with live fish. I suggested to Chris the extremely novel idea of fish tanks as presents. These were no ordinary fish tanks, as they were designed to be built into a wall. They were quite expensive but Chris loved the idea (not so much spending the money). Together we chose fish and tank décor, weed, etc. We set all three tanks up, complete with fish swimming away, on a catering trolley. We then covered them with a tablecloth so they could be revealed accompanied by champagne and a thank you speech from Chris. (The ceremonies had now become more private in the green rooms and crew were rewarded separately.)

The novel gifts were gratefully received, except Jeremy donated his to me which I was most excited about and my boy loved. James did love his but had real trouble fitting it in his Porsche, so it was arranged that Bas or JCP would take it back to the office and arrange delivery to James's home from there.

Another crazy ceremony in London was when pizza bases had been used in the show as JC's fireproof pants. Chris came up with the idea that Gemma, myself and the newly recruited Katie (my assistant, and a friend of mine) should be dressed in pizza base bikinis to hand over the gifts. Making such outfits and sourcing original gifts along with often printing and framing pictures of some of the crazy antics that had gone on in that particular stage of the tour could be incredibly time-consuming. It was now part of my job to think of, organise and manage my newly appointed and unsuspecting runners, to gather and assemble everything we needed.

In Dublin, there was a Christmas fayre attached to the show which provided the perfect shopping opportunity for buying gifts for the presenters and creating a closing ceremony. When Chris and I got together, our crazy creative minds could go mad. We came up with the idea, as it was so close to Christmas, and slightly inspired by *The Late Late Toy Show*, of creating a Santa's Grotto for the occasion. The boys would be invited to meet Father Christmas and receive their gifts.

The idea grew and grew as we were inspired by loads of Christmas crap at the fayre. We bought a Christmas tree, decorations, lights and candles to transform the spare portacabin we had next to the green room. We bought antlers and red noses for Gem and me and a Santa suit for Chris. We made fake snow and a beard for Chris out of cotton wool. We used the hampers that Donnybrook Fair had given us and filled them with loads of 'special' presents for Jeremy, James and Richard. I wish I could remember them all because there were a lot of specially chosen, very funny, individual gifts for each presenter.

What I can remember was a toy megaphone for JC, which Father Christmas (Chris) gave to him as he felt he needed help projecting his voice; a toy firefighting kit for James in case anyone should set fire to his newspaper again; and a tin of baked beans for Richard as that was all he wanted one night when we were at a Michelin-starred restaurant. (Another mad moment, when as always, the restaurant staff were desperate to please their celebrity guests, so a member of staff was sent off to the nearest corner shop for beans so Richard could have his wish of baked beans on toast.)

And so another great show came to a successful end, and Chris and I met and praised the presenters as usual, rewarding them with a drink of their choice, back in the green room. Having managed to keep our Christmas Grotto a secret, we then announced we were taking them somewhere special for the closing ceremony. Chris left the room explaining he was just going to see if the car was ready, and after a planned five-minute delay I ushered them into the Rolls Royce Phantom that was ready and waiting outside. They were then driven all of about five yards to the door of the spare portacabin, where Gem and I greeted them with reindeer antlers on our heads and flashing red noses strapped on (I, having run around the back of the Rolls, dressing up as I went).

Inside, the rest of the Bubble and our travelling crew had assembled as a Christmas choir around the tree and were singing carols. The laughter began as soon as the Phantom stopped just five yards away and two 'reindeer' greeted the boys. I don't think I've ever seen the boys laugh so much, I mean proper joyous, tearful, hysterics. It was bloody brilliant to be part of, as one by one each presenter was called up to sit on Father Christmas's (Chris's) knee. Chris was a bloody genius at performing in this idiotic way, with brilliant improvisation, relevant to each individual. The tears of laughter rolled on. This closing ceremony went straight to number one in the closing ceremony charts.

And so to the airport to catch a private plane. I, loaded up with Donnybrook Fair delights, a large polar bear I had smuggled out of a Christmas display from a whiskey distillery that had entertained us for our crew party, and of course my 'Ming' vase that was so kindly presented to me on the way over.

Johannesburg, Sydney, Auckland, Hong Kong

Proper international touring

This was exciting. I have always loved travelling and have in fact been lucky enough to visit Africa a few times but to be travelling with three international celebrities, who I now considered my friends, as were the rest of the Bubble, was a bit special. I was reaching my 'career' goals, travelling, working with friends and most importantly having a bloody good laugh in the process. To be honest I have never really had any goals. I had just drifted into all this like a happy accident.

I had several planning calls with Gemma prior to our departure for South Africa. We were now firm friends and allies. Gemma had not long joined Brand Events, *Top Gear Live* was one of her first projects. She was thrown right in at the deep end trying to manage three quite unmanageable celebrities, well Jeremy in particular. Her main job was Brand Management, Marketing and Communications for this crazy motoring theatre show around the world.

Obviously, with the fame and following that *Top Gear* and our famous trio had, marketing it was a relatively easy task. It was managing to pin down any member of the trio to fulfil PR requests of TV, radio, editorial interviews and photo shoots that was challenging, as well as coordinating all their travel logistics, which could get very difficult as the live shows were being squeezed in around their already incredibly hectic filming schedules for *Top Gear* and their other individual projects. That also involved travel all around the world. A little-known fact is that if you work abroad as much as these guys did, you can have more than one passport, so one can be away getting a visa while another can be with you on your current trip. But another thing we always had to check and double-check was that each presenter had the right passport for the right trip. And yes, sometimes mistakes were made, but guess what, when you have a face as famous as our three boys and you fly first class or by private plane, you can get away with it.

I remember vividly meeting Gemma for the first time on site in Birmingham when she had to approach Jeremy to request him to do an interview to promote the forthcoming shows, something he hated and always argued that he had never had to promote his incredibly popular TV show. Why did he have to do this? Mmm, well it was a bit different when you don't have a media giant like the BBC busily promoting that for you. But you don't argue with Jeremy, you just have to try to persuade him gently or ask Richard and James to do it.

On this occasion Gemma approached me before stepping inside the Winnebago to confront the 'Bear'. She asked me if now was a good time. She was very anxious about approaching him as he was not always very welcoming, and also about whether he would say yes. She was under pressure from Chris, her boss, to get the job done. Having known Jeremy for nearly ten years by now, I was never afraid of approaching him. I was a good judge of his mood and he was usually polite and amenable to me. I offered to ask him for her. We decided our approach was for me to go in first to see if it was convenient for Gemma to talk to him and then she would follow accordingly. There was success on this occasion but this is how we continued. Gemma was really grateful for my insight and support. We became a great support to each other over the years and crazy times ahead and I was very grateful to have her by my side.

Anyway, back to preparation for Johannesburg, and one of my biggest responsibilities was to feed back any information on our three celebs' needs and preferences and to make sure I had about my person my now infamous essential kit bag with all their preferred medication, sweet treats, fags, lighters and nicotine gum, etc., etc.

For this leg of the tour it was just Richard and Jeremy. I think it was a combination of budget restrictions and also James's reluctance to be involved that there were just the two presenters. James claimed he hated the live shows, and to add more work and travel to his already hectic travelling and working schedule was not appealing to him.

To be honest we didn't really miss James. No disrespect to James but I think he would agree he really didn't like performing in the, what he described as, 'panto' style performances. He was generally quite morose in our Bubble apart from the rare outburst of frivolity. As he was often sat with shoulders slumped, head down and long grey hair hanging, Jeremy gave him the nickname of Eeyore. In fact, on recalling this I remember there was actually a big discussion in the green room, in London one year, deciding who would be who out of A. A. Milne's characters. Jeremy declared he would be Tigger, (annoyingly bouncy, loud and demanding?). Richard was either Roo or Piglet (for obvious reasons, although the anxiety of Piglet doesn't match RH; he should've been Roo – cute, cheery and small), and Chris would of course be Pooh, as both he and Pooh would stop at nothing for food.

My weekly shop at Tesco included buying all the special things for the boys. The checkout person must have thought

I was hosting a kid's birthday party and I was a huge nicotine addict as I piled up bags and bags of sweets and cigarettes. Gemma had emailed schedules to me for the whole trip and arranged for a car to pick me up to take me to Heathrow where we would all assemble. Gemma always arranged special services to escort all of us through security and into the first-class lounge. Although Gemma and I flew cattle class in the back, we were usually allowed to accompany Chris, JCP and the boys in the lounge.

We could then run any last-minute errands, such as shopping for razors, shaving foam, etc., therefore saving our celebs from enduring a fan-invading nightmare of a shop in the busy airport. Jeremy absolutely hated airports, what with the crowds and the security kerfuffle, which Chris also hated, so things could get quite stressful.

Comfortably ensconced in a luxury lounge, usually in a quiet corner, the silliness would begin. It was like being on a school trip except you could drink champagne, which Jeremy proclaimed you could drink any time of day on the occasion of flying. We were all more than happy to join him. Whilst drinking, eating and whiling away the time, there would be a lot of banter. There wasn't usually much talk of work, even though Gemma and I were at the ready with schedules and scripts jammed into our already overflowing bags. There were always arguments over what time we should leave to board: Chris and JCP would want to lead the charge and not take any chances in case we missed the flight, but Jeremy for one was adamant about not going too soon and therefore spending more time on the plane.

On one of our many trips, whilst hanging around for a flight, after having gone through the stripping-off and invasion of privacy procedure through security, Jeremy came up with the idea of setting up his own airline, called 'Take Your Chances Air'. His fantasy airline would provide an efficient service where you only had to arrive a maximum of an hour before you were due to take off, check in your hold luggage if you had any, and then move swiftly straight through the airport, with no security shenanigans, browse the shops if you chose to, or board and make yourself comfortable on the plane. A plane that would not be miles away from where you had arrived. Chancing that all your fellow passengers had no desire to kill themselves or anyone else by blowing the plane up.

This potentially great idea would lead to hilarious discussions and debate with Chris wondering why on earth security were worried about passengers carrying large bottles of moisturiser: 'What do they think passengers are going to do? Take over the plane by smothering the pilot in Nivea!?' Chris would demonstrate exactly what he meant when talking by huge gesticulation and acting out his ideas or tales. He was hilarious, very quick witted and imaginative. Jeremy would often remark that he was the funniest man he knew. We as a group were so often in tears with laughter.

Boarding the plane, Gemma and I would turn right and the others left to have a lie-down and more champagne. Gem always had heaps of work to catch up on and I just delighted in sitting still having someone wait on me and watching a whole movie. Life at home for me was in huge contrast to my work adventures. My boy, Alfie, who suffers from autism, never 'slept like a baby', as they say. I was constantly sleep-deprived and he was extra work compared to a neurotypical child. To get on a plane for a long-haul flight was a huge treat for me.

Upon arrival in Johannesburg, we were met by Denzel and Clinton, our security and drivers for our stay. Denzel had driven for the boys before, the last time they were in South Africa, and doubled as our security too. When he wasn't driving for VIPs he was a policeman and in South

Africa they are armed. The boys loved the fact that he was packing a Glock. (That's a pretty deadly handgun for those of you not used to dealing with arms. I am now but more of that later.) Clinton came on board as a trusted friend of Denzel's, and as far as I remember his other job was in IT but he was a great driver and generally a great and useful guy to have around.

We were swiftly driven to the venue, the Coca-Cola Dome in Johannesburg, a similar structure to our Millennium Dome (O2 Arena) and a venue that is as well known in South Africa for hosting big name events as Wembley is to us. The boys were excited to be back as they loved South Africa and this venue made it feel like real rock and roll touring.

We were greeted by the lovely Paul Edmunds, who headed up Brand Events in South Africa. He and his assistant Alex made us very welcome and showed us up to the green room, which was guarded by a security man who became known as 'the incompetent racist'. He was a very tall, intimidating, moustached chap, I assume of Afrikaner descent (they are known for their bluntness). To the boys' annoyance, he would not let in any of the catering staff, who were local black people, but would allow random, business-like white people to enter without question. Hilariously and bizarrely, he would often not recognise Jeremy or Richard (who were definitely not business-like), and would ask them for their passes, which they never had.

What became even more amusing was that during this visit to Jo'Burg, the door to the green room actually came off its hinges and the security man had to literally lift the door out of the way and then replace it once you were through. He rarely spoke and looked very miserable. The door remained broken throughout our stay, which summed up how difficult it was to get anything done in a hurry. Something that was largely due to the wonderful, laid-back culture of South

Africa, but that is very frustrating and difficult to work with when you are trying to put on a huge production and keep its stars happy.

Talking of stars, to make up for the absence of James and have some local influence, the show recruited Sasha Martinengo. Sasha is the voice and face of Formula 1 in South Africa. As well as TV presenting, he is a well-known club and radio DJ in South Africa. Jeremy and Richard really liked him and he fitted into the Bubble really well.

On this trip, which I felt honoured to be on, I kept my head down and got on with helping out wherever I could. It was, by our standards, a fairly sensible trip. The boys moaned about how they were kept in a darkened room with no windows, which they were. So I found a space outside that they could get to without going through the exhibition halls and being held up by fans. I was chuffed with my find, and I sourced sun loungers, chairs, tables and umbrellas for shade. All I had to do was clear what turned out to be quite a lot of dog poo from our proposed slice of paradise at the edge of the Dome. Not one to shy away from getting on with it, I stole paper towels, used by the mechanics for dealing with oil spills, etc. backstage, and bravely cleared the grass area by hand. Just as I was finishing off, Gemma led the boys out for a break. Having asked me what I was doing, and consequently laughing at me, they named their outdoor rest area 'Dog Shit Park'.

Once the mess was cleared up, the boys were very happy with their new space, where they could soak up the sun and smoke in peace. I had scored a few brownie points, that was, until the Saturday, the first full day of shows, when we quite quickly learnt that the huge audiences arriving and leaving the venue did so by walking across a flyover that went right over 'Dog Shit Park', turning it into something very similar to an animal enclosure at London Zoo, except that they weren't viewing gorillas, just something similar: *Top Gear* presenters. Excited fans couldn't believe their luck when they realised and started taking photos of the intriguing creatures below, relaxing eating pizza and drinking fizzy pop. The boys did see the funny side, naturally, and as usual we had a lot of laughs over it, mainly at my expense.

In contrast to Dog Shit Park was our home for the next few days, the Palazzo Montecasino Hotel in Sandton. Sandton is known as a safe and affluent area of Johannesburg, although, because it is known for being affluent, it isn't completely safe and is a great place for local muggers to take advantage of unsuspecting wealthy tourists. We were briefed accordingly by Denzel, who had a direct line to the police on duty and would report if there was anything going down, as they say. Denzel often got the heads-up on any shooting incidents that might affect our route to or from the venue.

The hotel is set in a huge resort area which includes a Las Vegas style casino and shopping mall, styled like a faux Italian plaza, which you could walk through to other, less starred hotels. Gem and I were staying in one of those, but we went over to the Palazzo for all our meals and to look after the boys.

There were the usual mad nights out and we were joined by Mindy, Richard's wife, who had flown out with their two girls to enjoy a short African adventure. Accident-prone Richard was actually hopping along with a crutch on this trip as he had fallen off a horse and injured himself. Doesn't seem to matter what sort of horsepower he messes around with, he still gets himself in trouble. Jeremy was as sympathetic as he always is and enjoyed having something else to jibe about, at Richard.

On this trip I was introduced to Patrón, which is Sasha's favourite after-dinner tipple accompanied with espresso to help you become 'flying drunk'. This became a favourite for all and fuelled us, after dinner, to endure another crew party which was a bit pitiful so don't go thinking it's rock and roll all the way. This crew party was not the best, despite having man about town Sasha on board. Somehow we ended up with the worst DJs in town, who looked like the characters Vicky Pollard and Lou Todd (Wheelchair Andy's carer) from the comedy sketch show *Little Britain*.

The only other memorable event from this trip was when Gemma was awarded her official tour nickname, 'The Boy'. Poor old Gemma had got food poisoning or a general stomach upset from somewhere (another downside to touring and one that affected most of us at some point along the way). All of us had a strong work ethic, and Gemma, stronger than most, had kept going until she could no longer and was confined to her bed and hotel room.

Chris, could be ruthless and harsh but deep down he had a soft centre, quite a large one actually, both physically and mentally. He was very fond and could be protective of Gem, who he valued a great deal. He demonstrated this by making a big effort to take time out from his busy business schedule to visit Gem in her hotel room and make sure she was OK, delivering her some comforting supplies. Which was lovely and very thoughtful of him.

When Gem was back on form and had joined the Bubble once again, Chris, true to form, then began to recall his visit to her and began explaining in detail to us all how he had uncovered her true identity and that she was in fact a boy! The evidence of this was largely based on the fact that she was watching football whilst trying to recover in her room, but Chris went on to embellish the story convinced that he'd seen her 'manhood' that had been exposed out of her dressing gown. Oh my God, poor Gem, Chris went on and on 'stuck on idle', as Richard would say, describing the scene in Gem's room and what he thought he had interrupted upon entering her room – you can imagine.

There were tears of laughter once again, accompanied by 'aww Chris!' as he went too far, as he so often did, in creating a crude picture of what he actually hadn't seen at all. Despite the shocking images he had put in our minds that we would probably sooner forget, Gemma became affectionately known as 'The Boy' from then on.

Another half a dozen successful shows over, it was time to fly home again and we were delivered safely back to Jo'burg airport by our ever-diligent duo, Denzil and Clinton, who helped fast-track us through the airport and carry our luggage. They loved us as much as we loved them. They were good solid guys, very professional and always there when you needed them, armed and ready in Denzil's case. Luckily, on this trip, no shots fired.

I say we flew home again, but actually it was just me that came home, while the rest of the Bubble flew onwards, sideways, backwards or whichever, which way, to Sydney, Australia, and then further down to New Zealand. Chris wanted me to do the whole section of this tour but he knew I had my boy, Alfie, to think about, so between us we decided I would leave the tour after Jo'burg and rejoin in Hong Kong about ten days later.

The boys would have to accept an Australian Horse. I was now always referred to as 'Horse', and anyone who took my place was referred to as 'Australian Horse', 'New Zealand Horse' or basically Horse, preceded by whichever country they were working in. Oh, apart from Katie, my friend, who had helped in London and who stood in for me now and again, and was known as 'Foal' because she was young and Chris decided she was actually my foal (just another little insight into Chris's mad mind). It was reported that no one was ever as good as the original Horse.

I would like to claim that, in the absence of my calming influence, all hell broke loose in Sydney. At a press conference, which many of you may in fact recall as it became worldwide news, Jeremy, whilst being interviewed by Australia's Jono Coleman, called our then prime minister, Gordon Brown, a Scottish, one-eyed idiot. This of course went down like a lead balloon with many.

Chris Hughes was rudely awakened in the middle of the night by the powers that be at the BBC, back in the UK. The senior and business members of the Bubble assembled to 'fight ever growing fires' for a good twenty-four hours or more. Jeremy, as ever, was reluctant to apologise. There were calls by the RNIB and others for him to be banned from performing. There were a few sweaty and tense moments for Chris. To be fair, it would have been pretty catastrophic for him and most concerned if the show could not go on.

I have been around Jeremy when he's been in trouble before with the world's press after expressing his controversial views, and it's not pretty. Although perfectly happy to shout out his outrageous opinions, he then does get into quite a state when coming under attack from those he's offended. Although his comments are so often on point and very amusing, he does tend to push the boundaries just a little too far. The ripple effects are huge and he detests being hounded by the paparazzi, which is one inevitable side effect.

He did eventually apologise for referring to Mr Brown's one eye, but in his defiant, schoolboy way, refused to apologise for calling him an idiot. Anyway, in the background, it was not only JC who received a telling-off from the BBC. Chris Hughes, who was accused of risking the *Top Gear* brand's future by putting Jeremy out there unleashed and unedited, had to accept new rules from then on. Our tour Bubble would never be the same. We would always be accompanied and watched over by a BBC official to make sure we never allowed Jeremy Clarkson to say or do anything controversial.

This was very annoying and also pretty pointless. Was anyone ever going to stop Jeremy doing or saying what he liked?

Of course, as the saying, goes, 'There is no such thing as bad publicity.' I think there might be, but in this case it did give *Top Gear Live* great exposure and so the tour rolled on to Auckland, New Zealand, and don't worry, you are not missing out on too many amusing stories because by all accounts things were a little tamer after the furore in Sydney, and of course New Zealand is a very conservative, well-mannered country so a perfect setting for the Bubble's behaviour to calm down.

Things weren't too calm behind closed doors, or on a private island in this case. The Bubble had some R & R in a secluded house with its own beach, pool and a boat at their disposal. The competitive sport of 'Girl Throwing' was invented. A game carried out in the swimming pool (would have been a bit harsh on land). The Bubble now had the lovely Meghan, part of the Oz/NZ ticket sales team, and Naomi, who became lead horse in my absence. These two game girls joined Gemma in this exciting new contest, getting launched across the pool by *Top Gear* presenters, the winner being the one who could throw their girl the furthest. Now there's a new TV show idea. (Of course, in this PC world of ours it would have to be 'Any type of person throwing'.)

Now in the full swing of rock and roll touring, including controversy and drama (they had a near-miss helicopter incident with a bird), the calming down was only going to last for so long. Whilst thinking up stupid games and luxuriating in their private beach house, there was unfortunately, for Chris, a chance for our hyperactive, naughty, schoolboy-like divas, to get bored. They demanded that the game of *Risk* be delivered to the house as soon as possible, and so there it was, the point at which there was no going back for the Bubble to never not act on the boys' every whim. A helicopter was sent from Auckland to land on the private beach and deliver *Risk*.

And so on to Hong Kong where I joined the crazy gang again. I remember this trip really well, starting with the fact of juggling life on my own with Alfie and never having enough sleep and therefore not being terribly organised. I packed in record time of forty minutes, literally zipping up my bag as the car arrived to pick me up.

Anyway, I made it and relaxed into another long-haul flight with an undercurrent of great excitement; one because I hadn't been to Hong Kong before, and two because I couldn't wait to get back amongst the Bubble and all the madness.

Hong Kong is brilliant for a Brit to visit as you have the wonderful experience of a totally different and quite unique culture, but due to it being under British rule for over 150 years everywhere is signposted in English, and there are huge numbers of ex-pats there and British influence all around, which makes for a very welcoming and easy arrival. This was a huge relief to me as I had to make my own way on a train into the city and the familiar luxury of the Grand Hyatt Hotel.

This hotel was one of the most amazing we stayed in throughout all the years of touring. It overlooked the famous Victoria Harbour and had the most ridiculously oversized foyer and reception. Jeremy and Richard had huge suites with their own butler and there was the most beautiful outdoor pool, spa and dining area, not on the rooftop where you might expect it, but halfway up the hotel's skyscraper building. The phrase coined by Richard, I believe, to describe Hong Kong was 'They don't fuck about.' Everything they built, cooked or provided as a service was brilliant and delivered with super efficiency, like the Star Ferry, with its quaint, old ferries linking Hong Kong Island to Kowloon. And of course any of the hundreds of tailors in the backstreets who could turn out a bespoke suit within twenty-four hours.

When I arrived, the Bubble had been there for a day already and enjoyed an adventure out on a chartered boat around the harbour, which I don't know much about because I was literally not interested – this is another Bubble phrase coined by Jeremy and used frequently, especially when Chris was delivering information about their itinerary, which often included his dreaded PR interviews. I am using it here, because if I wasn't there to enjoy the fun, I did not want to know.

I was soon part of the fun again, and upon my arrival I had to make a quick turnaround, freshen up and change ready for a night out. I was most excited for obvious reasons but also because I had some new shoes in the latest most fashionable style. I made my way down to the foyer to meet everyone, feeling rather good about myself as you do when you first wear new shoes.

'What are you wearing?' was the first thing I heard from Jeremy, swiftly followed by Richard, 'Oh my God!' and that was it, straight into an evening of cruel jibes about my shoes from everyone – well, actually, just JC, RH and Chris Hughes, who decided they were special needs shoes like the ones designed for those unfortunate enough to have one leg shorter than the other. In case you're interested, they were what I thought was a classy stone/donkey brown colour, but described by my 'abusers' as NHS brown or hearing aid beige. They were quite high, with a contrasting, fashionable black rubber wedge. The teasing went on all night.

Firstly, we enjoyed a cocktail at a hotel, right on the water, where we could watch the nightly, yes nightly (part of Hong Kong's not fucking about strategy), laser and firework display along miles of the waterfront. A display that could blow Sydney Harbour Bridge's New Year's display out of the water.

We then went to dinner at the top of one of Hong Kong's many skyscraper hotels, where we were all treated like superstars and were escorted up a spiral staircase to an exclusive bar which could only just fit all the Bubble in. After enjoying another cocktail we were then invited into a private dining room, like no other (until we got to Russia). It had the largest chandelier I have ever seen, central to a huge oval table, with chairs fit for royalty. One wall was floor to ceiling glass enabling incredible views over the harbour and the lights of the city's skyscrapers.

We were all quite overwhelmed and stood for a while aghast, which was shortly followed by overexcited giggling. Once we had settled into our luxury environment (not quite looking the part, Jeremy and Richard were never out of jeans, whatever the occasion, and obviously I was wearing my shoes!), we ordered from the incredible menu. We had advice from JC's friend, the late and very missed A. A. Gill, the *Sunday Times* food critic who Jeremy called – well you would, wouldn't you?

As we left, which was hard to do, given the surroundings, the usual incredibly discreet bill paying was done. So discreet that it often felt like we just left without paying, hence the boys coined the phrase 'Chris Hughes's cashless holidays'. This had a seriously bad effect on me. I got so used to just walking out after dinner that I once, whilst travelling alone to meet the tour, walked out of one of Gordon Ramsay's airport restaurants without paying, after enjoying a delicious meal and very agreeable large glass of wine. Sorry Gordon.

My first VIP evening in Hong Kong ended with Chris Hughes insisting he wore my shoes which was a terrifying sight, but none the less very funny.

The rest of our stay in Hong Kong was the usual whirlwind of nights out, lunches, sightseeing and of course performing. The pace was quite ridiculous. Jeremy and Richard were incredibly professional at bashing out changes to a script to make it more current and appealing to the nation they were performing to. By this time the scenes in the show were often familiar to them as they had been used elsewhere on tour. The challenge in Hong Kong was to work with a local, Marchy Lee, a well-known (in Hong Kong, anyway) Formula 3 driver.

Marchy couldn't speak or understand English very well so was accompanied by a friend who was his interpreter, and his girlfriend. They all arrived in a slightly diva-like way, much to the annoyance of the boys and the Bubble in general. Anyhow, once their hackles had gone down, Jeremy and Richard set about going through the script and rehearsals with Marchy. It did not go well.

Marchy clearly wasn't as experienced as JC and RH but had a lot of confidence so appeared onstage in true racing driver dramatic style, but too late, and then would jump in over Jeremy who was filling in for his lateness. When he did deliver his lines at the right time, it was very hard for JC and RH to know when he had finished as he was speaking in his native language, which was meant to help get any natives in the audience onside. It may have done, but it was hard to tell as the audience in general, including a lot of ex-pats, was not very expressive at all. They were the smallest audience the boys had played to so far and their lack of enthusiasm added to making the shows the most difficult to date for our presenters.

It was quite fascinating as a spectator to observe the reactions of different cultures around the world. South Africa was at this stage in the tour by far the best, hugely expressive, reactive and loud throughout the entire performance.

Australia was running second and London was definitely in last position until now. Trying to cope with a lacklustre audience and the incredibly cocky but amateur Marchy, and without any onstage chemistry between them, made our boys quite tetchy.

After a testing first performance, it was back to the hotel driven by the worst driver in the world, Edward ('but you can call me Eddie'). Eddie was a huge fan of *Top Gear* and was so excited to be driving for the boys but really couldn't. He was ever the professional with his meet and greet. He greeted the boys with a bow and was keen to point out that there was cold water available for them and sweets, every time. He tried very hard to contain his enthusiasm of being in the presence of JC and RH but couldn't help himself now and again and in very broken English expressed his joy at watching certain episodes of the TV show and tried to ask the boys questions. The boys were fond of him but not his driving.

I travelled with them as usual to and from the venue and these became the most amusing journeys. Richard would sit in the back with me and give a running commentary on Eddie's driving, with Jeremy chipping in now and again. Poor old Eddie was none the wiser as he didn't understand English well enough. I would be in belly-aching hysterics as Richard talked us through Eddie's dreadful gear changes with the poor old car's engine screaming out, followed by us passengers being flung backwards and forwards upon Eddie's totally unnecessary emergency braking. He drove like a racing driver who suddenly felt he was breaking the speed limit. When Chris heard about our experiences he said, 'Right we'll fire him.' The boys immediately protested, 'No you can't, we love Eddie.'

After a tough first show followed by a comedy drive back to the hotel with Eddie, Gemma told the boys they had time to freshen up but had to meet her in a conference room to give an interview to a few media peeps. There was a lot of moaning from the boys. I was told to meet them back in the foyer and escort them to the conference room. I was always in contact with the boys on my mobile and I got a text from RH confirming he'd made his own way, so I just waited for JC and we headed up to join him. On arrival there was only one journalist there, an attractive lady who was chatting to Richard. But as soon as JC walked in, in his bombastic way, she immediately turned her attention to him, literally following him to the coffee machine and around the room. After about two minutes, RH stomped off slamming the door behind him. By this time Chris had joined us and he sent me off after Richard and told me to take him to the bar for a drink and try to placate him before we were to get a quick supper.

I caught Richard up just as he was getting in the lift to disappear. It was just me and him, and I asked if he was OK and what had upset him. He launched into quite an angry outburst ranting on about Jeremy and most memorably declaring, 'It's not my fault I'm so short.' I found myself shrinking down against the lift wall as I felt I was towering over him and this would not help his mood. Plus I was quite scared as we were in such a confined space and he was not happy.

Richard and I ended up having quite a heart to heart as we had done on numerous occasions in the past. He always said I was just like his wife, Mindy, but twice the size! Mindy and I shared a passion for horses and the outdoor life. We were both a bit tomboyish but could glam up, like the best of them. I managed to pacify Richard, sympathising with him that he was tired, missing home and fed up of being antagonised by JC. Their relationship was like brothers, the bigger, older one picking on the smaller younger one. It was a love–hate relationship.

Unfortunately, the drama did kick off again later that evening as Chris had yet again pushed the boys to their limit by getting them to do a live Q & A as an after-dinner entertainment for the main sponsor of the show.

To be fair to Chris and JCP, who was always by his side, it was tough making the tour financially viable with all the costs of shipping cars, sets and crew around the world as well as the huge fees for the presenters and the rock and roll luxury lifestyle. It was often quite close to the wire and tensions ran high. To sell in a package to a sponsor of a dinner with exclusive access to the boys was a necessary evil.

The boys dutifully perched on bar stools, with Marchy Lee too, in front of hundreds of corporate guests, and answered questions. As usual JC dominated and led the proceedings, and I never knew what was said but all of a sudden RH was off again, exiting the stage at speed. JC smoothed things over and brought the questioning to a slightly premature end. By this time Chris and JCP had shot off after Richard. Gem and Bas were left looking after the sponsors and their guests and I went after JC who was now equally as riled as Richard.

Oh the drama. All tired, stressed, jet-lagged, homesick, hungover. A good hour went by trying to diffuse a huge Bubble family bust-up. Chris and JCP were with Richard and I was with JC in the gardens of the hotel trying to stay away from other guests. Eventually, after a few drinks and fags (RH was now actually on e-cigarettes and we did all wonder if that was affecting his mood. Richard also suffered from extreme tiredness, and memory loss after his infamous high-speed crash, and we all genuinely worried about him.), Chris walked RH back to his room for a good night's sleep and then joined the rest of us for the end of the party with the corporate guests, whereupon we let off steam having a gel-ball fight using the hundreds of gel-balls that filled the vases of the table decorations. These Malteser-size balls were totally harmless and bounced off your target's head at great speed. Another school trip moment to end the rather fraught day.

Thank goodness, the next day was a day of leisure until needing to prepare for the evening performance. Richard had a big lie-in and a very gentle day. I accompanied JC who had arranged to do a day's filming for the TV show, part of a review of the BMW X6.

We went to the beautiful Peninsula Hotel, where we met a cameraman who had organised a helicopter shot to be taken on the roof of the hotel. Another surreal day. We were treated like true VIPs and taken to the departure lounge on the top floor where we met the pilot. JC and the cameraman discussed how they were going to film. Although JC only needed the helicopter as a backdrop and for a short scene of the view flying over the vast skyscrapers, the pilot offered to give us a flight around all of Hong Kong's numerous islands. It was amazing! How lucky was I! Jeremy was also very grateful, and in contrast to when he was spending Chris Hughes's money, he did not want to abuse the pilot's generosity. Much to my frustration, as he turned down extending the flight to fly over the giant Buddha on Lantau Island. He could be surprisingly humble and conservative at times. That or he desperately wanted a fag.

To top it off, on our return we were taken to the opposite end of the hotel to be shown the record-breaking fleet of fourteen Rolls Royce Phantoms with extended wheelbase and a 1934 Rolls Royce Phantom II restored to its former glory. OMG, Hong Kong really doesn't fuck about!

Completing his workaholic's day off, Jeremy and I then went with the cameraman to film a very quick shot of Jeremy with a BMW X6. Forever thinking about work, he had come up with the idea, whilst on tour, to take advantage of being all over the world. With his usual creative genius he created a story on the new BMW. He filmed with it in many different countries with the premise of working out where it belonged and its purpose. This involved many short clips of him in Spain, Sydney, the highest ski resort in the Alps, Hong Kong, of course, and ending in Barbados, where he was making the point that he'd rather spend the money on a holiday there than purchase an X6. The finished article was introduced in true *Top Gear* style by James May saying, 'Our instructions to Jeremy were very, very specific, keep it cheap and simple.'

Apart from completing another long weekend of shows, we managed to fit in lunch on the beach, shopping, sightseeing, a night at the horse racing, and a monumental crew party and closing ceremony.

Our night at the races, whilst filled with the usual hilarity, had presented us with a new challenge. There was a dress code of no jeans, but jackets and collared shirts were a must. Jeremy was OK, because he usually travelled in a formal jacket and he had in fact packed a special one he had previously had made on a trip to Asia. He coupled this with a new pair of beige combat trousers. Although not terribly stylish his look would gain him entry. Luckily no ties were needed (one of his pet hates).

Richard on the other hand was only ever seen in jeans, T-shirts and a leather jacket. I was tasked with going shopping and finding him a suitable outfit, while they were performing. There was a lot of advice about what I should buy, from JC and Chris, you can imagine.

I was so tempted to have a laugh with my choices, but given that Richard was a little fragile at this time, after his little outburst (for which he apologised, by the way), I played it reasonably safe. It was tough enough anyway given that a formal shirt and casual slacks were not his style. Off I went, armed with cash and Richard's measurements, to have another surreal moment – I'm in Hong Kong, shopping for Richard Hammond. He was quite accepting of my choice and we had a great night out. Jeremy's tailor-made purple silk jacket clashed beautifully with Richard's new shirt and Bas's tropical number.

Chris decided to have a huge crew party and closing ceremony to celebrate the end of the first successful, proper tour. Gemma and I were tasked with booking the poolside bar area exclusively for us, at our hotel, for a champagne reception. There, Jeremy and Richard would award every crew member with a present and a personal thank you. The moment was to be captured in true ceremony style with a commemorative photo, also awarded to each crew member. The ceremony was of course hosted by Chris, who had thought of something to say about everyone. He was a genius at that.

The presents were belts, which Jeremy had found on a shopping trip and Chris had been inspired by. They had digital screens fitted to them into which you could type a message. After a runner was tasked with purchasing dozens of them, our poor tour photographer/techy was tasked with entering all the special messages that Chris had come up with, into each belt. I obviously can't remember them all but I know mine said 'Horse'. Gemma's said 'The Boy', Richard's said 'Dick', and JC's said 'C**t' or something similar.

Gem and I, along with our local hosts, sourced a nightclub that we had exclusively until 11pm when members of the public would be allowed in. There we were entertained by a band that had been briefed and was prepared to accept what became known as 'band-jacking'. Jeremy and Richard would take over the drums and bass guitar, while Chris would get on vocals, accompanied by Gem and me as backing singers.

That was a night and a half. Despite monumental hangovers, the boys went on to perform their finale for this first tour. Spirits were high but there was a sense of 'We wanna get home now.' A few pranks were being plotted and I was party to all. Jeremy and Richard were planning their farewell, parting line, and Chris was planning a special message for the boys, to be delivered whilst they were performing.

An urban myth had been created about James Cooke-Priest, who was the sensible, handsome, well-dressed, urbane one amongst us. James was often tucked away in an office at the venues, managing the finances, etc., or out meeting potential new sponsors or hosts for the show. If he was out and about, he was often seen charming attractive ladies and it was constantly joked about that he stole Chris's chances.

The myth was that he lured women back to his hotel room, never to be seen again, and that he was actually a serial killer. In the green room or at our numerous dinners this story was embellished more and more, mainly by Chris and the boys. It now was suggested that he had a van which he used to dispose of bodies, some of which he had supposedly skinned. Through all these crazy tales being created, the phrase 'Get in the fucking van' had been coined. It was imagined that James would have to shout this out to Chris, who he normally travelled with, upon leaving a city or country. According to the myth it was in order to avoid being caught for his murders. The phrase had been adopted by all of us, to be used in any situation that you needed to get out of, in a hurry.

On the back of this, whilst Jeremy was trying to think of a fitting last line on which to end the show and the first official tour, I suggested that both Jeremy and Richard shout out, as they walked offstage from their final performance, 'Get in the fucking van!' As a special surprise, for all the Bubble. Nobody else, of course, would have a clue what they were talking about.

None of us from the Bubble were going to miss this finale. We had reserved a whole row of seats to enjoy the show together, which was a rare opportunity as usually one or more of us was needed elsewhere.

Meanwhile, Chris had planned to deliver a special message to the boys and he commandeered Gem and me to laminate sheets of A4 with letters that would spell out 'YOU C**TS'. He then handed them out, in order, to the rest of the Bubble. On Chris's cue, just as Jeremy and Richard had arrived onstage and finished their hellos, we all held up our cards spelling out the special message which of course only Jeremy and Richard could see. It was a classic moment to see them both stifle laughter and stumble through their intro. We were in tears of laughter once again.

And then Chris whispered to me, 'We haven't organised a closing ceremony.' I said, 'We've had one.' 'Well yes,' he said, 'but we can't end without a bit of a party, backstage.' So off I went, and within fifty minutes, with the amazing help of the venue staff and their 'We don't fuck about' attitude, I had organised for a bar with champagne, dressed tables and chairs, and food to be served out on the balcony where the famous ceremony of Chris Patten handing over Hong Kong had taken place.

I got back to my seat just in time to enjoy the 'Get in the fucking van,' final line. Mass hysterics broke out from the Bubble as a bemused Hong Kong audience looked on.

Whilst racing backstage to greet the boys and guide them onto the balcony for a much deserved glass of champagne, Gem and I decided we could dress in our kimono style dressing gowns that we had been given to present Jeremy and Richard with their end of tour gifts.

Chris decided he wanted to present us, presenting the gifts and ordered us to hide on luggage trolleys covered in tablecloths, to provide a further element of surprise. What a way to finish an epic start to our world touring. In much laughter, champagne and emotion.

It's such a shame Hong Kong has changed so much since then.

Back to Reality

London, Birmingham and Dublin again

The next time the Bubble reassembled was for what had now become our annual October/November visit to London and Birmingham, having had a much-needed seven-month break from touring. From the end of October 2008 till the end of February 2009, the boys had been on the road almost permanently, as when they weren't in the Bubble of *Top Gear Live* they were filming for their individual projects and of course the TV show.

During that first tour they had performed over fifty shows to over 280,000 people. The shows continued to evolve, with a combination of Rowly and his team, Andy Wilman and the boys' imaginations coming up with more ridiculous ideas to continue to entertain their huge fan base.

Amongst these crazy ideas was Reliant Robin racing, which I loved watching every single time. It was hilarious. It started out with six Reliants, with JC, RH, JM, Paul Swift and some of his team racing round an oval in the arena. However, this became unsustainable as the Reliants rolled over so easily that they would often pile up and hold up the racing, so this evolved into just the three presenters racing with the Stig. This allowed for the comedic rolling over of the Reliants to occur, but only one or two would go at any one time, enabling backstage crew to roll them back onto their wheels again, which was a spectacle in itself, to see two burly crew flip the Reliant the right way up while a Clarkson, Hammond or May wobbled about inside. Meanwhile, the others could carry on racing.

Generally, this was not choreographed, so every race was different but would always include a lot of contact and shunting into one another. Jeremy even managed to lower the tone by suggesting he was mating with Richard Hammond as he got literally up RH's back end, with his Reliant bonnet under RH's back wheels so they were conjoined (what a hideous thought, Jeremy and Richard mating). The boys were miked up so any incident like this was commentated by all three of them. In this instance you could mainly hear Richard shouting 'Stop, stop it, I don't like it,' whilst Jeremy shouted, 'Children, look away.'

The only attempted choreography was Jeremy throwing himself into the last corner so he ended the race on his side and the camera that was filming the whole stunt went close in, on Jeremy's fat face in a helmet almost filling the whole Reliant's windscreen (which had been removed, along with all the other windows, for obvious safety reasons).

The boys did generally enjoy this racing, but not after the twenty-seventh time, with many more to go, after being soaked in petrol (as often happened) and bashed about as they were, despite neck protection, full racing harnesses and helmet. It was hugely amusing to watch.

Other more gentle races were created for scenes where the story was that the presenters had been challenged with inventing vehicles using alternative sources of power, and with varying themes such as the garden machinery challenge, the smallest car challenge and the household appliance challenge.

These challenges saw the birth of Jeremy's Flymo-powered hovercraft, Richard's strimmer-powered 'Easy Rider' motorbike and James's chainsaw-powered sun lounger, the latter being the most comedic to watch as James raced around the arena in a very relaxed way, literally lounging on his lounger, with his hair flying behind him.

The smallest car challenge brought to life Jeremy's jet-powered car designed in the shape of his trademark jeans and jacket that he climbed into so he looked like he was wearing it. Unfortunately, the incredibly loud and powerful jet engine brought with it a whole heap of troubles, so it was soon abandoned and replaced by another vehicle – based on a mobility scooter – that you may well have seen on the TV show.

James's was the most successful, a motorised suitcase, basically a suitcase that opened up, had extra wheels fitted to it, a seat that could be dismantled and stored in the case, and was powered by a very small engine. Richard's was based on a child's trike, which was later replaced by just a basic plastic chair, like the ones you find in a doctor's waiting room. The basic bucket type seat was mounted on very small wheels barely off the ground and had steering controls made of power drills.

My favourites of all these vehicles were those derived from household goods. Jeremy's was the biggest of course, a huge dragster style vehicle made of twelve food blenders in a 'V' formation, three fridges lying end to end, microwaves and a Dyson ball on the front for steering. It was ridiculously long, which was one disadvantage to getting around the relatively small circuit. As Jeremy said at one point, 'I'm winning and losing at the same time' – he would have a nose in front of the other two but it took him ages to get the whole vehicle to catch up. The second disadvantage was it had to be plugged in and had a hugely long power cable. In fact, thinking about it, I don't know how they managed that race without getting tangled up, but of course they made it work.

Richard lay flat out on an articulated ironing board, powered and mounted on food blenders and steered by irons. I do remember that there were moments when he was nearly decapitated by Jeremy's cable. One of the lines in the scene was about the potential for him to have a catastrophic accident trapping his manhood between two of the boards as he lay face down hurtling around corners.

My favourite, James's, was made out of washing machines that he sat in. You could only just see his stupid face peering out of a top loader, with his hair flowing behind him once he got his speed up. The wheels were made out of washing machine drums. The whole thing looked like something out of *The Flintstones*. He finished the race but was still shaking away in the machine and he had to ask Richard to press the off switch, to which Richard replied, 'I've never operated a washing machine before.' However, he dutifully stepped forward and pressed a button at which point James whizzed off, shouting, 'You idiot that's the fast spin cycle.' Bit of a pantomime but very comedic to watch. The scene ended with loud clattering and banging coming from backstage where James had disappeared to.

Most of these vehicles were put together by a very talented group of mechanics headed up by Steve, who had started out by creating a jet-powered bicycle for Jeremy which was extremely temperamental and dangerous. After several incidents of Jeremy nearly having his backside set on fire and the jet engine refusing to start, despite the huge comedic appeal as JC hurtled across the arena on a jet-propelled bicycle, there were too many failed starts or near misses, so Steve and the bike were sent on their way. Nobby and Dave and their amazing team took over for the rest of the tour.

In the Bubble things carried on as usual, with nights out in top-class restaurants with private dining, plus the usual heavy drinking and hilarity, but it was noted that being in London or Birmingham was not as good as looking out over Sydney or Hong Kong Harbour in the sunshine.

I helped Gemma research alternative accommodation in Birmingham, as now the tour had raised its game we needed to keep the boys happy and keep them onside to endure the next tour. We looked into hiring whole houses and employing chefs, or going further out of town to country house hotels where the likes of Take That had stayed. However, we settled on a boutique hotel in the city centre which was apparently where Simon Cowell stayed when he was in Brommyville.

The funniest story I can remember from this visit to Birmingham was when we had a logistical problem getting everyone from the NEC back to the hotel for dinner one night, so instead of using a professional driver I was nominated to drive the boys in the Range Rover that we had for the duration of our stay. (The Range Rover press office were very good to us over the years. Of course, they were delighted to have the boys using their vehicles as a great PR opportunity; nevertheless, they went over and above to accommodate our demands.)

Having worked in the motor industry for many years and driven dozens of different cars, I was not daunted by the prospect. The boys had experienced my driving before and complimented me, which was praise indeed. The only concern I had was finding my way through the centre of Birmingham; however, Jeremy was already on it and sat up front taking on the task of setting the satnav that even he struggled with as they are constantly updated.

Off we went, James and Richard in the back, who started bickering over cars. Both of them were often on the lookout for new 'toys' and were frequently carrying a car or bike mag around, to browse through. Their debate got rather heated. Meanwhile, Jeremy had set the satnav in his preferred style, not mine, and I found it hard to read and anticipate when to turn off at roundabouts and slip roads. I pointed this out to him and asked if he could change its format as it was confusing me. Not one for taking instructions, and adamant that his way was the best, he left it as it was. I missed a turning. I felt mortified as it was getting late and it could take ages to get back on the right road again. Jeremy told me not to worry and just let the satnav work it out. But I noticed we had passed a road that was familiar to me and was sure it was part of the route back to the hotel. Jeremy and I got into a bit of an argument, as did Richard and James, who were still ranting on in the back. I eventually got the giggles as the satnav took us deep into a council estate in deepest darkest Birmingham. I said, 'God, this is like a family trip with the kids arguing in the back.' We were definitely lost but at least we didn't stand out too much – three very well-known faces in a brand new Range Rover!

Not afraid to speak out when necessary, I told them all to shut up and stopped the car. I checked on my phone again for the postcode of the hotel. It became apparent that Jeremy had put the wrong postcode in. Turns out he's not always right. He blamed it on being deaf. Soon we were on our way again and safely arrived at our luxury hotel. Another surreal moment, I'm sure you will agree.

In early December we were off again to Dublin, this time taking a private plane from Oxford Airport. The Bubble reassembled in the tiny airport lounge and the laughter soon began. Soon we were up and away with James sat up front as he was a flying fanatic (he has his own plane). James loved to observe all the instruments and the route plan and often sat right up front with headphones on talking directly to the pilot.

Meanwhile, the rest of us enjoyed a light in-flight snack, and a few drinks of course. It was dark outside and Jeremy suddenly exclaimed, 'There is something following us, there is a plane bloody close! Oh Christ I bet it's bloody paps.' We all stared and strained our eyes to try to see what he was seeing. A few of us becoming anxious, not about the paps but the fact that another aircraft might be flying so dangerously close.

Much to our amusement, we soon realised that what Jeremy was seeing were lights at the end of our plane's wing. OMG, did he get a ribbing for it. The usual hysterics commenced with both Chris and Richard coming up with ideas of how exactly a pap might be following us. Such as, the pap had obviously attached a ladder to the wing and climbed up with a long lens and flash. I loved these moments when even Jeremy was in tears of laughter. Yet again we were enjoying our own very special private party.

We were met at the airport by the same driver, Eddie (not the one from Hong Kong, this Eddie could definitely drive), in his wonderful Rolls Royce Phantom. Once again, the boys travelled in ultimate style and Chris, JCP and I went ahead in a Range Rover. Gem and Bas had arrived a day or so earlier making preparations. We headed once again to the Four Seasons to make ourselves comfortable.

Next day at the venue, there was a slightly different set-up. It had a Christmas fayre again, but alongside that outside was a small funfair with bumper cars, a big wheel and all the usual food and drink outlets to accompany what had been branded The *Top Gear* Funfair. This was our first problem.

Since the drama in Australia with 'Gordongate', we were now accompanied by at least one representative from the BBC. Here in Dublin we were joined by Duncan and Adam from BBC Worldwide. The funfair had been branded illegally and not to the usual high standards of the BBC. Immediately, there was tension and panic as Chris got it in the neck from Duncan and Adam, heavily bolstered by a very agitated Jeremy who was always very protective over what had effectively become his brand. He hated Chris threatening it and was not shy in letting him know.

The atmosphere had changed dramatically from our little jolly on the plane. The situation was quite quickly rectified with Chris and James Cooke-Priest getting rid of anything that wasn't appropriate. In fact it wasn't actually Chris's fault. It was the Irish host that had taken liberties but of course Chris was ultimately responsible. Situations like this were quite frequent along the way. The Bubble was continuously on a roller coaster of emotions.

During times like these I kept my head down and I was being ably assisted by Foal, AKA Katie, who was my brilliant right-hand woman. One of her shining moments on this leg of the tour, and possibly her most surreal moment so far in life, was successfully completing a mission to set off with Eddie in the Roller and collect fresh oysters and McDonald's for lunch for our hard-working trio in a very short space of time.

Eddie was a legend who shone on several occasions. He was prepared to loan his Phantom to become part of the show and have graffiti style words with some innuendo message stuck on with special tape, which was then removed so it could return to its usual duty as a beck and call chauffeur service.

The Bubble's most epic night out on this trip to Dublin was back to Lillie's, with me in tow this time and with strong intention to catch up where I'd missed out before. The evening ended with more jamming, I think with the drummer from U2, but I'm really not sure, I was too far gone. The morning, however, I do remember. It was a morning of probably some of the worst hangovers so far, within the Bubble. Even the hardened drinkers that the boys were, they were seriously suffering.

I was travelling with the boys in the Phantom for some logistical reason. I was in such a bad way that it was suggested I travel up front to try to decrease my nausea. I ended up having to hang my head out of the window and was praying to not be sick.

However long the journey was, it was too long. I seriously got in a panic when we hit traffic. The traffic was our own audience arriving. We usually arranged our schedule to avoid this happening, but as you might imagine we were running late, and it wasn't just my fault. We were now at risk of being late for the start of the show.

We had no need to fear: Eddie came to the rescue and pulled a cheeky stunt. He drove the wrong way up a slip road to get ahead of the trouble. The boys couldn't believe it and loved his boldness. I guess if anyone was going to get away with it Eddie was, with three very famous people on board desperate to get to their own show. I still had my head out of the window.

We made it, but only just, and we had to run up several flights of stairs to get to the green room and get the boys miked up. I still felt drunk and was giggling in between feeling like I might throw up at any moment. I did. I managed to save myself from further embarrassment by swallowing it. I immediately shared my experience with the boys expressing my thanks to Richard for inspiring me as I recalled one of his finest moments in Earls Court.

Richard was introducing the first show of the day with Jeremy and Tiff. Whilst Tiff was delivering his line Jeremy noticed Richard looking uncomfortable with his head down and his shoulders slightly convulsing. Jeremy asked RH off-mike, 'Are you OK?' 'I am,' came the reply, 'I've just been sick in my mouth but it's OK I've swallowed it.' Jeremy pronounced that this was the height of professionalism and had new-found respect for his small co-presenter. And the band played on.

In Dublin, Jeremy, Richard and James fuelled themselves with Berocca, coffee, Nurofen or paracetamol, whatever it took to get them onstage. I being a lightweight had a lie-down. I don't know how those boys did it, barely sober from the night before, continuously gathering themselves to get out onstage, shout and laugh, whilst driving around in circles at speed. They were true rock and roll heroes.

The closing ceremony was created accordingly. It was early December so we went with a Christmas theme again, but with a very gentle approach, given the hangovers and general exhaustion after a very busy year or so. It was decided to create a relaxing 'family Christmas'. Foal and I set up the green room with a cosy Christmas feel including a Christmas tree and presents for all of the Bubble, so we could all sit around the tree and unwrap them together with mince pies and sherry. We sourced a suitable movie to watch after Chris's speech (instead of the Queen), and the comedy came in the form of Christmas onesies for the boys. Jeremy looking the most ridiculous of them all.

It was perfect, an incredibly funny sight to see Jeremy, James and Richard in their onesies, cosy, content and relaxed.

Meet Beau Vas Deferens

After Christmas at our respective homes, we were soon out on the road again, in January, to Amsterdam. James had opted out again so it was just the tallest and the smallest presenter scheduled to entertain the Dutch.

On arrival at Schiphol Airport there was the usual kerfuffle, with Chris, panicking over whether Gemma and I had made sure there were no hold-ups exiting the plane. To assist this process, the talent always had the front row of seats on the plane and we prearranged for VIP Services to escort us through security and passport control, to make things as smooth as possible with as few hold-ups as possible. Jeremy was not very tolerant of hold-ups, especially when his endless need for nicotine was not satisfied.

The usual routine was for Chris to march ahead with the talent, flanked by security. Meanwhile, Gemma and I would collect all the luggage, often leaving me to manhandle trolleys and carry all I possibly could (a duty which fortified my nickname of Horse), while she leapfrogged ahead and checked that the convoy of Range Rovers was in place and that the highest-spec one was assigned to the presenters. I travelled with them as usual, taking note of any new requests to keep them happy. Chris and Gemma took the lead Range Rover, making last-minute phone calls to check all was ready at either venue or hotel, depending on where we were heading.

On this occasion we went straight to the venue and were met by the local event team, who showed us to the green room. Amsterdam was one of the most well-equipped and stylish green rooms we had had all tour. The room had been created within exhibition space, backstage of the main arena. It was dressed with white muslin drapes, and fitted with contemporary furniture and lighting, a decent and fully operational coffee machine, and a large surround sound TV. The Dutch had got it right, much to our celebs' delight. There was also a superb and amusing accessory, a smoking booth – a futuristic-looking cubicle, like a very modern looking Tardis, with top to bottom clear panels so the needy smoker could step in, lean on a built-in shelf with ash trays, but not feel cut off from everyone as he could still see and hear everyone in the room. Meanwhile, his smoke was sucked out through some kind of extraction system. Genius! Of course, after the initial novelty wore off, our famous smoking duo were too lazy to move from their agreeable chairs and, in their rule breaking way, puffed away *in situ*.

After a quick fag and coffee it was time to view the arena and give the other stars of the show, the cars, a once-over. It was routine for the presenters to arrive 'onstage' in the arena at speed in supercars, and then there was a whole cast of stunt cars and novelty vehicles, such as the Roman style chariots pulled by a herd of motorcycles as alternative horsepower. The boys never failed to be excited by some new supercar or one of their old favourites in the motorised cast that was part of what was known as Car Porn, a regular feature in all the shows.

This backstage area was always pretty much the same. We often had to remind ourselves of where we actually were in the world. A dark, black-curtain-lined, fume-filled mixture of garage, pit stop and prop store was created and precision managed by the incredibly hard-working crew, headed up by the unflappable, amazing Simon Aldridge who endured the tour from start to finish along with a core crew.

As the boys perused the car porn and boys' toys, there was more kerfuffle as the local presenter appeared, accompanied by their entourage. They were usually easily recognisable, dressed in slightly flashy designer clothes and shiny shoes, topped with highly coiffured hair, most unlike our famous trio who were in their usual jeans and abused shoes, with hair which wasn't sure which way it had been dragged through a hedge. Credit where credit's due: Jeremy, despite his well-worn bottom half, come showtime would have a freshly pressed clean shirt – clearly not pressed by him but amazingly, packed with care, so at least a small part of him looked presentable.

The 'new boy' would often be hovering in the background for a slightly awkward amount of time, waiting for the nod from Big Chris allowing the approach towards our 'Messiahs'. Showing a mixture of excitement and fear, in awe of meeting his idolised new temporary colleagues, the 'new boy' would move in for what was actually a polite handshake and perfectly normal introduction. Dear Chris was so often the cause of a kerfuffle through his desperate anxiety of not wanting to upset the main men.

Here in Amsterdam, the local talent was a very handsome, tall, shiny jacketed Beau van Erven Dorens. Known affectionately to the Bubble as Beau Vas Deferens (google vas deferens to get the gag).

Time was spent in the green room going through the script, and Beau's important role was to provide local knowledge, current news and cultural insights to help create a bespoke performance to get the Amsterdam audience onside. After a few hours of laughter, comedy translation, espressos and fags, there was a smooth transition into a few beers and a call to get the Range Rovers ready to head back to the hotel.

Although the local presenter was there to provide any necessary translation, in Amsterdam the show was mainly delivered in English, but the boys would always take time to learn the local language for their big entrance. This often involved a comedy twist, such as Jeremy introducing Richard, in Dutch, as a 'big penis'. Richard, blissfully unaware, would graciously and humbly accept the huge applause, mingled with what he thought was friendly laughter.

After a quick freshen-up at our quirky and incredibly expensive boutique hotel, Chris, Gem, myself and the boys headed out for dinner in the usual VIP style. As all was under control at the arena we would later be joined by the remaining Bubble members; Bas, James Cooke-Priest and Rowly.

On this occasion we were taken out of town to a unique farmhouse-style restaurant, probably Michelin starred. It was a cosy setting and we had a large table taking over most of the restaurant, which was more like being in someone's private house. We were joined by our Dutch hosts, two businessmen and Fascal, who you may remember had visited Birmingham to find out what the show was all about and beat me at arm-wrestling. The businessmen had formed a partnership with Brand Events to put on the show.

I can't remember ever having an evening without laughter. In fact we were often instructed by the Piggy-Eyed Businessman to make sure we were upbeat and to encourage laughter, disguising any negative issues such as low ticket sales or broken show vehicles. Traditionally, the first night in a city was usually a reasonably quiet one. However, this first night the boys were well oiled, literally, having been on the road so much, and now had no fear of making a night of it especially as the performances had become so familiar to them. If there were new scenes, they were brilliant at learning lines and getting to grips with new props and vehicles. Even with a hangover, that's what I call a true professional.

Over dinner I can actually remember it being quite civilised at one point, playing on a 'name that bird' app, surprisingly the feathered type. Believe it or not, Jeremy is quite a twitcher, while Richard is a country boy at heart and had introduced the app to the table. Maybe it was the appearance of a Shag, a sea bird, that got us lowering the tone. Somehow a game, Celebrity Sex Shop Sweep, was created. Having abused the kind, extended hospitality of the restaurant, we ordered our fleet of Range Rovers to drop us off in the middle of the red-light district, where we were given fifteen minutes to visit a sex shop and buy a present for a colleague. This was one of those moments when you thought, 'Well I didn't see this coming during my careers talks at school!'

Surreal, there I am jumping out of a top-of-the-range Range Rover with Richard Hammond and Jeremy Clarkson, running into a sex shop late at night to choose a gift for my colleague. I can't actually remember what I bought – my mind has blanked and been scarred by the ones I do remember. We headed back to the hotel, where Gemma had put a last-minute call in to book a conference room, complete with flip chart which was used to draw diagrams to explain some of the toys. With plenty of booze flowing, we began to present our gifts one by one to each other. Gifts such as the Master of Anal Authority, a very large silicone cone, gifted to Mr Beau Vas Deferens, I believe. Richard Hammond was given a head harness and gag with a large penis attached. Jeremy received, from the Piggy-Eyed Businessman, a package that was labelled 'Yes we did it, Anus and Vagina!' A large silicone set of buttocks with two access points. When awarded your gift, you had to unwrap it and talk through it. (See photos – Richard has always worried he would be blackmailed with this one. I haven't blackmailed him. I've just printed the photo.)

Dear Bas was left to clear the conference room of our new toys, as we all headed to the hotel restaurant. It was closed, but in true rock and roll style we demanded a nightcap, which was duly served. (When I say 'we demanded', I mean our Tour Manager, AKA The Piggy-Eyed Businessman, Chris, would order myself or Gemma to leave the current party and not accept anything but a Yes from the hotel, whether it meant large cash tips to the night staff or an order to add any extra charge to the company account. A No was never acceptable.) By the time the now drunk and jolly presenters arrived, the restaurant was cleared of the following morning's breakfast settings and was rearranged and ready, candles and all, as a drinking den. There we spent the next few hours demanding bespoke snacks from the kitchen and sinking nightcap after nightcap, which Bas eventually joined in on, having stashed the majority of our sex toy emporium in his room.

Sadly, in the early hours of the morning, when we had all finally retired to our rooms, Bas had a call from home. A member of his family, having battled with illness only had days to live. Bas got on the earliest flight home that he could, after helping to set up the extensive array of supercars in the exhibition and show that he had diligently worked twenty hours a day to organise whilst touring the rest of the world. He was torn, but family won out and he headed home.

That morning demonstrated the family-like camaraderie we had. After one of the funniest nights ever, with many tears of laughter, Bas's family news was felt by all of us. There was no moaning about hangovers, just tears of sadness and hugs all round.

Gemma, a good friend and colleague of Bas for many years, arranged for the hotel to pack his bags and have them put into store, in order to release Bas's hotel room and so he could set off direct from the venue as soon as possible. Gem and I would then ensure that his remaining luggage was on our return flight.

The next few days and sequence of events are not entirely clear but I know the script run-through and dress rehearsal went ahead, followed by what was secretly referred to as a full rehearsal but was in fact the first show. Dear Beau unfortunately went down like a lead balloon with the audience. It was as if Judy Finnigan had been sent out, not ideal for hungry for it, beered-up *Top Gear* fans.

Fortunately/unfortunately Beau was called away to another job involving a charitable commitment of his which meant he couldn't perform in the next show. So quite swiftly, it was decided that Beau, who was effectively standing in for James May, was 'let go', as Chris put it. Whilst discussing with RH and JC what to do Chris acted out the 'We are going to have to let you go' scene by raising an arm and opening his fingers as if letting go of a balloon. As the tour went on he used his unique sign language as a threat if you were about to let him down or had indeed made a mistake.

Next, or possibly during that first show, an emergency call was put in to James May and he was somehow persuaded to come and stand in for his stand-in Not just while he was off doing his charity stint but to stand in for his stand-in for the rest of the weekend.

So despite Beau only actually performing in the first show, he was 'let go' of quite amicably and joined us on that evening's novelty night out, prior to James's arrival. We were driven by Range Rover, of course, to a barge on one of Amsterdam's infamous canals. It was exclusively for the Bubble and was suitably loaded with supper and enough alcohol to sink a barge, of course!

And so we set sail. Spirits were high and heightened still by this fun, novel way of having supper whilst taking in the night-time, illuminated sights of Amsterdam. I don't know if you have ever been on a traditional barge but it's actually not the best way to see the sights, especially at night, as you are relatively low down and the windows are small. There is very little outside space except for walking precariously around the narrow edge of the entire vessel which is around 100 ft in length.

However, our new, now 'sacked', boy was not down about his downfall and proceeded to demonstrate the way to maximise our sightseeing. He leapt, like a gazelle, onto a table, opened a hatch and invited those willing and able, to join him for a guided tour. Standing on tables and viewing the sights, beer and fags in hand, was the way to go. However you needed to be ever vigilant for low bridges, which could quite literally decapitate you. This jeopardy just added to the frivolity and there was much laughter, oohs and aghhs as plenty of near misses played out.

Beau decided to step up the excitement and had now ventured onto the roof of the barge, followed by Richard Hammond. As the next bridge got close, Richard laid low commando/coward style, as us onlookers screamed at him to remain low. Meanwhile, Beau made a brilliantly timed leap onto the bridge, well not quite onto, as he had to haul himself up over the wall and run to the other side, where he planned to finish his party trick by lowering himself back onto the end of the barge, which was slowly gliding like a swan, appearing out of the pitch black with Richard still lying low, having narrowly avoided being scalped.

Hilariously/alarmingly, our shiny jacketed Dutch 'stunt presenter' didn't quite get his timing right and was left hanging like a chimp above the dark, extremely cold waters below (it was January). A mild panic broke out as some of our Dutch hosts screamed at the barge man/driver, whatever you call them, to reverse as swiftly as possible. If you have been on a barge, you will know that there is nothing speedy about them.

Luckily, due to Beau's well-invested time in the gym, he hung in there long enough and was rescued. This slightly dramatic event did not dampen Beau or the Bubble's party spirit. In fact I think it only served to fuel the flames of our unending passion to party. Literally, as it turned out.

Before we were actually asked to leave the barge for good, Richard, running on alcohol-infused adrenalin, tried to set fire to Chris's trousers as he stood unaware, with his head out of the hatch, bantering with Beau. (There was often an underlying hateful tension between presenters and the Businessman as said presenters perceived Chris as just swanning around, basking in their talented glory, whilst making vast amounts of money on the back of their seemingly endless performances This was, in fact, far from the truth, but the playground, boyish banter infused with alcohol could turn nasty.) Thankfully, as smoke was seen drifting from the hem of Chris's chinos, Hammond was guided away by one of us girls then bellowed at by JC, and Chris was spared.

This was one of those moments like at a children's birthday party when the sugar high has kicked in and Billy is about to stamp on Harry's head before a gentle but strong mother diffuses the situation and separates the boys whilst turning down the music. Gem and I represented those mother figures and forever on duty, drunk or sober, put the call in to the Range Rover drivers to ensure our safe return to the hotel.

There were other memorable moments in Amsterdam, low ones, when the sugar-high, overtired 'children' had tantrums, and Gem, I, Bas or James Cooke-Priest were whisked in to prevent things escalating, and bedtime was encouraged.

Nevertheless, Amsterdam was conquered, with thousands of *Top Gear* fans and their families having been extraordinarily entertained and made happy. Plans were made for our three musketeers and their merry management team to return.

Come the final curtain we were once again whisked off by our convoy of Range Rovers with extra luggage of gifts from our local hosts and fans – china windmills filled with local tipple, clogs, pickled herring, etc. My special souvenir was a cowhide rug that had been part of our contemporary green room, and Jeremy insisted that I have it, knowing full well that our Dutch hosts, whom he'd come to despise as he deemed them to be milking his celebrity for everything they could, would have to pay for it, and in true *Top Gear* style it would give me a problem trying to get it home. I felt a tad awkward trundling through Schiphol Airport with a six-foot roll of dead animal but, travelling with my infamous colleagues, no questions were asked.

Dear Bas on the other hand, having arrived home ahead of us to support his wife and family, once reunited with his luggage, had to explain to his family why he had a suitcase full of sex toys! Some pretty extreme ones at that. Imagine what the porters thought when they cleared his room. Despite the tragic circumstances this story brought much laughter to us all.

Richard, You're Fired!

Cape Town, one of my favourite places in the world. First of all, you can travel there and back with no jet lag because it's on the same time line as the UK. Secondly, it's beautiful and has a wonderful climate. Thirdly, it has wonderful wildlife, and maybe I should have prioritised the fact that I have family there.

Anyway it was the next stop on our World Tour. Richard accompanied Jeremy again, and Sasha from Johannesburg joined us, along with our brilliant drivers/security Denzel and Clinton. Security was a necessity everywhere we went now. There had been one too many incidents with crowd control and celebrity harassment. It was 2010 and the boys were reaching the height of their fame. They were recognisable around the world just like Coca-Cola and Man United. It was quite unbelievable, especially for me as I had effectively grown up with the brand and still viewed them as just motoring journalists with a schoolboy mentality. However, they were now appealing to young and old, male and female.

Jeremy was very happy in Cape Town, which meant that we all were. He was now known, affectionately, as the Maharaja. (This nickname was given to him by Chris after Jeremy appeared, for leisure time, in a white Indian/kaftan style shirt, and obviously for his behaviour now and again…) Wherever we were going and whatever we were doing, saying

115

or eating had to be run by the Maharaja first. Richard was generally more easy-going and in fact often his only demand was to have or do something simple, like pasta or a baked potato for dinner and a run or a trip to the gym for his leisure time. At the end of the day, Jeremy was effectively The Boss. Without him there was no tour.

Our hotel for this stay was the Mount Nelson, another favourite with Jeremy and in fact all of us. It was set against a backdrop of Table Mountain, amongst palm trees and beautiful gardens. It was a very elegant, colonial style hotel with attentive, good old-fashioned service. The wonderful staff also turned a blind eye to our ridiculous behaviour, like swimming fully clothed (or naked) at midnight and luggage trolley racing.

This was after yet another boozy night, following dinner at a charming restaurant where they served, to our amusement, 'brick flattened BBQ Chicken'. This bizarre description of a dish provided much amusement as we imagined exactly how that might be prepared. To top off the stupidity playing out at our table, I had actually found a brick in the ladies' loos that I brought back to the table. Once again we were in hysterics as we imagined, and Chris acted out with the prop I'd found, a chicken literally being flattened by a brick. Maybe it was, but I don't think, as customers, we needed to know!

Anyway, in a very jovial mood the Bubble arrived back in our Range Rover convoy at the hotel. The boys lit up a last fag of the night, and whilst keeping them company Chris came up with the luggage trolley racing idea and proceeded to push one to the top of the drive ready to launch himself back down at quite a speed. It didn't take long before Richard and the rest of us joined in. The incredibly polite doormen and concierge just looked on trying not to laugh, as that would have been deemed unprofessional. Just another night out with the Bubble.

On the journey to the venue for rehearsals, the boys often asked how ticket sales were going. One of their biggest fears was to be playing to empty seats, whether it was a few rows or a half-empty stadium. It could really affect their mood and obviously the whole show's atmosphere. They also looked out for local advertising, such as banners, posters and screens promoting the show. If there wasn't any evidence, then Chris and Gemma never heard the end of it. As we turned into the approach road of the venue, the boys noticed a very small, probably A5 size poster on a lamp post. Well that was it, Gemma got ripped to shreds, in a comic way but with a distinct hint of serious accusation. She was then given the name of Publicity Mouse, which Richard acted out just how she might go about her ad campaign in a very squeaky, quiet voice saying things like 'Sorry to bother you but would you like to come to our show?' Again, Chris and I, who were as usual on board in the lead Range Rover, were in tears of laughter. Chris's laughter was slightly more nervous than mine.

The boys needn't have worried as the audiences were packed, and in fact we had to add seats and put the row of disabled seats closer to the front of the arena. That was another interesting thing to observe worldwide: the health and safety policies varied considerably in each territory. In Australia you couldn't get away with adding seats at the last minute or too much dry ice, and when it came to pyros, you could barely get away with lighting a match. Contrary to that, here in Cape Town the pyros were big and loud and if anyone needed a seat, then a way was found to squeeze them in.

The crowds were awesome in Cape Town and the boys were quite overwhelmed with the huge, very noisy welcome they received upon arriving onstage and in fact throughout the duration of the show. It was so lovely to witness, Chris and I would often get emotional at these times. I was very proud of the boys and felt so honoured to be part of the team.

However, a slight problem became apparent in the first show: the pyros, which were used to add to the drama of one of the scenes, used to make me jump, even when I knew they were coming. But as they went off, the front row, consisting mainly of disabled people, many of whom were in wheelchairs, were nearly blown out of them. A huge shock to them and a big one to Chris Hughes. Thankfully, no one was hurt in any way, and arrangements were swiftly made to rearrange the audience and move the disabled seats back.

The boys were unaware of this, but Chris in his usual theatrical way described the scene to them after the show and went on to recite an imaginary complaint letter in the voice of Stephen Hawking, 'Dear *Top Gear*, after your show I have now lost my one remaining sense...' Another unforgettable moment as both Jeremy and Richard were reduced to tears of laughter, as were the rest of us.

We generally had a fantastic time in Cape Town including a rooftop lunch at the Twelve Apostles Hotel overlooking the Atlantic, where we watched huge pods of dolphins playing. It was decided that it would be too troublesome to go to the top of Table Mountain as it was impossible to avoid long queues, so we chartered a helicopter for a trip around the cape, spotting shark and whales and viewing the whole of Table Mountain, the Twelve Apostles, the Lion's Head, the Cape of Good Hope and Robben Island in one easy flight with no moaning from a giant presenter in a queue.

Back at work the shows were going down incredibly well and the boys would come offstage quite high, especially after an explosive game of Car Football between England and South Africa. The crowd went nuts for this. The whole venue was near perfect for the Bubble as everything was in close proximity, and they had a sunny garden to relax in with no dog shit. Even the crew had a large outdoor area with marquees for sheltering out of the sun, which made a welcome change from being in a darkened, fume-filled, often too-hot or too-cold exhibition hall.

The green room was comfortable, until that is, there was a visit from half a dozen South African rugby players including Springboks Bryan Habana, John Smit and Schalk Burger. There were more but I'm so sorry guys I can't remember your names. One of them was over 7 ft tall, making for a fantastic photo opportunity with Richard Hammond, like a scene out of *Game of Thrones* or *Lord of the Rings*, or indeed me meeting Warwick Davis.

I was the only other one to be the subject of ridicule, when it was spotted that my pants showed above the top of my jeans, when I bent down to fetch drinks from the fridge. Richard and Jeremy thought this was a great opportunity to keep making fun of me by announcing, 'Here it comes, another episode of Pippa's Pants.' Apparently, they used to do this to some poor researcher who worked on their show. However, I was not going to take it for too long. During a performance I snuck off to the ladies with a permanent marker and wrote 'F**k Off' at the top of my pants, so the next time they looked they would receive a special message. Another ordinary day at the office.

Talking of which, the closing ceremony for Cape Town was a bit of an epic one. Up there with Dublin's Christmas Grotto. Richard had been on tour with us over several months now, but after Cape Town he was leaving for home and James was to replace him in Johannesburg.

Chris came up with the idea of firing him, *Apprentice* style. Genius, but oh my God did Gem and I have to gather a lot of props, most of them from around the venue, to create a board room, where Chris would play the part of Alan Sugar.

James Cooke Priest covered his hair with talc to play Nick Hewer and Gem wore a long dark wig to play Karren Brady. I had a ridiculous blonde curly wig and wore huge pants over my jeans (making reference to my pants showing) to play the receptionist. I had a phone, even though I was in the same room as everyone else, so I could 'call' Chris AKA Alan to let him know Jeremy then Richard were there to see him.

Jeremy was obviously not fired and was given words of praise and ordered to sit down at the other side of the board room. Richard was then commanded to take a seat directly in front of Chris, who was sat on a ridiculously high chair (bar stool) behind a desk alongside James as Nick and Gem as Karren. From there, he reeled off all of Richard's faults, such as being short and talking too much about helicopters (Richard did that a lot). To accompany Chris's comments, and to demonstrate his point, he had produced charts and diagrams which Gem and I had framed and were displayed on the wall. One, entitled 'Height Is Power', had columns depicting the average height of presenters on the World Tour. The other was entitled 'Chopper Schwaffling' (derived from the Dutch word *swaffelen*, which we learnt whilst in Amsterdam. If you are over eighteen, google it). This pie chart depicted the percentage of people interested when Richard is talking about helicopters.

Our security hero Denzel was also involved and stood 'on guard' throughout until Chris bellowed those immortal words 'You're fired!', at which point he drew out his gun (unloaded I'm told) and aimed it at Richard. By this time all of us were in hysterics once again. Gem and I presented Richard with his leaving present – a giant, and I mean giant – about one metre in diameter – clock. Richard had to take it home. Those were the rules. And he did.

Richard flew home, as did I in order to pick up my single mother duties again. Chris, Gem, Jeremy, JCP and Chris's

The Olden days and not a grey hair in sight. Entertaining a soldier with an amazing leg. The boys doing their bit to support Tickets for Troops in an extremely basic green room, Birmingham, 2007.

Richard Hammond visiting "Santa", aka Chris Hughes, in Dublin.

Preparing for snorkelling just off Hamilton Island, Australia with "Shane-O" Jacobson who declared we were the new "Incredibles".

A night at the races: JC sporting a silk number to clash beautifully with his combat trousers, RH striking a pose in his new ensemble purchased by moi. Dear Bas in something that was fashionable at the time!?

Absolutely smashed: Chris attending to the Maharaja, doing his best version of subservient, using the shoeshine facilities outside the Palazzo Hotel, Jo'burg.

Amsterdam: A very special conference after Celebrity Sex Shop Sweep. Yes, Richard does have a gag in his mouth and a penis on his head.

Me – aka Horse – there just happened to be a horse mask at our holiday home, Waiheke Island, NZ.

Aboard the Super Yacht, The Flying Fish – "Nursey" taking two of her best behaved "inpatients" out. Sydney, Australia.

James May going for another World Record: How many adults can you get in a Wendy House without spilling your vino.

Me, Gem, RH and JM popping out for lunch at The Cradle, Cradle of Humankind, Jo'burg.

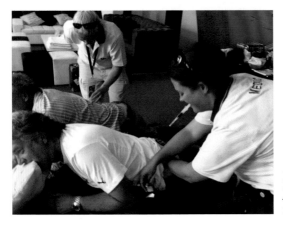

Hangover cure in Kyalami, Jo'burg: B12 injections – not in the eye.

Possibly the worst boy band in the World. JCP, Chris Hughes, JC, JM, Rowly.

Motorcycle juggling in the Thunder Dome, Kyalami, Jo'burg.

Last Supper, Oslo: The boys sporting their Norwegian gifts with me and Gem.

Chris Hughes in Vigeland, naked statue park, Oslo. Nothing to see here.

RH pulls a moose, outside The Ritz, Oslo.

Warsaw National Stadium: The Greatest Show on Earth (I thought).

Durban: "MC Hammond", "Mother Fu**er", "Beyoncé" and a monkey with blue testicles.

The Final, O2, London: Mindy Hammond, Gemma, Me, RH on bass, JC on drums, Chris Hughes on lead vocal, Dan Richardson of Rockaoke, JM on keyboard.

"Evolution": Thank goodness for our guide, the Professor, who proves we have managed to evolve beyond Clarkson.

wife went on a mini-break by private plane to a safari lodge. I never quite understood and was intrigued about how the business afforded all our luxury accommodation and leisure time. This little jaunt would have cost a fortune. I am no businesswoman but I do not know how the tour made money, and sometimes I know it didn't but it kept rolling on.

Often Chris and JCP would go into a quiet huddle and Chris would take phone calls and excuse himself from the room. The boys would always tease or provoke him and claim it was the bank on the phone again. If ever we didn't have the highest spec of Range Rover, or the restaurant we were eating at was not quite the usual standard, the bank jokes would start up. It was quite an extraordinary business relationship between the boys and Chris. I know Jeremy had stipulated that touring had to be fun and a certain standard had to be upheld, otherwise he wouldn't do it. I think Chris was very much on board with those demands but JCP was often trying to rein in Chris.

After the safari break, the streamlined Bubble moved on to Johannesburg to meet James May, who was to replace Richard for this leg of the tour and would present alongside Sasha and Jeremy. Their leisure time here included a rather mind-blowing meet-and-greet with the iconic Nelson Mandela.

Back in Cape Town, the lady that helped PR the shows in South Africa was involved in Nelson Mandela's charity, 46664. The boys had done a Q & A at a fundraising dinner that took place after their performance. A lot of money was raised and it was arranged for Jeremy and James, escorted by Chris, to have tea with Mr Mandela and for him to give them a personal thank you. It was also a great PR opportunity for both the charity and *Top Gear Live*.

It was a huge honour, and Jeremy and James were humbled and very excited to have such an opportunity. However, it did not go quite as they had expected. Mr Mandela was by this time in his nineties and was clearly suffering from some memory loss and confusion. There was a huge case of mistaken identity. He thought that Jeremy and James were American astronauts. To be fair to Mr Mandela, he was due to meet the astronauts that day, and as Jeremy himself reported afterwards, he probably had never heard of himself and James. The meeting had only come about because of the donation made to Mandela's 46664 charity. Jeremy, not quite knowing how to handle the situation, decided to just go with Nelson to be polite and answered Nelson's moon landing questions as if he was an astronaut.

Unfortunately, Jeremy chose to report the slightly comical event in his *Sunday Times* column including his inappropriate question to Mandela, 'Have you ever had a lap dance?' Jeremy blamed his inappropriate questioning on the fact that he was overwhelmed when invited to ask such a legend a question. As we know, Jeremy does like to push the boundaries and shock his audience. To be fair, it is usually with good intent to entertain, and when asked by Mr Mandela what the moon was like, he replied, 'It's rocky and dusty and there is not much gravity.' A little disrespectful but the usual schoolboy humour prevailed.

Despite the large amount of money raised by Jeremy and Richard supporting the fundraising event, Jeremy's report of the meeting did not go down well at all with Mandela's people. Jeremy Clarkson was yet again in hot water and caused further stress and drama for the Bubble and its extended family and colleagues. Fighting fires and Clarkson dramas were events that came with the job and were becoming the norm.

In stark contrast to tea with Nelson Mandela, they also saw Eddie Izzard perform in his one-man show and had some celeb-meets-celeb backstage time. Never a dull moment.

And there's an important point: there really was never a dull moment and the pressure grew on Chris to continually come up with something fun and original to entertain the boys in their downtime. Although they did enjoy the odd lazy morning and some time to chill, those creative minds were always on the go and got bored easily. Like hyperactive children they were hard to keep up with and manage.

Anyone for Cricket?

On to Sydney, where I was to join the party once again, and what a reunion. I flew the twenty-odd hours with a brief break in Dubai (literally off and on the plane again) and was met at the airport to be driven to our five-star luxury accommodation at the Park Hyatt, in prime position, on Sydney Harbour. I literally dropped my bags at reception and went out to the jetty at the back of the hotel where the Bubble were just disembarking from their superyacht, *The Flying Fish*, which was at our disposal for the duration of our stay.

The full Bubble reassembled, less Richard Hammond, and headed back to the hotel to freshen up for dinner. Dinner was a big affair as we were joined on this trip by a lot of BBC management. I think this was partly to watch over us after Jeremy's last trip down under when he caused trouble with his remarks about Gordon Brown, but also to renegotiate a deal with Channel Nine, the big Australian channel that produced the Oz version of *Top Gear* with its own presenters.

Andy Wilman, Adam Waddell and Richard Porter (script editor and author of *And on That Bombshell*) were amongst the BBC entourage. After dinner, a few of us ended up taking over the small hotel bar. No other guests were up except for Brian Johnson from AC/DC.

What a lovely guy. I think the band was on tour and playing in Sydney. Andy Wilman was a huge fan of Brian's who is coincidentally a huge car enthusiast too. After a few drinks in the bar he was invited to join us the following evening on our superyacht, *The Flying Fish*.

My first experience of *The Flying Fish* was the next morning as we took a leisurely cruise to the venue. It was stunning. Upon boarding, you were politely asked to remove your shoes so as not to damage the immaculate, polished teak of the deck. We were served breakfast in the open air, at the stern of the boat.

The trip took an hour or so. Jeremy and Richard went through the script adding a few topical lines. JCP, Chris and Gem ventured to a top deck for a business meeting. I was left to keep an eye on the boys and had a chance to explore the 32-metre-long floating palace. It was like nothing I'd ever seen before – even the luxury hotels we'd been in couldn't match this. Every single room was luxurious and immaculate. I've since learnt that a yacht's crew is on duty twenty hours a day, if need be, with their duties including very, very high-standard cleaning. The decks are cleaned every single day, as much as is required if guests are on board, as are the crystal, the silver and the most lush carpet ever.

We had access to a couple of cabins which had more lush, seriously deep pile, velvety carpet, silk sheets on the bed and the fluffiest towels for anyone needing a shower in the equally luxurious marble shower room. It was truly stunning. Outside on the top deck was a Jacuzzi and somewhere, I was never quite sure how it fitted in, was a helipad. In true James Bond style, the boys' co-presenter, Greg Murphy, arrived by helicopter. Greg is four times winner of the Bathurst 1000, a 1000 km touring car race, and had worked on the live shows before.

After a tough start to my working day, we made our way on land to the Acer Arena for the usual run-through/dress rehearsal. The show itself was the same as the boys had been doing in Cape Town and back in Dublin and England with the huge, loop-the-loop, hotwheels style track as a backdrop. The finale of the show was the Stig performing a record-breaking 360-degree stunt in a Rage Buggy. Poor old Greg had his work cut out to get familiar with the set, the lines and of course all the cars. As with poor Sasha back in South Africa, you could sense Greg's stress and angst while our boys breezed through yet another what they called, 'Pantomime'. They were, however, professional to the end and supported Greg, as any other guest presenter, to get through their first few performances.

Even though the boys were pros and made performing look easy, the first day of rehearsals and first show made for a long day with a few stressful moments when car, props or co-stars went wrong, so to alleviate any stress and celebrate getting through the first show a BBQ was arranged by our Aussie hosts headed up by the lovely Tim Etchells, who knew how to throw a party. The year before he had arranged a party in a private house filled with supermodels. I wasn't there so I'm literally not interested and have nothing to report.

It was no ordinary BBQ. It was set up on a private beach, just a half-hour cruise from the hotel on our superyacht. The five-star catering crew had gone ahead by boat and set up tables with white cloths and flowers and a fully stocked bar. As we and all our guests including Brian Johnson and members of his band, as well as, quite randomly, cricket commentator Mark Nicholas (a contact of Tim Etchells) arrived, we were met by the catering crew's tenders (small boats) that helped take us all to shore. Superyachts are too big to get right to the beach.

One of the Bubble's best nights ever was getting underway. After a few beers, burgers and prawns from the barbie, a *Top Gear* vs AC/DC cricket match was declared. Absolutely epic! The atmosphere was awesome – we even had team picking, you know, like the ones at school when you were so desperate to not, not be picked. AC/DC obviously had to have some of our crew make up their team. What a laugh! Mark Nicholas commentated on the match and there were some great moments, the best of which was James May running for a catch. Determined not to give up, he didn't let the sea put him off and dived in fully clothed to emerge, like a drowned spaniel, not having caught the ball but also realising he had his mobile phone in his pocket!

The fun didn't end there. We had to leave the beach, but back on the yacht it was time to warm up in the Jacuzzi and drink some more. Didn't see that coming – sitting in a Jacuzzi on a superyacht with AC/DC, a cricket commentator, a Bathhurst Champion, Jeremy Clarkson and James May. A rare moment indeed.

And so the madness carried on. We had to disembark a short drive from the hotel, I think because no large boats were allowed to dock close to the hotel past a certain time at night. As we pulled up alongside the rather unglamorous quay, I noticed a vintage fire engine parked up. Of course, this was perfect for our ride back to the hotel.

Could it get any stranger? I was now riding in the back of a fire engine with Jeremy Clarkson, Gem and others with James May riding up front in just his underpants (his jeans hadn't dried out). We pulled up outside the Park Hyatt where Rowly, who had been working, was having a quick fag. His face was a picture, as he had first thought, 'Oh shit, the hotel is on fire.' What was more of a shock was to see James May exit in his boxer shorts. Just another night out with the Bubble.

The shows went ahead with no drama other than our most gentle presenter, James May, thinking he was having a heart attack. He was suffering from chest pain and generally didn't feel great after an afternoon performance. Paramedics were called to the green room and he was given some privacy to have a check over. Luckily for all concerned he was not having a heart attack, but not surprisingly he was clearly suffering from stress and the effects of a not so healthy lifestyle. After a snooze, he declared he felt better and he would go ahead with the evening's performance.

As a *Top Gear* presenter, you were not allowed to be ill and certainly weren't going to get any sympathy, even if you were close to death. Jeremy and James joked on this occasion, as they always did, if one of them was potentially facing death, about the promise they had made between the three of them, that the first word after announcing publicly the death of any of them would be 'Anyway…'.

Anyway, all's well that ends well. James was still alive and they completed three more days and nights of successful shows. On the last day in Sydney, Gem and I were frantically preparing for the next leg of the tour in New Zealand, which was to start with a short break for the Bubble on Waiheke Island, not far from Auckland. Whilst trying to put in a huge online order of supplies, for our extraordinary family, to be delivered upon our arrival to our luxury holiday home, we were also expected to prepare a closing ceremony.

With the help of our colleague Meghan who worked for Brand Events in Oz, under Chris's direction we created a Bruce Forsyth *Generation Game* style ceremony – I don't know why. In the green room there were black drapes cordoning off a storage area, and we used those as the curtains to disguise the beginning of the conveyor belt (created out of trestle tables and powered by our hands) that would deliver all the special gifts to Jeremy, James and Greg.

Chris dressed up in traditional Aussie costume, in a grubby vest (he always had spilt food down him anyway), shorts and a hat strung with corks. He suggested Gem and

I got into beachwear, which we did but kept our dignity by wearing sarongs tied around our necks. This kind of request/demand from Chris, our boss, went into our imaginary file for our case of sexual harassment in the workplace. This file became huge. It was of course in jest, a running joke throughout the tour. I must also report that the visual image I have portrayed of Chris must not in any way detract from the fact that he is an excellent businessman and great chap, and most importantly Gem and I were happy to dress up ridiculously.

The gifts included plenty of cuddly toys. For those too young to remember, Brucie's *Generation Game* was a Saturday-night family game show which ended with the contestant watching dozens of prizes going along on a conveyor belt that then disappeared out of view. To win the prizes you had to remember and recite everything that you had seen. Including a cuddly toy that was always there to win.

Other gifts were a plastic cricket set, a wooden bridge (bridges were a bugbear as we couldn't get as close to the arena as we would have liked on our superyacht, because it was too high to fit under certain bridges en route), a make your own lightning kit (we experienced plenty of terrifying lightning on our superyacht), a plastic boat to remember our superyacht by and plenty more silly things to amuse us all. Including a very expensive bottle of Glandosane, which is a throat lubricant especially used by actors to prevent or ease a dry throat.

Glandosane had become a necessity for Jeremy by this point in the tour, as not only was he using his renowned gravelly booming voice so much, but he was, as you might have guessed by now, seriously burning the candle at both ends and in the middle, along with smoking sixty a day. God knows how he's still alive.

ANYONE FOR CRICKET?

After the inevitable hysterics, farewell drinks with our Australian hosts and celebratory champagne, it was time to move on and prepare for the next territory to be conquered. Piling ourselves into the mandatory Range Rover convoy with cuddly toys, cricket set and all, we headed to the airport once more.

Jeremy Gets Married Again

After a relatively short flight, our exclusive little entourage made its way into the arrival hall in Auckland to be greeted by a Maori welcome of half a dozen Maori ladies doing their thing in full Maori costume, grass skirts and all. This had in fact been set up as a PR stunt to promote the forthcoming shows. Once Jeremy and James had fulfilled their obligatory questioning by the press we were all whisked off to waiting helicopters to take us to our private house on beautiful Waiheke Island.

After the incredible opulence of *The Flying Fish* superyacht, landing by helicopter on the lawn, at the edge of our own private beach, had just trumped that experience. Much more to my personal taste, our new home for the next three days was far more simple and rustic, but equally as pleasant. It was a wooden bungalow, almost ranch-like in appearance, with its own private bay, complete with jetty and a motorboat for our use. It had an annex where Gem, Naomi (who was NZ Horse in my absence the year before) and I slept.

With the bungalow's accompanying pool, sun loungers, tennis court and large front terrace overlooking the bay, we were all very happy to be there. It actually wasn't all holiday for us girls as we were responsible for cooking and cleaning for the duration of our stay. At this point I must confess I am no domestic goddess and certainly could not cook anything marvellous for large numbers. Our Bubble numbers were up to ten, as Rowly and his now girlfriend Naomi Lynch (another Naomi) joined us for our special holiday.

Naomi had been auditioned by Rowly for the shows a few years before as an exotic dancer/flame thrower to add some sexy glamour to the shows. She was a very sexy performer and created some amazing flame-throwing stunts which got more impressive as the shows evolved. She was nicknamed by the boys, and introduced as, 'The Girl with Petrol Pumps for Arms'. There were a whole raft of amusing stories created by the boys and Chris, about her family, featuring characters such as Great Aunt Kerosene. The boys had imaginary concern about Rowly's safety when he was due to meet the family for the first time and for subsequent dinners. They imagined flame-throwing incidents resulting in him being hospitalised, or worse still fully cremated, and perhaps that was the reason Rowly had no hair. These ridiculous stories just added to the soundtrack of our travelling circus.

Highlights of our holiday were late nights by the pool and the Girl Throwing competition (created the year before), along with the 'name game', in which we all sat with post-its on our foreheads with well-known names given to us for the others to guess. It ended up with Chris and Jeremy left in. Chris was Napoleon and JC was The Wicked Witch of the West. Other games included acting out well-known adverts in the large kitchen window looking out over the terrace, to represent a TV screen, and the After Eight game, which involved getting an After Eight from your forehead to your mouth without using your hands. All these silly games created a typical family holiday feel with incredibly eclectic family members.

A low point was Jeremy and James deciding to give Chris a birthday surprise of a strippergram, after dinner one night. This treat cost them a fortune as two girls had to travel a huge distance including getting a ferry to and from the island. It was hilarious but slightly uncomfortable to see the usually bombastic Chris Hughes ridiculed and squirming with discomfort especially as he was really suffering with sunstroke and certainly didn't want anyone stroking his 'on fire' red head let alone a glamorous topless girl gyrating in front of him.

The following morning I was on breakfast duty and was from that day forward constantly ridiculed for my terrible catering skills. A constant repertoire came from my diners of, 'coffee then milk, bacon then egg, toast then jam' as I failed to meet their demands. After the slightly disastrous breakfast was eventually over, we packed up and boarded the boat, reluctantly heading back to Auckland to get on with what we were there for.

The shows were staged in the slightly unusual setting of the Auckland agricultural showgrounds. The stage was set in a large cattle shed. It had more of a County Show feel to it than a Motor Show, but with that slightly rural feel came the finish line to a vintage car rally that had driven the length of the North Island to kick off the start of the shows. However, instead of a local vicar opening the show, we had New Zealand's prime minister. Another normal day on tour.

This bizarre village fete type setting and atmosphere was actually the beginnings of a bigger festival type event that was growing on top of the motoring theatre. Around the cattle shed were huge tarmacked areas that provided great settings for Stunt Driving School, Drifting demonstrations and Power Tool Drag Racing, to name a few, along with the original motor show displays of highly polished performance and vintage cars. Visitors could also buy upgrade tickets that gave them backstage tours to see all the cars, crazy inventions and props used in the performances. If you were lucky, you might even get a glimpse of our worn-out, slightly sweaty presenters as they headed for a break in the green room.

We were now staying in a four-star hotel in Auckland that was a little too business-like for our Bubble, so excursions were made to entertain our presenters in ever more ludicrous, budget-blowing ways. The boys, especially Jeremy, would love to push Chris and his budget as far as he could, and here in Auckland he decided that he wanted proper fish and chips, wrapped in paper, on a beach, with a scenic helicopter ride there and back. To be fair, he was offered the helicopter, that or a motorboat for the day, but I don't think Chris had planned quite so much airtime. James for some reason was having a bit of an Eeyore-like low day and did not want to join us. So another crazy day began, choppering into a tiny coastal village with a fish and chip shop. We landed on a grassy area right opposite a tiny parade of about four shops, much to the surprise of the dozen or so locals. Greg Murphy was with us and advised on the NZ fish shop speciality, hapuka. We then wandered across the road to enjoy our picnic on the beach.

I do not know how but we were then invited to have a cup of tea at some millionaire's beachside mansion which the helicopter landed at on our route back to town. All very pleasing, not like the evening that was to follow.

As usual there was a local team who helped source and arrange anything we needed. Chris had asked for a novelty dinner to be arranged, and the girl assigned to help us had sold him the idea of going to a contact of hers for a beach BBQ at his beachside residence. Chris bought into the concept as the guy offering his hospitality was part of the winning NZ America's Cup sailing team, clearly worthy of entertaining our superstars.

After the last show of the day was over, we bundled into our convoy of cars. Unusually, we actually had a Maserati Quattroporte, 4.2 V8, to be precise. The boys loved it and we had a good old Range Rover for the others. We had to order a couple of taxis to bring the rest of our Bubble members to this exciting beachside location.

Chris, Gem and I had been told that it was about a forty-minute drive away, much further than we would normally drive to get our tired and hungry presenters to a place of relaxation for the night, but we were assured it would be worth it. After thirty minutes, there was complaining from Jeremy. After forty-five minutes, trouble was brewing and JC asked me to call Chris, who was in the Range Rover behind, to find out what was going on.

We drove for close to an hour but at last we could see, just about, as it was getting dark, huge expanses of empty beach and coastline. The Maharaja was slightly pacified but was hungry and on the verge of getting hangry. I was beginning to feel increasingly anxious as to how this was going to end, especially as we now had to change direction away from the coast.

We had a call from Chris to say we were minutes away, which was a relief, but that feeling didn't last long as we reached a highly populated residential area and pulled into a small driveway that led to a slightly scruffy small house with a ute (pick-up truck) outside.

Chris was panicking. He jumped out of the Range Rover and met the barefoot hippy beach bum who came out to greet us, beer in hand, followed by some feral children. There was quite a bit of swearing in our car. The very friendly beach bum came to explain that he would light a BBQ on the beach and the boys could have a muck about in his ute on the sand.

Oh dear. There were some cross words had with the girl, whose name I genuinely can't remember, who had set this up. Jeremy was going mad and even the placid James May was not happy as he was so hungry and tired. Chris got Gemma and JCP on to finding an alternative venue to eat, as quick as fucking possible!

Our convoy backed up sharpish as we withdrew from the *Neighbours* type setting and headed back to town.

This is where my humour and placid nature helped out big time. I started to get the giggles and suggested that when we did get to dinner we all drew what we were expecting to arrive at. I still have an idyllic vision in my head, a wooden, simple but stylish beach house with candles lit, BBQ and roaring fire on the beach, with us reclining on beach chairs, relaxing, taking in the view. The boys did start to see the funny side and decided that what had been lost in cultural translation was that the man whose house we'd just turned up at had sailed a boat once and had a coffee cup with an American flag on it. Peace and stupidity had returned to the Bubble.

Gem, thank God, had come up trumps and we got into a quayside restaurant in town. The hysterical laughter ensued and poor Chris, whose birthday it was, had his chocolate birthday cake smeared all over him, by JC. Plus, as you can imagine, a lot of verbal abuse for cocking up the evening plans. The girl responsible for the evening was sacked. Maybe a little unjust, as in her eyes she had offered good old-fashioned NZ hospitality with one of her nation's sporting heroes. She just was not up to speed with the standards our Bubble demanded, which if I'm honest were starting to get a bit out of hand.

As the tour became more demanding on all of us, so did the high standards of private dining, private air travel and novelty entertainment. So often, all of it had to be delivered at high speed and at the last minute. Gemma and I used to joke, as we ran through logistics and schedules that were constantly changing, 'and have you got the tickets for Barbados?', referring to the fact that we could literally be asked to get anything at any time. We didn't know that one day, that request would actually come to fruition.

As we left a hotel or house at speed, trying to thank all the staff and hosts of that particular city, that we had swept through, in our demanding ways, Gem and I often felt like raping and pillaging Vikings.

Whilst stomping around Auckland, we had one wonderful night, in a very, what I would call, 'Ta Dah!' restaurant. We had exclusive use of the top-floor, open-air terrace. There must have been nearly twenty of us as an extended Bubble, with Rowly and Naomi and our New Zealand hosts. The tables were set up to fill the whole terrace in a large open square. We had full-on silver service and the staff choreographed the delivery of food, some of which was covered in a silver dome. Hence, my 'Ta Dah' reference, as when those silver domes are whipped away, that is what I think should be said to finish off the delivery.

The Bubble adopted my thinking and there were many 'Ta Dahs', much to the waiting staff's amusement. There were lots of 'oohs' and 'aahs', too, as we were all presented with incredible culinary delights. Nights like these, which of course we had a few of, between the McDonald's and fairly regular hotel food, were always appreciated and really enjoyed by the boys, so whilst you might think they were getting spoilt and brattish, they weren't just yet.

It was late that night when we finished eating. As usual, the convoy of cars were standing by but it turned out we were only about a one-mile walk from the hotel. The boys chose to walk home to enjoy the warm evening and walk off the enormous amount of food they'd eaten. There was a little panic and fluster from Chris, as if we were about to move royalty who should never walk on soiled public ground. To be fair, it was a risk this late at night when drunk revellers would be piling out of bars and restaurants. As I've said before, the boys could get mobbed, and when there was alcohol involved tempers could get frayed.

Anyway, we made a plan along with our driver/security Nigel who was over 7 ft tall. He knew the best route, and once Chris had calmed down, the fun side of him returned. We were instructed to board Nigel's 'walking bus'. This was genius as it provided humour, and safety too, as we snaked past a few bars closely following one another. This ridiculous approach confused the 'enemy', who weren't able to clearly identify our celebs with Jeremy travelling up front in Nigel's shadow and James tucked in between us 'normal' Bubble members. By the time anyone recognised the boys, we were well on our way listening to the distant voices exclaiming, 'Did you see who that was?' and the odd 'Jezza!' and 'Captain Slow!'. We then reached a safe zone alongside the quay, where several expensive yachts were moored up. Childish, drunk giggling was in full swing as Chris started a 'Ministry of Silly Walks' competition inspired by the incredibly tall Nigel, who Chris claimed could in just one step reach Australia.

The stupidity went a little too far after Jeremy had fallen over and was in a giggling mess on the floor and the more able of the party had jumped aboard one of the very expensive yachts and were bouncing up and down on its trampoline-like sunbathing area at the front of the boat.

Nigel stepped up his security role and encouraged everyone off and into a nearby bar for a nightcap. Yes, we needed another drink just to wrap things up for the night.

The next day, another ridiculous closing ceremony was cobbled together which didn't go incredibly well. Jeremy wasn't in a great mood and don't ask me why Chris, who had dressed up as Nelson Mandela, was throwing stale bread rolls at him. There had been some kind of incident reported on the news of athletes, I think, having things thrown at them in some form of protest. Chris was making a comedy reference to that. Jeremy did not appreciate it.

Time to move on, after a rather awkward end to the NZ shows. Never fear, there was another big party planned to mark the end of another long leg of touring. The whole crew were invited, with drinks and food all paid for, and we took over what was normally a sedate community hall. Don't imagine our UK type hall – this was a simple but stunning rustic building surrounded by wonderful ferns and tropical plants, with a huge outdoor area lit with flaming torches and lights strung in the trees on the edge of the beach. No one else was around.

For some reason, Chris had decided that the Bubble would create a wedding style line-up to greet the crew on arrival and hand out champagne. I mean literally wedding style. Jeremy dressed as the bride with a piece of white netting over his head, carrying a hydrangea bouquet, pilfered from the venue's garden. JCP was the groom in black tie, and James, Greg, Gem and I were bridesmaids. Chris was the icing on the cake dressed as a Dick Emery style vicar complete with false buck teeth and hamming his role up beautifully. I don't know why! But it was very funny and greatly appreciated by the incredibly hard-working crew who worked at least twice as hard as all of us in the Bubble and didn't get all the perks.

We had a band who I have no recollection of at all. I can only remember Jeremy getting on drums, Chris leading yet another rendition of the tour classic, 'Mustang Sally', and James really finding his rock and roll touring feet going mad on percussion, eventually dancing like a lunatic on the tables outside and also trying to fit himself, JCP and a couple of the girls in a small Wendy house. This was a turning point for James. It was great to see him really letting his hair down and he became an expert at going mad, pulling off stunts, like fitting the highest number of people in a Wendy house, without spilling a drop of wine.

With another monumental hangover it was time to head home. Back home I got my first taste of *Top Gear* fame when Jeremy chose to mention me in his review of the Maserati Quattroporte in the *Sunday Times*. The double-page headline read: 'Lie Back, Leggy Phillipa, While I have some Fun'. Thanks Jezza.

Rabbits

NO ENTRY

Back in the UK, the Bubble had a few months off, but there was no rest for our favourite trio. They were busier than ever with the enormously successful TV show that was now a huge hit with men and women alike and had begun to be a family favourite on a Sunday night, due to the unique and amusing dynamic between what were now the most famous motoring journalists in the world.

Come October 2010, a big relaunch promoting the World Tour was scheduled, and I was involved in the planning of it. A press day was set up at the *Top Gear* track at Dunsfold. We used the decommissioned Jumbo Jet that lived at the edge of the runway/track. This giant 'monument' was bought from British Airways to be used as a prop in films and TV. It was the perfect setting for our press launch.

We branded the plane as if it was *Top Gear Live*'s own airline (not too far from the truth as the number of private flights we took was increasing). I and another girl were roped in to dress as air hostesses/extras for the promotional films that were made with the boys boarding the plane and making themselves comfortable up front. It was a novel idea to lure the press out for a day at the track and in return promote the next leg of the tour.

And so the next leg began, with a repeat of London, Birmingham, Dublin and then on to new territories in Oz, Brisbane and Melbourne. It was much of the same in London, Birmingham and Dublin but we did change tack with accommodation in Birmingham and took over a small country hotel, where a game of drunk Laser Quest was the highlight of our entertainment. Everyone ran riot through the whole hotel whose staff were incredibly tolerant.

On the whole, we were welcomed with enthusiasm by hotel and restaurant staff around the world. As you might imagine, having Clarkson, Hammond and May as guests was quite exciting to most and a potentially great PR opportunity.

However, on arrival in Brisbane at the Palazzo Versace Hotel, the one used for *I'm a Celebrity… Get Me Out of Here!*, it became evident quite early on that the staff wanted our celebrities out of there as soon as possible. Chris Hughes had been told to stay away from the piano and the staff generally were not amused by our sense of humour and antics.

The disapproval was mutual. The pompousness of this completely over the top resort was not enjoyed by any of us. I arrived late to the party and was commended on my work ethic as I landed, showered, joined the breakfast table and went straight to work after another non-stop flight. At the breakfast table the usual pranks were being played. Chris had gone to the loo and while he was away we surrounded his breakfast plate with every piece of cutlery from all twelve settings. Apparently, Chris had kept complaining about all the cutlery, which he said he found confusing and totally unnecessary. My laughter therapy had begun.

I was then warned about the kamikaze helicopter pilot who had been employed to fly us all to the venue from a helipad on a jetty near the hotel. I was not laughing quite so much as I walked to board our flight to work. Charlie, a Vietnam War veteran pilot, looked as though he wasn't long for this world. Jeremy and James, who had been joined by the wonderful and very funny Shane Jacobson (film star and generally great bloke – check out his feelgood movie *Kenny*), were acting out Charlie's flying skills and bumbling in-flight commentary. Apparently, he flew with his head lolling forward and down. Shane (who shall be known as Shane-O from now on, because he was) impersonated him brilliantly and acted out him holding on to the joy stick and seemingly nodding off mid-flight only to be suddenly awoken, jolting the helicopter to a higher flight path.

I was feeling very anxious but thought I shouldn't complain and would just have to trust that we'd be OK. Charlie had already given the boys a couple of frights including narrowly missing some power lines. On this flight we crossed major flightpaths and the terribly unnerving thing was that you could hear in your own headphones the conversations between Charlie and air traffic control. We all heard him being told to keep left or fly north, to which he responded by flying in the opposite direction. We were all terrified and sooo glad to land safely, having narrowly missed power lines again that surrounded our landing spot. I prayed for bad weather later so we would be forced to drive back to the hotel. I didn't care how long it took or how grumpy any presenter got.

After this experience, the boys had come up with a phrase to constantly annoy Chris with if things weren't going according to plan or not up to standard: 'What would be the cheapest…?' In this case, helicopter pilot. The reality was that this was the case sometimes. Gem, JCP and I spent a lot of time when booking boats, hotels and helicopters trying to get the best deal. The Cashless Holiday did have a budget even though it was often blown. I had previously experienced pre-helicopter flight anxiety back in South Africa when a helicopter was needed for an extra excursion. Chris literally asked me, 'Is there a cheaper one?' The cheaper one was the one I had to book. I found myself imagining my boy being motherless after the cheap helicopter I was on fell apart mid-air. I was mightily relieved to land. I never imagined that a stressful day at work could entail having to go on a helicopter trip around the coast of South Africa against your will.

I had actually arrived for the last day of shows in Brisbane and so after another finale it was a quick 'bounce', as we called it (quick exit straight offstage), and back on 'Charlie Air' for another eventful flight home. Charlie couldn't find the hotel, and we could hear him mumbling to himself: 'Is that it?', 'No', 'There it is, oh no'. He could not hide his uncertainty at all, especially as he started descending into a residential area, terrifying both locals and us. We became delirious with giggles, out of fear as well as amusement. We then all started to help Charlie identify where the Versace was. To add to the hilarity we could hear him muttering 'elephant tusks'. Oh my God, I was about to burst with hysterical fear and laughter. Meanwhile, Shane was giving a running commentary, impersonating Charlie as if he was confused and was on an elephant hunt in Africa. James was about to wet himself. This truly was one of the most surreal moments of the whole tour.

Dear old Charlie was right – there were actually, in true Versace style, a huge pair of ornamental golden elephant tusks at the end of another jetty by the hotel and there to the right of them, much to our relief, was the helipad. I really, really, never wanted to fly Charlie Air again.

With no time to dwell on the shock of a dodgy helicopter flight, it was straight off to the 'last night Bubble party'. Knowing that the hotel would not tolerate our antics, Chris had decided to hire a house for the evening – as you do. It was stunning: an incredibly modern, immaculate pad on the beach with amazing interiors including a cinema, high-tech gym, pool and drum kit – perfect for JC – the drum kit, that is.

Naomi and Meghan, our Antipodean extra 'horses', had prepared a load of food and drink, and Chris was about to add to our 'sexual harassment file'. He actually took me into one of the bedrooms and said, 'Get your clothes off.' I should quickly explain that he actually meant could you change into your bikini for the closing ceremony, which I was forewarned about and earlier had been given the job of finding a rabbit costume for him. Another perfectly normal business meeting. Bikinis were obviously chosen as we were on the Gold Coast. The rabbit was chosen because a large amount of tour banter had been about all the rules and regulations of Australia. A real surprise to me. You'd think with their beach bum lifestyle they would be really laid-back but no. They are the worst. Jeremy hated it there, largely due to their no smoking rules and paparazzi who loved to hound him. Back to the rabbit costume: this was to symbolise our rebellious attitude towards all the regulation, as rabbits were illegal in Brisbane. The authorities weren't going to stop us from having fun, with a rabbit, at our party.

Our parting gift to the Versace Hotel was inspired by the black-and-white photos of various film stars and sporting heroes adorning the corridors. Sounds a bit TGI Fridays doesn't it, but no, these photos were quite stylish in their own way. Each star was half-naked, posing in a way to show their beautiful body off at its best. Chris and I had the idea of superimposing Jeremy's, James's and Shane's head onto stunning bodies, for example a ballerina or Calvin Klein underwear model. We originally presented the opulently framed beauties to our celebs to take home but then decided it would be very funny if we were to replace some of the superstars in the corridors, such as Madonna, Tom Cruise and Patrick Swayze, with our beautiful boys. I wish I'd seen the faces of any staff or guests that spotted our generous offerings.

It was now time for the Bubble to have another holiday before heading over to Melbourne. These luxury holidays were actually a necessary treat to enable the set and crew to travel and for the motoring theatre to be rebuilt at the next venue. As we were on the other side of the world, there was no point flying home and back out again, and in fact that cost would have been as much as what we did spend on our special treats. Well nearly.

We took a normal plane, with normal people, to Hamilton Island, where we were met by slightly sycophantic resort staff from the incredible resort, Qualia. However, instead of being met by Rolls Royces or Range Rovers, we had a fleet of chauffeur-driven golf buggies. No cars were allowed on this paradise island.

We snaked up the hill rather slowly in a comical-looking convoy with the likes of Jeremy and Shane-O not quite fitting into our new mode of transport (Shane-o is built like an oversized Barney Rubble. However, despite our low-key vehicles, our accommodation was out of this world. The Maharaja was appointed the largest and most beautiful villa with a teak-clad living space opening out to an infinity pool overlooking the ocean. We were all in awe until we were shown James's dwelling, which was like the butler's quarters over a little wooden bridge and down some steps directly below the Maharaja's villa. It too was beautiful and right on the water's edge, but it was about a third of the size of JC's palace. This obvious difference made us all feel a little awkward.

James, slightly miffed at first, soon stepped away from his ego and embraced his very beautiful but slightly humbler abode, although he did make it known that he was not happy about having to walk past Jeremy's place in fear of having to face a naked Clarkson first thing in the morning. Chris, anxious to dispel any upset, turned on the humour, suggesting James was Billy Goat Gruff and he would have to ask the Troll, JC, at the other side of the bridge for permission to cross every time he wanted to go out.

It was decided we would all meet at JC's for pre-dinner drinks. We were all assigned our own golf buggies to get around the stunning and serene resort and tropical paradise. The serenity did not last long.

We each had a villa. I was absolutely blown away with the luxury I had landed in. After testing out the free-standing bath, veranda, living area, minibar, bed and shower (needed to rinse my hair after a bath) at high, overexcited speed, I set off in my golf buggy in search of Jeremy's palace. All the villas were linked by narrow brick lanes that were actually very slippery especially after a tropical shower. They were lined with dense flora and fauna which was home to wallabies and possum that could surprise you at any time, as could Shane-O coming at you at high speed looking like Barney Rubble completely out of control.

Shane-O had discovered he could take a corner on two wheels in his buggy. We became accustomed to the screeching of his tyres before he threw it sideways to stop. The excitement was palpable within our totally overindulged Bubble. After drinks at the Maharaja's villa, we all set off for dinner. I don't know how I stayed on the road as I was in hysterics with tears of laughter blurring my vision as seven of us created a golf buggy Grand Prix to dinner.

We all parked up, Shane-O in his dramatic stunt-like way, and were promptly warned by a hotel manager that the buggies would be taken away if we drove too fast or damaged any of them. Not so sycophantic now. I felt very sorry for anyone who had been enjoying their dream honeymoon or holiday before we rocked up.

After dinner in what was probably the best dining setting I had experienced so far, up high in a luxury treehouse adorned with vivid tropical flowers, water features and the sound of tropical birds, with views looking out to sea, we made plans for the next couple of days.

The boys did actually have to do a couple of radio interviews which they were both really reluctant about. Somehow, a deal was negotiated between Chris and Jeremy that he and James would do the interview if while they were doing it, Gemma and I were massaging each other in the same room. Another page in our 'sexual harassment' file. Fuelled by pre-lunch cocktails, Gem and I did 'perform' for a few minutes for a laugh and to get the boys started on their call promoting the next leg, Melbourne. To be clear it was an interview over the phone.

Between some actual relaxing, which was rare with our hyperactive performers, we had a couple of excursions just to keep the budget up to its max. We chartered a boat and crew to take us snorkelling. As was a certainty with the Aussies, there was a full health and safety briefing, much to the annoyance of the Maharaja. Part of the briefing was to inform us that we had to wear full wetsuits including hoods and gloves as there was an infestation of deadly jellyfish in the area. You can imagine how well that went down. 'I've been snorkelling all my life, I have never had to wear that!' ranted the big man.

He conceded, and as the rest of us squeezed ourselves into the full gear, he joined us and posed for one of the funniest tour photos. We looked like a very eccentric mime act. You can imagine the unique silhouette that Jeremy formed in the bright Australian sunshine. We became used to this overgrown toddler/teenager losing it now and again, reassured by the fact, that like kids do, he would eventually get over it and conform.

Our next excursion was what Gem and I would describe as a terrifying jet-ski safari. Jeremy got into a bit of an ego-off with the young instructor. He unsurprisingly did not want to sit through yet another health and safety briefing but was made to, so by the time we got out into the open sea he was ready for battle. A pretty tragic-looking jet-ski battle commenced between a middle-aged, balding, pot-bellied man and a young Adonis, leaving the rest of us, including Gem and me who were complete novices, desperately trying to keep up through rough seas.

It was thrilling but terrifying. There was more terror than thrill for my liking. I held on for dear life as I descended into trough after trough of waves as everyone else seemingly disappeared. Us girls looked out for each other but the instructor's health and safety ethics had long gone, as had any chivalry of Jeremy's. They and their egos were battling it out way ahead of us.

As we returned to dry land, my knuckles were white as they were almost welded to the handles. I wasn't sure I could actually dismount as the rest of me had turned to jelly as the adrenalin drained out. When I did make it, I was literally wobbling as my brain tried to work out that we had come to a standstill. I could have killed Jeremy and the instructor for putting us all at risk as they carried out their twattish sea race. However, I was quite chuffed I had survived something I would never have pushed myself to do ordinarily. Not at that speed anyway.

Meanwhile, Jeremy was all puffed up and bantering with his new juvenile friend who had conceded that this old man was quite good.

However, the Maharaja did not look quite so James-Bond-like when he arrived for breakfast the next morning. He could hardly walk and felt so exhausted he actually arrived in his complimentary resort bathrobe. The smug smile was gone, but not ours as we failed to contain our laughter. The big man was down – but not out, as he was soon leading the next golf buggy Grand Prix when we headed out for dinner off-resort.

After arriving back for nightcaps on our own reserved terrace, in the tree-house style dining area, Chris pushed the boundaries one step too far as he drove his golf buggy right in through reception to the steps of our private terrace. After yet another disapproving frown from management, the buggy was removed and the keys confiscated, it was time to move on.

Next morning, we headed back to the tiny airport with a fond and relieved farewell from Qualia staff. In full rock and roll style we had a private jet, a proper jet, waiting for us on the runway. The boys were dead chuffed and all of us were overexcited and not rock and roll cool as we took pictures posing with our luxury beast.

It did not disappoint inside: you could actually stand upright on the luxury deep-pile carpet (unlike on the cheaper, private planes we had experienced before), and we each had a first-class, bulging with comfort seat. For a more leisurely moment you could lounge in the lounge area or even crash out in the bedroom. We were really reaching the dizzying heights of our tour literally as we sped through the air to Melbourne quaffing champagne in crystal glasses.

On arrival in Melbourne, we checked into a huge hotel in the city that included a casino and nightclub. It was a bit of a culture shock compared to the tropical paradise we had left behind. There were a few grumbles from the big man as he had concerns over crowds heading in and out of the casino harassing him. We headed straight out to recce the venue, the Melbourne Showgrounds, where a temporary racetrack had been set up for speed tests of rally cars and various supercars. Jeremy and James whizzed round in the latest Ford Falcon GT, which is basically a pimped-up Mondeo with an engine base taken from the Mustang. Jeremy loved it for the noise it made and the tyre it laid down every time you set off. He chose to drive himself to and from the venue in it, I think partly to have some time away from the Bubble and partly to have some fun throwing it around corners and making noise.

Jeremy was obviously feeling the strain of touring and a heavy work schedule. It was difficult to find a restaurant of the usual high standard he had come to expect, but we were assured by our Melbourne hosts that the Italian we were heading to served up a great steak, tasty traditional Italian dishes and was just a short walk away in a pedestrianised area behind the hotel.

We met in the hotel foyer as usual. It was generally quiet in the hotel, casino and along our route to the restaurant. As we entered the fairly simple, nondescript restaurant, a few heads turned to stare at our famous friends. Jeremy was immediately agitated, unfortunately having been so spoilt of late and especially at the idyllic resort we had just left, so it did make this rather bland establishment not very appealing. We also didn't have our usual private corner, let alone a private room.

Chris was panicking and trying to appease JC, who had grumbled off to have a fag outside. Gemma and I tried to get a better table, but there was no other option. Jeremy, having calmed down, accepted the table we'd been given, and we all tried to position him so he was shielded from other diners. JCP hastily ordered the wine to continue to calm the Maharaja who was truly acting up to his newly acquired name.

Unfortunately, a rather uncouth local was determined to get a picture of JC and was sneakily trying to get a shot from where he sat, through us Bubble members, despite us trying to shield the Maharaja. Meanwhile, James was just quietly getting on enjoying his vino and Shane-O was telling jokes.

Jeremy snapped, got up from the table and grabbed the phone out of the shocked fan's hand and an argument broke out which looked like it was going to escalate. Chris and Shane jumped up to intervene. Jeremy stormed out, swiftly followed by Chris. Jeremy launched into an angry tirade at Chris, protesting that he couldn't just walk him through the streets to a shabby restaurant without security or a private area. He was really angry that Chris seemed to have no idea just how famous he was and what it was like to be hounded for pictures and autographs. He then stropped off, on his own, towards the hotel, demanding that Chris get a helicopter to take him to the venue in the morning. I was sent after him to make sure he was alright.

By the time I caught up with him, he had phoned home and was considering quitting the tour for good. He continued to rant about how life was not fun being famous, and people were milking him to make money. At the same time I was receiving messages from Chris and Gem asking if they could do anything and confirming that they were booking a helicopter. I gradually talked Jeremy down and suggested that getting a helicopter was more trouble than it was worth as he'd need to take a car to a heliport and a car at the end of the flight to actually get into the venue. He eventually calmed down, and told me to cancel the chopper and that he just wanted to sleep.

After reassuring Chris and Gem and the rest of the Bubble that the Maharaja was just overtired and would be returning to work the next day, I turned in as well and tucked into a tube of Pringles, having missed out on supper.

Everyone was a little subdued the next day. Jeremy apologised but we all spent the day walking on eggshells. After a rather low day, a treat was in store for our evening entertainment. We were off to see Neil Diamond in concert.

We had the usual VIP treatment and arrived in our convoy of Range Rovers through a back entrance where we were taken to a VVIP area to be fed and watered. Neil Diamond's people had been talking to our people, and it was the boys' understanding that Mr Diamond wanted to meet them before the show.

We ate, we drank and we drank some more. The Maharaja was getting a bit tired of waiting, especially as Neil's VIPs were all keen to have a chat with him and James. I did feel sorry for them and realised the value in having our own private dining, transport, terraces and lounges wherever possible. If not, they could never really switch off for fear of photos of 'men behaving badly' or constant interruption from overexcited fans.

After a long and slightly tense wait, we were finally ushered into a side room which had an area curtained off. It turned out we were in a further holding area and the boys were briefed on what they could and couldn't ask, which I wasn't privy to otherwise I'd tell. It was a strange circumstance to see our celebs being treated like minions to meet an even bigger celeb who definitely had Maharaja tendencies, more so than our main man.

There was more, tense, waiting. The awkward silence was broken by JC exclaiming, 'I've got to have a piss.' Oh no. Panic broke out as a few of Neil's people said he's ready for you, can you wait? This did not go down well with the big man, who set off to have his piss, Neil Diamond or no Neil Diamond. James was left to be escorted around the curtain to meet Neil and have not much of a conversation as Neil had no idea who he was and was equally unimpressed when our Maharaja returned. JC was told he'd only have two minutes with Neil, which did not go down well either. I don't know exactly what was said between the three of them but it wasn't a lot. This was not going well considering we were trying to raise the mood of the Bubble and especially JC.

After a lot of grumbling and a verbal assault on Chris for arranging such a ridiculous meeting with someone who was literally not interested in *Top Gear* or its presenters, Jeremy gradually calmed down. Once Neil started blasting out classics like 'Sweet Caroline', washed down with a few more beers, the Maharaja was happy again, and so too, the Bubble.

Thank heavens for Shane-O. He was brilliant at cheering us all. If Jeremy did go off on one, James and Richard would quietly retreat to a corner, but Shane-O helped diffuse any awkward moments with his brilliant comedy. He had a great repertoire of stories and jokes but was very humble and knew when to speak up and when to quietly make a cuppa and find a corner. The next day, back at the venue, JC requested that the DVD for the afternoon rest period should be Shane's movie *Kenny*.

Shane's brother, Clayton, had produced and directed it, and several other members of the family starred alongside Shane in the lead role as Kenny, a family man who worked for a portable loo company. Kenny is described as the 'Dalai Lama of waste management'. It's a brilliant movie, both funny and heart-warming. We all loved it, especially the Maharaja. It bought out his softer side once more.

With another city under our belt it was time to move on. I can't actually remember travelling at this point in my tale, but I know we flew back to Sydney for one night and we ended up in Johannesburg. This is a definite black spot in my memory, which is strange because this was a pinnacle moment for the whole tour.

No, In Your Backside

After too much text bombing from the other side of the world from the whole of the Bubble, Richard joined us. The venue, Kyalami Grand Prix Circuit, and the huge motoring festival that was created there, were the cherry on the biggest most delicious cake with the finest ingredients – mmm? Maybe not the finest. It was March 2011: the boys were at the height of their fame.

Kyalami was a stunning and perfect venue for our once pokey panto style motoring theatre to evolve into an incredible motoring festival, with many of the greats from motorsport participating in track events alongside 4x4 courses, stunt driving schools, classic car shows and of course the boys performing in the largest arena yet, outside, in the *Top Gear Live* Thunder Dome.

The money spent on this was huge. I know there was a big sponsor involved, the owner of several luxury brands and a huge tobacco company. He clearly didn't impress me too much because I can't remember his name or any of his brands. I do remember he hosted a huge gala dinner that the Bubble attended and during which Jody Scheckter, former Grand Prix World Champion, now organic farmer, entered the dining hall in his ice cream van to serve up some of his delicious organic ice cream.

I digress. This festival was enormous. Jeremy, James and Richard had Tiff Needell and Sasha performing alongside them in the Thunder Dome, which was gigantic and allowed for stunts such as Sasha bungee jumping in a Nissan Micra from an incredibly tall crane, and James and Jeremy battling it out to fill giant inflatable dolls modelled on them. The blow-up Clarkson and May were attached to the exhausts of supercars which were mounted on 'rolling roads'. Jeremy and James had to rev the engines of their supercars in order for their dolls to become erect. Plenty of opportunity for innuendo, which was pretty much constant in all the shows and in fact anywhere the boys or Chris were (or me if I'm honest). Alongside the usual Car Porn parade and crazy races were incredible stunt teams such as a trial bike team who drove at speed up an enormous ramp, triple somersaulted, and twisted in all directions, like they were being juggled in the air, before landing and disappearing at speed backstage. This was by far the best show of the tour.

A temporary stadium had been created for the ever-enthusiastic South Africans to scream and holler as much as they liked. The giant backdrop was created out of scaffolding, accommodating a screen over 40 ft wide and 30 ft deep hanging above a wall of shipping containers, stacked three high, that were draped in black tarpaulin branded with *Top Gear Live* Thunderdome. The shipping containers created a tunnel for the entrance from backstage.

Backstage was a show in itself: backstage right had a pile of smashed-up cars from a stunt involving a moped being fired from the back of a monster truck. The aim was to hit the target of a car at the other side of the arena. The cars were already heading for the scrapyard. Back of backstage, the supercars were parked up and guarded for the Car Porn scene. Backstage left was the enormous crane and Nissan Micra in a metal frame ready for bungeeing, and beyond that was the huge ramp that was fitted to a truck for the motocross bikes to launch themselves off and that could be driven to centre stage when required. The original motorbike stunt team from France were flown over, and their giant colander must have been shipped over, too. They stood by, backstage left. Somewhere amongst all this were an incredible bunch of guys called the Soweto Wheelspinners, who put on an amazing performance of mind-blowing stunts jumping in, out and over the cars like parkour with fast-moving and donutting cars, choreographed to some heavy and very loud hip-hoppy street sounds. (I so don't know what I'm talking about with regard to the music.)

Our stars of stage and screen had a very basic hangout in the back of one of the containers. They also had a small area amongst generators and heaps of cables where a few camp chairs were set up by a huge cooler of cold drinks. All these performers, vehicles and props created quite a scene as the show started to take on a kind of Cirque du Soleil feel fuelled by petrol (and a bit of alcohol).

The Thunderdome was about a mile from the main grandstand where above the pit lane a red-carpeted, shaded terrace had been created for all the VIP performers, who included Eddie Jordan, Sir Stirling Moss, Nick Mason (drummer of Pink Floyd, and collector of Ferraris that had also been shipped out for the occasion), Sabine Schmitz, the aforementioned Jody Scheckter, Derek Bell (Le Mans winner and former F1 driver) and David Coulthard.

The Bubble itself was fully inflated, with Andy Wilman on board along with several of the *Top Gear* TV show's crew and other BBC execs. It was an amazing atmosphere and we all had full-on schedules, especially our three amigos who, as well as putting on at least two shows a day in the Thunder Dome, were appearing on the track racing against each other and the other motorsport celebs. They were also commentating, interviewing and appearing at the stunt driving school. For any downtime there was a large, well-equipped green room and plenty of great food.

Rather than our leisure time, it was the festival that became the highlight of this leg of the tour, although we still had amazing dinners, and we were staying at the Palazzo Hotel again, as was everyone else involved, so partying began at breakfast, minus the alcohol.

We did have a wonderful lunch at simply the best restaurant in the world, The Cradle, set in 7,000 hectares of World Heritage conservation area. Home to lions, giraffes and all the usual safari stars, it was incredible. (At the time it was owned by a friend of Jeremy's. Jeremy not only knows everything, he also knows everyone and had in fact given over half of his address book to help put the festival on.)

Gem, Jeremy, James, Richard and I were flown by helicopter to make it even more special. At the top of the path leading to this extraordinary establishment was a beautiful sculpture of a fallen angel, feet and wings reaching for the sky. The intriguing path led you through the bush until you reached the simple but stunning wooden and stone building which encompassed an incredibly stylish bar and restaurant area as good as the very best in Mayfair or Chelsea, but which led out to a charming rustic veranda like a film set from *Out of Africa*. From here you could watch the wildlife wander about in the bush below that stretched out for as far as you could see. This was my favourite lunch of the tour, with my best and most amusing friends and colleagues, spotting giraffe as we dined on the most delicious food.

After such a sophisticated lunch, it was hard to go back to work. I say sophisticated but as usual there was larking around and I have a great photo of the three boys posing as the three wise monkeys, hear-no, speak-no and see-no.

After the first day of rehearsals, JC was concerned that there wasn't enough content of himself, James and Richard larking about and came up with a brilliant idea over dinner. All three boys bantered away like schoolkids creating this new game. Imagine having a job where you get paid a lot of money for just messing about with your mates.

Rowly was summoned and had the task of sourcing a fleet of typical Jo'burg taxis, which were renowned amongst the locals for being heavily dented, barely roadworthy white minibuses that were overloaded and driven terribly, broke down a lot, and whose drivers failed to observe just about every driving regulation going. Jeremy had come up with the game of Splat the Rat (rats were also common on the streets of Jo'Burg). The plan was for Tiff and the three amigos to be chasing after rats – to be created out of remote-control cars that would be whizzing around the arena for the boys, in their taxis, to splat.

Rowly and his team pulled the 'rat out of the bag' once again, sourcing dozens of remote-control cars and a small fleet of taxis. The boys pulled off game after game of thrilling taxi driving madness. It was hilarious, especially in the rain, which we had quite a lot of. The crowd loved it.

The rain unfortunately was quite a big feature of the festival and caused quite a few dramas. We had to cancel some of the Thunderdome shows and time trials, etc. on the track and desperately tried to keep the audience at the festival for rescheduled shows. There was a lot of can we, can't we going on, as well as tension, panic and general upset as incredibly challenging rescheduling was planned and risk assessments carried out. This included weather predictions and wondering if the whole audience would be taken out by a lightning strike as they all sat in the huge scaffolding structure that formed the auditorium.

The lightning and storms were quite terrifying in such a prominent wide open space and sadly a marshal on the track was struck by lightning and had a heart attack. This incident did stop play, understandably, for quite some time.

Eventually, despite the rain, which was monsoon-like, the shows continued with our brave presenters poncho-ing up and performing to the smallest crowd ever, which was quite comedic in itself. The arena was treacherous despite backstage crew frantically sweeping huge puddles and rivers away as best they could. The spray created by the cars did enhance the spectacle of the show and added some unpredictability for all. We all suffered several drenchings. The green room looked like a Chinese laundry, with all three presenters' jeans, shirts and T-shirts hung out on a makeshift line between furniture.

However, the rain did not dampen spirits, and there was the inevitable crew party, which had the bar raised just a tad as we were entertaining a few extra stars. With JC's influence, the professional, wonderful Paula, sister of 'The Blonde' (A. A. Gill's wonderful wife) was hired to draft in more celebrity guests who had attended the festival and to provide top-class entertainment and catering.

The venue got a first-class upgrade too and was poolside and candle-lit at the Palazzo Hotel. It was stunning and very rock and roll, drinking and partying alongside legends such as David Coulthard (a party pro), Lady and Sir Stirling Moss (still got it although didn't last the distance), and Eddie Jordan (goes in fast and hard and knows when to pull out).

Jeremy gave a thank you speech, hijacked by Chris Hughes who can't bear to be silenced and itches to get on the mike, wherever possible. There was a very talented George Benson style singer and his small band who didn't mind the inevitable band-jacking. Who wouldn't mind moving over for Nick Mason to perform? Even if he was accompanied by

Chris Hughes on vocals backed by yours truly, Mrs Mason and Gem.

James May continued developing his rock and roll skills and although he started off slowly, quietly drinking in a corner, he was becoming renowned for attracting small groups of women with his gentle ways until later on in the proceedings when, as in New Zealand, he came right out of his shell and was stage right of Chris crooning along with him. Still requiring a lot of sleep and often peaking too early with his drinking tactics, Richard had disappeared relatively early, wobbling off with someone reminding him of his room number (a regular job for Gem and I, and an occupational hazard for someone who had suffered a severe head injury followed by heavy drinking and world touring).

Another brilliant night stretching into the wee small hours, interrupted briefly for me, as I was pushed in the pool by Adam Waddell from the BBC. It did not finish me though: after a quick visit to my room for a change of clothes, I was back to catch up where I'd left off.

The next morning was tough. Dark glasses were a must, as were plenty of fluids for most, apart from the legend that is Eddie Jordan. I asked him how he managed to have that same familiar energy and enthusiasm. He shared his secret of being the life and soul of the party early on in the proceedings, then quietly exiting on a high, early doors.

Our famous trio were not feeling quite so chipper, and nor was the party king, Chris Hughes. He had been reported asleep in a large chair just outside the lifts, in the wee small hours, much to the entertainment of most of the Bubble, his tubby little body slumped with one arm propping up his head as he sullied a beautiful, ornate chair, more suitable for an elegant, elderly lady to rest upon while waiting for the lift than an old drunk. We just left him there until he was eventually escorted to his room, to be woken up fully clothed by his alarm a few hours later.

Unlike myself, Chris was a trooper at getting going again and holding the fort no matter what. I can only remember one time when he had to disappear to his room in order to carry on for yet another evening of buoying up the boys for a late show and after-show celebration. There was constant speculation that he would drop dead due to his terrible lifestyle, and especially his diet. As I've said before, he was not named 'Piggy-Eyed Businessman' just for his love of money. I once witnessed him, at yet another tempting and delicious restaurant, order a spare meal as he couldn't decide what to eat. He ate both.

On arrival in the green room, more hangover cures were demanded. Jeremy, James and Richard were actually seriously concerned how they would perform their races on track, due to start in less than an hour. I was genuinely worried as this wasn't like larking about in the arena. This was proper racing around a proper track. I quickly remembered that the paramedics who had been on duty at all our other events in South Africa had offered Vitamin B12 injections in the past to help with hangovers and tiredness. I knew first-hand about these, having had them for health reasons. They give you an immediate pick-you-up.

I suggested the B12 to the boys. Jeremy said, 'Yes, good idea' and sent me off in search of the paramedics to see if they had any. I came back into the green room to report the good news that the paramedics would come up to administer the injections. Jeremy asked, 'Where do they inject?' 'In the eye', I said instantly with my best poker face knowing that JC had a massive aversion to anything to do with eyes, which we all knew about when he had a sore eye and had to brave a few Optrex drops. The room fell apart with laughter.

The injections were actually delivered into their backsides, which Richard opted out of. He had youth on his side and went for his trusted recovery option of Berocca. James and Jeremy were up for it, especially as the paramedic was a rather attractive blonde. They had no shame and lay face down on the giant bean bags with pants down for all of us to see. I think this scene at least matched that of Richard with a gag in his mouth and cock on his head in Amsterdam. Especially when James stuffed a cushion in his mouth.

Unfortunately, unlike my experience of the great B12 high, because the boys were pumping adrenalin so fast as they sped around the track, they experienced a dramatic low as the effect wore off towards the end of their laps and had to mask their staggers as they exited their cars to be interviewed.

However, I was instructed to add B12 shots to my bag of essential things to be available for any hangover emergency.

Sadly, the rain didn't let up and continued to hinder the shows, but luckily both crowd and performers were not deterred. Sometimes the motorbike stunts had to be rescheduled for fear of them killing themselves, but other than that with ponchos on, umbrellas up, we soldiered on.

After Chris's heavy night, the boys thought he was sloping off for snoozes. In fact he was busier than ever troubleshooting constantly throughout the enormous site. The boys were keen not to let him skive off and put out a request over the Bubble's walkie-talkies to come immediately backstage as there was a problem. Around twenty minutes later, Chris appeared looking ready for his first heart attack, whereupon James complained in his sultry tone that Richard had crushed his beef Hula Hoops. Chris's response as the boys were in hysterics was, 'You fu**ers!'

There were a lot of practical jokes, as you might imagine, none larger than, probably the ultimate one, when the boys decided to really stitch Chris up. All three boys plotted and schemed to buy an old transit van and have it sprayed on both sides with our special phrase 'Get in the fu**ing van!' They then arranged for it to be delivered to Chris's family home in Marlow, out of the blue.

Genius! One ordinary day, away from touring and travelling, after his usual daily commute to and from London, Chris arrived home to find an old transit parked annoyingly close to his driveway. His wife had already had complaints from the neighbours and enquiries as to where it had come from. Imagine his horror when he read what was on the sides. He then had to arrange to have it towed away and scrapped. Brilliant.

Assembled once more with the Bubble to recall the story, all he could do was laugh and say, 'You fu**ers!' Just another day in our extraordinary Bubble, drinking champagne, in hysterical laughter waiting for the next flight.

Kyalami, despite the torrential rain, was a great success. The boys had created the largest crowd of car fans ever in Africa, performing to over 60,000 people over three days. All three of them genuinely loved it and had really settled into touring life with all its trimmings, which were much more fun and luxurious than when filming for the BBC.

Chris and I came up with the perfect gift to commemorate this leg of the tour and created a CD of relevant tour tracks complete with bespoke album cover of the three of them and Tiff dressed in matching ponchos performing to an almost empty stadium, entitled *The 'Take the Weather with You' Tour*. This included the Rock-a-saurus's tour favourite, 'Turn the Page' by Bob Seger, 'Red Wine' (to represent the consumption of and UB40 being from Birmingham), 'Gimme Hope Jo'anna' by Eddy Grant (for a tenuous link to Johannesburg) and so on. Not forgetting our crew party anthem, 'Mustang Sally'.

The joy showed on their faces as we bundled into a Range Rover, straight out of the Thunderdome and were driven at speed by Denzel to avoid our own traffic and catch our flight home. Jeremy, James and Richard were overwhelmed by the huge number of fans who were corralled the other side of a fence cheering and waving as we departed.

Richard Pulls a Moose

Carrying on with our trio, or as I now referred to them, the three Am-egos, we headed to Oslo to start conquering the people of Scandinavia. After an eventful flight that involved being diverted from Oslo to a tiny country airport as two hang-gliders had flown into Oslo's airspace, I eventually made it and joined the Bubble at the venue to start rehearsals. Although Kyalami was amazing, it was quite nice to be back to working with the simpler routine of performing hour-long shows in one confined arena, especially as it was minus something outside and knee-deep in snow.

Doing these short hops to Europe was reasonably stress-free, especially in Norway as the Scandinavians were generally a polite bunch who didn't harass our stars too much, and paparazzi didn't really exist. So we thought.

Our home for the next few days was at the Ritz in central Oslo. Although a little too staid and old-fashioned for our liking, it did provide a lovely rooftop terrace (linked to bar/nightclub in the evenings) to soak up the winter sun. We also had a private breakfast room, which helped provide a relaxed start to our mornings.

We had a great welcome to the hotel with a real tour feel to it as a crowd had built up, ready to catch a glimpse of our heroes. We literally had to jostle our way through after leaving the comfort and security of the Range Rovers, though as I've said, the Norwegians were very polite and the boys enjoyed this rather civilised mobbing from fans.

Things were fairly civilised in our leisure time too. James and Richard went off to shop for clothes and visit a museum, and I suggested that JC, Chris, Gem and I went to Vigeland, the naked statue park. I had been taken there before in my teens and remembered a huge phallic-looking column that was made up of stone, naked bodies entwined around each other. I thought the others might enjoy some culture and art (titter, titter).

As expected, it was not a very cultural trip with Jeremy and Chris in tow. To start with, reminiscent of school trips, Chris had forgotten his coat, quite unbelievably considering everywhere was covered in snow. Our young driver offered up his, despite being half the size of Chris, and I lent him my hat. He looked, once again, like Dick Emery.

Once amongst all the stunning and slightly provocative statues, Chris proceeded to act up, eventually stripping down to his waist and poking his finger through his fly posing like one of the statues. Jeremy did not need any encouragement and took an extra interest in all the breasts available to inspect, cupping some for size. Gem and I did find them very amusing, especially when they both performed a rendition of Morecambe and Wise dancing down the steps of the park. Luckily, there was hardly anyone around, so when to top off their schoolboy behaviour Jeremy took a pee in the bushes, due to lack of facilities, no one saw us.

We had our usual great nights out, with a rather weird crew party on a terrace on top of a shopping centre, complete with band for band-jacking, and there were the usual antics in the green room, like Jeremy chatting to James with a banana poking out of his fly, while James had a cushion cover on his head to create a nineteenth-century artist kind of vibe. I don't know why but it was funny.

We made use of the very convenient small nightclub on the roof of our hotel. Norway was where I introduced Baileys to the Bubble. I've always liked it as a winter treat – it's like pudding and a nightcap in one. Jeremy pulled faces and made disapproving comments in his snobbish way. However, once he tasted it he joined in with the rest of us and so another Bubble ritual was born. Trays of Baileys were ordered as we huddled outside on the terrace under blankets and patio heaters till late into the night.

Turns out as smooth as Baileys is, it doesn't help smooth over a hangover. The boys groaned their way through the journey to the venue and Richard dragged himself into the green room, immediately asking for a Berocca. I headed to the fridge for the water to make one, but he insisted he'd do it so I passed him the Berocca, which he duly added to a glass of sparkling water. If you've never tried this before, it makes a wonderful spectacle as Berocca is effervescent. Richard, the fridge and the floor were decorated with orange bubbles. Richard gave up and let me take over while he lay on the sofa.

As usual, the shows were performed whatever condition the presenters were in, and as ever they were well received. I was sent on my usual shopping spree for gifts for the presenters. Chris had decided to create a special game of charades and a quiz, which would be in place of the usual closing ceremony. This would also act as some entertainment as we had a bit of a wait before we could set off for the flight home. The winner of the games would receive a special gift which he wanted me to find, something that represented Norway.

I found it: the most enormous stuffed toy I have ever seen and it was most appropriately a moose. A huge blue one dressed like Superman – of course. It was as tall as me and twice as wide. It had actually been on display in a random toy and souvenir shop but I'd persuaded the shop owner to sell it along with some classic Norwegian jumpers and woolly hats.

Chris had begun to build up the amazing prize that was on offer to the winner of his parlour games tournament. But between us we planned to rig the competition so that Richard won. At the end of another successful run of shows, we snuggled into our makeshift living room at one end of the green room and everyone was kept happy with snacks and champagne and beers.

Our three Am-egos were given prime position on the sofa together. They were presented with their gifts and Richard and James sat with their silly Norwegian flag, woolly hats on. They may have looked stupid but all three of them were taking the competition seriously as they had really been taken in by Chris's lure of a big prize.

The charades game was hilarious. Chris had given each of us scenes from all our touring adventures to act out for the boys to guess. According to plan, Richard was winning and he was loving it. Despite Jeremy's and James's desperate and extremely competitive attempts to beat him, they couldn't as Chris was rigging the whole thing including the questions of the quiz that followed.

After some ridiculous mimes and shouting through quiz answers, Richard was declared the winner. He was so pleased with himself, as pleased as the others were disappointed. Chris left the room to retrieve the much-awaited prize, returning of course with the moose that was twice the size of Richard. There was a little bit of swearing from Richard and much laughter from the rest of us. As *Top Gear* rules dictate, if you are given a prize or present, you have to take it home. And carry it back to the hotel and pack, and carry it out of the hotel and into the Range Rover and out again at the airport, and through the airport, through security into the lounge and onto the plane.

Chris hadn't been quite clever enough as he ended up having to buy a business-class seat for the moose!

Back in the UK, the Bubble dispersed in time for the annual *Top Gear* break of two weeks with no filming or touring over the school Easter Holidays period. I think all concerned were pleased for the break and time with their families.

Unfortunately for Jeremy and me, a bomb went off as we were outed by *The Mirror* for having an affair. There is never a good time to tell your family that you are leaving them, but for it to be speculated and broadcast all over the tabloids is really not ideal or pleasant for all concerned.

As you can imagine, there was quite a lot of stress and upset for both of us, and Jeremy's family, especially. Eventually, the tabloids got bored and we kept a low profile as a couple so as not to fuel it.

Going back to the Bubble was a little strange but everyone was very supportive and nothing really changed. We were both there to do a job and that's what we did. Chris was the most confused. He said, 'I don't know whether to call you Horse or First Lady?' I answered, 'Horse'.

We were back in Birmingham again and this time decided to hire a whole country house with a chef and housekeeping. It was hilarious, as it had eight bedrooms and looked like a haunted house from *Scooby-Doo*, making the perfect setting for a crew Halloween party. Apart from being a bit spooky and a bit tired, with wallpaper from the seventies and carpet to match, it provided a real homely resting place for an ageing and tired Bubble. We were all starting to flag a little and definitely felt we had exhausted the nightlife of Birmingham.

Tiff Needell and Vicki Butler-Henderson were with us too, creating a welcome extended Bubble family. Vicki is like a long lost sister to me, she was part of the original *Top Gear* line up, now a presenter with Tiff on *Fifth Gear* and is married to Phil Churchward a long suffering and very talented *Top Gear* and now *Grand Tour* director. I have worked and 'played' with Vicki and her brother Charlie, also a racing driver and stunt driver, for over twenty years as they live local to me. Vicki completed my favourite dysfunctional family bringing some very welcome sisterly comfort to me on this leg of the tour.

The show had become more festival-like for the first time in the UK and a track had been set up at the NEC, where Tiff and Vicki performed along with other stunt drivers. Several celebrities made appearances, taking part in time trials in the Reasonably Priced Car. They were known petrolheads like Shane Lynch (former member of Boyzone and brother of Naomi, the Girl with Petrol Pumps for Arms), chef James Martin, Paul Hollywood, Carl Fogarty and Gethin Jones to name a few.

It was not as big as Kyalami but had a great atmosphere in a more intimate setting and provided a great day out for *Top Gear* fans, where they could enjoy seeing the boys live and uncut, make their own additions to the cool wall and have their picture taken on the car seats of the infamous *Top Gear* set, as well as get up close and personal with many of the cars that had been used in the crazy *Top Gear* challenges on TV.

The show itself took on an Olympic theme to start celebrating the London 2012 Olympics. There were some great additions to the show including what I thought made the best entrance for the boys. A replica of the stage and seats that they delivered the news on, in the TV show, had been motorised with a mini engine. (As JC had a constant need for speed, this was very quickly upgraded to a 5.7 V8 engine.) It had been modified with steering wheel, accelerator and brake pedals in front of JC's seat. It was fast and noisy, and very funny to see the boys hurtle around the arena, hair flowing, holding on to their seats as Jeremy threw it around corners making his perfect entrance.

Their entrances constantly entertained Chris and me. We would faithfully race to a seat to view them at every show, which was a must in order to give praise and feedback to our stars. Each presenter would introduce one of the others and they entertained themselves by making intros up on the spot in true *Top Gear* style:

JC – 'The most interesting man in the world, James May, live!'

JM – 'One day he'll be reincarnated as a whelk but for now he's live, it's Richard Hammond!'

RH – 'A welcome please, as unnecessarily enormous as he is, ladies and gentlemen, Jeremy Clarkson live!'

JC – 'Look who we've got here… His favourite recording artist is Vera Lynn. His favourite food is winter warming soup. His favourite year is 1953—' ('Get on with it,' interrupts James. They are all laughing.) 'Ladies and gentlemen it's, James May live!'

JM – 'It's like a hideous plastic novelty fallen from a satanic Christmas cracker, Richard Hammond!'

RH – 'It is a Sunday and nobody should have to look at that [pointing to JC], but nevertheless it is here and we should acknowledge that fact. I give you, and you are welcome to it, Jeremy Clarkson!'

It was actually written into their scripts:

Richard – Jeremy insult
James – Richard insult
Jeremy – James insult

They loved to catch each other out depending on the mood in the camp. If they were hungover, there wasn't so much effort made. They loved to unnerve each other or outdo each other with their incredible wordsmith skills. Each time they went out they had no idea what the other one was going to say about them, which made for some genuine spontaneous laughter between them.

The Olympic theme inspired an opening ceremony with a pimped-up black cab and open-top red bus roaring around the arena, around and under the motorbike stunt team from Kyalami, interspersed with huge pyros and a thoroughly British Aston Martin. All this was randomly followed by the tour's longstanding stars, the flaming Subarus.

The ceremony led into the first event of motorbike limbo. One of the stunt motorbikes jumped off a ramp between two giant walls of polystyrene that were lowered from the ceiling. Each jump became more challenging as the gap between the two walls became smaller. The bike was out of the game when the driver took a chunk out of the wall with his helmet. It looked way more impressive than it sounds.

Another Olympic classic inspired the game of car curling, which involved Richard and Jeremy competing in modified hatchbacks that, when a lever was pulled, came off their wheels and then rolled on a frame of castors, like those on shopping trolleys, allowing the cars to move in all directions. The boys had to pull the lever at the right time in order to direct them towards a bullseye-like target on the floor. The second car to go would aim to hit the other off the target. To add to the authentic curling experience, James was on a quad bike fitted with road sweepers. He whizzed around sweeping the course between games. This game created some great moments, such as when Jeremy rammed into Richard so hard his car limped off smoking, and he had to run to a spare to complete the competition. There was always a fine line between really wanting to destroy each other and sporting showmanship.

Thanks to Rowly, Paul Swift, his stunt team and the team of amazing mechanics, unique and crazy games were constantly being invented and evolving.

On our last night in our cosy family home, we arrived back from the NEC to a Halloween surprise. Some of the Brand Events staff had gone all out to dress the house ready for a small crew party. This was with permission from the rather eccentric owner, who would pop in from time to time with the proviso of checking all was OK, but I'm sure it was to befriend his rather popular amusing guests. Anyhow, he was very accommodating, and our team had cleared out the living room and set up a bar, as well as booking our favourite tour party band, Rockaoke. The team had carved out dozens of pumpkins and dressed the place in fake cobwebs and skeletons. We were welcomed by them made up as zombies lying on the floor and up the stairs, as if they were dead, which was quite impressive.

Unfortunately, Jeremy was not amused, just tired and hungry, as were Richard and James, but Jeremy made the most noise about it. We had put in a special request to the chef for lamb chops and mash, the boys' choice for a bit of home-cooked comfort. We all sat in the seventies style pine-clad kitchen instead of the grand dining room. It was just like a regular family Saturday night in, except that we had three rather grumpy presenters on our hands. I don't know why. I think they were just really feeling tired. The cracks were beginning to show.

Meanwhile, across in the other side of the house, the party was getting started with other members of the crew. The next thing we knew was Chris came bouncing in, accompanied by Paul Hollywood who was up for a party and very excited to hang out with the boys, as a fellow petrol head. The feelings weren't mutual. Awks. Big time.

Chris picked up on the vibe and ushered Paul out of the kitchen to show him the party room. JC summoned Chris and made it clear that he and the boys were not there to be shown off to prospective new clients of Chris's. It was a tense half an hour while Gem and I kept the boys happy with drinks in the kitchen and Chris tactfully tried to arrange for poor old Paul to get a taxi back to his hotel. (Paul, if you're reading, you missed nothing but three middle-aged grumpy presenters). A diva moment from our boys followed by a pretty tame party by our standards. The boys did get in the mood eventually and the inevitable band-jacking took place. The boys from Rockaoke, who had played for us several times before in the UK, knew our preferred playlist and were very accommodating when it came to a band-jack.

The tour rolled on to the new location of London's ExCel, where more of the same was performed alongside Vicki and Tiff and further celebrities such as Rupert Grint and Chris Evans (the ginger one not the Hollywood star). Who knew he would, somewhat controversially, end up presenting *Top Gear*. It certainly wasn't on the cards then.

Starting a new year, it was time to conquer a new territory altogether, Moscow, followed by more of Scandinavia, Sweden and Denmark. For reasons I cannot remember but I'm sure there were many, I didn't go to all these locations. Life for JC and me was pretty complicated at this point and we wanted to minimise the impact on anyone else, both in our personal life and professionally. And we may have fallen out. We did that a lot.

In fact we did travel a lot personally and I also had other work including working with Chris and more Brand Events crew at *CarFest*, another motoring extravaganza but with glamping not five-star hotels. Obviously, I had to be a mother from time to time too.

Get Me a Range Rover and Some Bear Stew

I was soon back with the Bubble to experience Finland, which was very grey. On arrival, as we travelled in our Range Rover convoy, Gem, AKA Publicity Mouse, came in for some stick. James and Jeremy (no Richard on this leg) noticed a lot of direction signs for the show along the side of the main road into Helsinki, which at first sight they were celebrating, impressed with the Publicity Mouse's efforts. Unfortunately, it became apparent they were facing the wrong way. A few panicky phone calls from Chris to Gem, to get onto the Finnish hosts, and problem solved.

But there was another problem. We didn't have the top-spec, long-wheelbase Range Rover that the Maharaja expected. There were the inevitable moans from JC. Gem reassured him that there would be one ready for the morning. The diva-like demands were becoming a little ridiculous and this was a prime example. Gem and Bas had searched the whole of Europe and beyond with the ever-diligent help of Range Rover, but there simply weren't any available. In the end one was sourced from Russia and driven all the way to Finland to be of service for our four-day stay. I asked Jeremy if it was really necessary to demand such detail. His reply was he had to keep reminding Chris of his value. A lesson we all need to learn, to value ourselves, but to that extreme? I'm not sure.

Jussi Heikelä was the local presenter to join JC and JM. He had already been 'interviewed' back in England by James and Jeremy, who had asked crucial questions like 'Do you smoke?', 'Do you mind being put in a shopping trolley and being hit by a muscle car to act as a bowling ball?' and 'Have you ever driven a chariot pulled by mopeds?'

Finland was dark or grey the whole time, so unsurprisingly the people were pretty miserable. They were the least reactive crowd in the whole world. In fact, to make it worse, as our presenters made their usual dramatic entrance, a few of the crowd appeared to be giving them the 'finger'. This leg of the tour became affectionately known as the Fu** You Tour.

Thankfully, Jussi was a bright young soul with a slight wild side. He explained that in the depths of winter no one really went out, but he helped us create our own fun, which included taking over the small nightclub that was within our hotel.

We had a free bar, courtesy of Chris Hughes's Cashless Holiday. We were fuelled by two enthusiastic cocktail barmen and we opened up the seemingly 'closed for winter' nightclub. We literally turned on all the lights and got the sounds going. It wasn't long before James with his newly acquired tour spirit was dancing on the tables with Jussi and the Rock-a-saurus. The night ended with the now-inevitable several rounds of Baileys.

The upside of Finland was that we caught up on some much-needed sleep as it was dark much more than light. The highlight of our limited leisure time was going on a cruise. Not on a superyacht this time, but a former Finnish navy warship. On first sight, in its original dark battleship grey livery, sitting in the cold grey waters against a cold grey sky, it did not look very inviting. However, there was plenty of warm hospitality on board including a hot tub and sauna. Quite frankly, it was too damn cold to be taking your clothes off but a brief look around the Helsinki archipelago was interesting and the boys of course loved the novel form of transport.

We went on to warm up for a typical Finnish lunch. We descended into a basement setting that looked like a Disney theme park's attempt at creating Snow White's log cabin, complete with staff dressed in traditional Finnish costume (Snow White-like and lederhosen). I was waiting for the Maharaja to kick off. However, humour got the better of him and he embraced yet another bizarre tour treat. We were ushered into a very cosy corner of a near empty restaurant. I think all the locals were at home contemplating suicide. (Apparently, Finland has very high rates of suicide, which is tragic, but not surprising given the lack of daylight.)

There were a few giggles as Jeremy gave Chris grief for taking us to lunch in some freak's shed. Gem, trying to make light of the situation, dressed up with a napkin on her head to fit in and tried to fathom out what some of the strange ancient artefacts that decorated the place were actually for. Jeremy was very happy once he saw the menu with Bear Stew and seven-day-old Reindeer Stew and was not disappointed. So thank you to the lovely, cosy, quirky basement restaurant somewhere in Helsinki, with very friendly staff and delicious stews. I had reindeer not bear – that seemed more acceptable?

Perhaps feeling deprived of luxury, Jeremy and James decided they would like caviar on blinis to celebrate after the last show. I think they got a taste for it after their earlier trip to Moscow, and Jussi had encouraged them by mentioning that it was widely available in Finland. However, not on a Sunday. A local runner had been sent out on a mission to find some. After several phone calls trying to explain that she thought she had found blinis but they were big, which I said would be fine, we can cut them up, the extra-large blinis arrived. They weren't blinis at all but some kind of potato cake. A small panic broke out worrying about the Maharaja's reaction.

'Don't worry,' I said, 'let's just get on and create tiny potato cakes.' As backup we got some plain crackers. We had a small production line going frantically trying to get our celebratory spread ready. The mood of the boys was not great as the crowds were so hard to perform to, with their strange sign language of appreciation (Jussi had assured Jeremy and James that is what they meant), made worse by a warehouse type venue with terrible acoustics. There was just no atmosphere. We desperately wanted to lift their spirits as much as possible.

We failed. We might as well have been serving the caviar with dog shit. Jeremy was not happy and even James moaned as they suffered their way through a few servings of caviar on not-blinis. Time to leave in our special-order Range Rover, not before I shoved down a few spoons of neat caviar. I hate food wastage at the best of times.

Onwards and upwards, well kind of sideways, we headed to a nightclub that was actually open, though I think it may have just been opened for us and all our crew. The Bubble made itself at home on a balcony, outside, so our presenters old and new could smoke. Chris, the Ring Master, ordered up gallons of Baileys, which were delivered on huge trays with a bucket of ice to provide as much or as little as preferred with our favourite winter tipple. As more and more was quaffed down, Jeremy preferred to surprise Chris and Rowly by tipping the ice bucket over them. Although shocked and very cold, they did see the funny side, thankfully, and the laughter continued.

It was time to leave this dark corner of Scandinavia, except for James – he stayed in order to film something for the TV show. As often happened, the schedules for all three of our stars crossed over, and with the help of Andy Wilman, slightly reluctantly, both tour and TV production somehow got squeezed into the calendar. But it was getting tough. That year alone, Jeremy had been to over twelve countries.

There was more of the same for the following year including Moscow, Amsterdam, Belgium, Sydney, Durban and Poland. The tour had dropped London and Birmingham for the time being. Amsterdam and Belgium were part of a new tour strategy to do one night only in each city and keep time away from home, or *Top Gear* filming, as minimal as possible.

Is That James May or Arnold Schwarzenegger?

Moscow was a real adventure for me. Although I love travelling, it is not somewhere I would chose to go to, but to go within the safety and luxury of the Bubble was amazing. I mention safety as there seemingly were risks, so we were assigned Olag, a former KGB officer and a member of the Kremlin's security team. Olag was with us all the time. The boys had met him and he had been of service to them before, so he gave us a warm but formal welcome. He totally looked the part with incredibly neat hair, straight face at all times and was dressed in black from head to toe. Oh, and he came with a gun. And a magic badge.

Olag's badge, which became a bit of a joke and an object of fascination within the Bubble, could be whipped out anywhere and would grant us immediate, no questions asked, access. From the reaction of anyone that had the badge waved at them, we imagined Olag had licence to kill. We joked that it was a Blockbuster card, but with a hard stare from Olag, and a flash of his weapon, no one would dare to argue with him.

We were staying at the very comfortable and luxurious Ritz, with amazing views over the city, very close to the Kremlin and Red Square. Even Jeremy and Richard still got excited about exploring a new city, which was lovely and endearing to see given they were so well travelled.

Moscow felt exciting and glamorous. However, there was nothing glamorous about the venue, and the green room took a massive U-turn in our green room travels. It was small and incredibly dark. It actually could have been a museum exhibit showing how we used to live (loved that series when I was at school). It was perfect for a scene in a 1950s film. On the classic fifties dining table was a display of sweets, fruit and pastries as if your nan had invited you around for tea. Everything was presented on a paper doily. The wooden-framed, uncomfortable sofas were dressed with plaid woollen blankets, and the incredibly dim lighting was ever so slightly enhanced by a wooden standard lamp topped off with a faux-silk lampshade with a cord frill. Everything was brown or beige.

Bless the Russian team, they were so welcoming and had obviously tried to make it cosy by even adding a dresser with teapots, ornaments and glasses on. Richard decided he liked it and between shows stretched out on the sofa and cosied under the blanket. Which he could, because he is short. I had to do some running around to find a large bean bag to keep the big man happy.

Moscow is a city of extreme contrasts, which was evident on our drive from the airport, through the city, past dirty rundown tower blocks and clapped-out old Ladas, and the like, battling for space on the road with top-of-the-range Range Rovers and supercars. In the places we hung out, extreme wealth and hideous amounts of new money were on display for all to see.

One of my jobs was to book a restaurant for one evening. I was sent out to do a recce of a couple that had been recommended. The one I chose was mobbed by Moscow's new money brigade. At lunchtime when I visited, I was entertained, while waiting to be seen to book a table, by very young women clad from head to toe, but certainly not covered, in designer clothing with matching designer bags and incredible real bling.

It was an amazing setting on the sixteenth floor under a cathedral-like glass dome, but I couldn't bear the clientele or the attitude of the staff. For the privilege of booking a table for the evening, I had to wait, as if for an interview, to put down the equivalent of £700 in cash as a deposit. A problem in itself, but never one to fail on a Bubble mission, I drew out cash from my own account to make up the petty cash I had on me.

It was worth it. In the good company of the Bubble, we had yet another great night out. However, even Jeremy, whilst he loved to watch the ladies in all their mini-skirted, boob-revealing finery, got pissed off with their attitude. He was shoved out of the way, with not a hint of an 'excuse me', by a clutch of such young women determined to get in the lift before him. The Russians aren't known for their manners.

The show itself was one of the least enjoyable for me, as half of it was presented in Russian. In all the live shows there was always a certain amount of film footage shown of old *Top Gear* TV shows. Throughout 2013 there was a great montage celebrating ten years of *Top Gear* but here in Moscow the whole thing was dubbed with Russian voice-overs, which kind of took the edge off it. That is, until the clip of James and Richard in bunk beds, sleeping out at the site where they were going to attempt to launch their Reliant Robin Space Shuttle.

The voice used for Richard, chatting to James, as he lay in the bunk above him, was like that of a prepubescent boy. Whilst James had the voice of a Russian Arnold Schwarzenegger from *The Terminator*. When he addressed Richard as 'Hammonddd' I think it was possibly the funniest thing I've ever heard, and the worst voice-over casting ever.

Chris and I found it funny every time. The boys had no idea as it was not broadcast through their earpieces. I got Rowly to play it to them on his laptop. Another hysterical moment back in the green room.

For the rest of the show, Jeremy and Richard were accompanied by two twenty-something Russian presenters Micha and Oscar, which didn't really work for Chris and me (probably the biggest *Top Gear* fans ever), but clearly it worked for the Russians.

Following on from the Olympic theme, some more sporting activities had been created. The boys were now playing Motorbike Sidecar Polo, which Jeremy hated as he hates motorbikes. He had to be instructed by Richard and constantly moaned, questioning why anyone would want to ride one, except for girls as there was a constant vibration between his legs.

Someone who had much better functioning legs than Jeremy Clarkson was Paul Joseph, who had recently joined our 'circus'. Paul is an incredible athlete whose speciality is parkour, or free running as it is sometimes called. He created a stunt especially for the tour which involved him running towards three go-karts that were driving towards him at speed. Incredibly, he jumped over each go-kart, one after the other, with split seconds in between. He then upped his game by running towards a Lamborghini Gallardo that was coming towards him at speed. He made a spectacular somersault over it. This had me on the edge of my seat and holding my breath every time.

The boys worked the least they had ever done on tour out in Moscow, as a huge portion of the show was delivered by the Russian presenters. However, Jeremy, never being one to slack, arranged to do a day's filming for a documentary he was working on about the Arctic convoys. I was lucky to accompany him and get a VIP look around the Kremlin.

We walked through Red Square and along the river beneath the walls of the formidable Kremlin. There was snow on the ground and the river was frozen. It was like being in a Bond film set. Moscow has a very unique skyline of golden-topped churches set amongst Gotham City style skyscrapers and what we called 'steam factories'. I never did really know what they were but there were loads of them – industrial buildings with tall chimneys constantly pouring out steam. What was really bizarre is we saw loads of trucks seemingly transporting steam, as it was pouring out of the top and sides of them.

Jeremy and I had to go through a security process before our arrival and were instructed to go to a certain gate to get a special pass and then be escorted to meet the film crew. As you would expect, I actually felt quite nervous with my continuing fear of Russians. I should not have worried. As was so often the case we were greeted by an overexcited, armed security guard who was much more overwhelmed by meeting Jeremy Clarkson than worried about checking our credentials. The big man seemingly had, worldwide, access all areas, even the Kremlin.

I had a double honour, of exclusive and private access to the Throne Room in all its gold and ermine glory, and the privilege of watching Jeremy work in a more grown-up and intelligent way. Jeremy's knowledge is phenomenal and I realised for the first time he really was wasted, in many ways, clowning around with cars.

Moscow was a success and plans were made to return and to add on a stint in St Petersburg. In the words of James May, we would be back!

Paparazzi

Next stop Australia again, but this time it was different, starting with the flight. Over the years Gem and I had been lucky enough to be upgraded on a few occasions because of our famous travelling companions, and also due to our frequent flying. Both Virgin and BA were very good to us over the years. On this trip, however, I was now the Maharaja's woman of choice, so I was given first-class treatment, which was amazing if a little embarrassing as I just thought of myself as one of the crew and especially didn't want to leave my wing woman, Gemma, at the back of the plane. Good news all round, as Gemma was rightly upgraded, too, along with her promotion in Brand Events. She now travelled business class, which in Gem's world was as good as first as she is even smaller than Richard Hammond.

Meanwhile, I was right up front enjoying the firstest of first class, even being able to have a shower in the biggest shower room I'd ever seen. It was quite a bizarre experience. I had to book a slot. It was strictly one person at a time. Apart from feeling a little vulnerable being stark naked with only a flimsy door that could be opened from the outside, it was a wonderful way to not feel as if you'd been on a flight at all. If you've got the money or somebody else's, I strongly recommend it for not taking days out of your trip suffering with jet lag.

The Bubble also changed its accommodation strategy to a private house, no ordinary house of course, one with a stunning view over the ocean, and enough luxury accommodation for all our Bubble family, although in this particular instance JCP had to make up a bedroom in the garage adjoining the house. It wasn't too much of a hardship, as he obviously had access to all the living areas, clean running water, sun decks and swimming pool. Another essential requirement was that it was just a short drive to a helicopter landing space.

The show's venue had been upgraded to the Sydney Motorsport Park to accommodate a Kyalami style festival with another extended cast including Shane-O, Steve Pizzati, AKA Steve Pizza, from *Top Gear Australia*, Casey Stoner, two-time MotoGP World Champion, and Australia's F1 hero, Team Red Bull's Mark Webber.

The show was all performed on track and included a small stunt plane taking off from the start line alongside Casey Stoner in a Red Bull touring car, both racing around the track (the plane obviously in the air). Jeremy Clarkson reversed a supercar at speed, racing against an Australian international athlete over a 100-metre sprint. Mark Webber performed doughnuts in an F1 car. There was the regular game of Car Football in Reliant Robins and a thrilling race between Jamie Whincup, Supercars and Bathurst Champion, in a V8 supercar, Mark Webber in an F1 car and Casey Stoner on his superbike. Perhaps most comical of all was Jeremy and James driving pimped-up Utes in a Ford vs Holden race. Jeremy was too fat (or too tall as he would say) to put the seat belt on and definitely too tall to put a helmet on. James May, AKA Captain Slow, was constantly getting lost on the track. Jeremy won, of course, and celebrated teenage style with doughnuts and drifting.

Before all this action, we had a couple of days to get over jet lag and for the boys to start scripting. What better place to do this than on *The Flying Fish*, the superyacht at our disposal once again for the duration of our stay, because of course one could get bored by a luxury villa with pool and ocean views. The other drawback of being out of town in a luxury villa was getting to anywhere else, so helicopters were a must. After a trip out somewhere, we headed back to a heliport to chopper back to the villa. And there he was, the man of my nightmares, Charlie. Oh my God! My heart sank. He was sat in the heli-lounge, glasses on, hunched over, looking more like an air-ambulance victim than a pilot. To make matters worse, he was actually reading the helicopter manual. Nervous laughter ensued as we greeted old Charlie once again.

You may think that all would be perfect in such luxury and idyllic surroundings, but in fact the Maharaja had been on edge since our arrival. He was very agitated by the presence of paps as soon as we were out of the airport. They caught us as we boarded the helicopter to fly to the villa, and he was convinced they were out on the water in small boats spying on the villa. He was incredibly irritable and made life tricky for all of us.

One evening we took a water taxi to a waterside restaurant, a Bubble favourite over the years visiting Sydney. As we were stepping off the boat, a small army of paps ran towards us with flashes flashing. It was really alarming and set off panic in the Bubble. I tried to get out of the way as soon as possible and made for the cover of the restaurant. James Cooke-Priest went into Bodyguard role and strode ahead of JC, blocking the paps' shots.

The paparazzi are really quite unbelievable and will stop at nothing to get the best shot. They were running backwards, bumping into other diners and anyone else enjoying an evening stroll by the water. Jeremy quite clearly expressed his opinion of them, as you might imagine. Unfortunately, JCP added to this and the whole thing was recorded. His words weren't favourable about Australia.

Meanwhile, in the restaurant, crisis management was taking place to move our party indoors to ensure our privacy. It was a horrible evening. JCP had a pop at me as the cause of the added interest in JC, who had disappeared trying to escape the whole situation.

After giving up on supper, I went out with Chris and Gem in search of JC. Our Range Rover convoy had been summoned and eventually we were all reunited to head back to the privacy and safety of the villa. There were a few tears including from the big man.

The mood was not good and was only set to get worse as the pictures came out on the front pages the next morning. JCP's tirade about Australia and threatening that *Top Gear* would never return caused huge tensions and trouble from the powers that be at the BBC. The BBC put out a statement that was broadcast and published all over the world declaring that James Cooke-Priest did not work for the BBC and that his opinions were not theirs. This was all necessary, of course, in order to protect the *Top Gear* brand.

It left the Bubble very fractured. JCP felt terrible, as he'd had a taste of fame and what it's like to be made a scapegoat. The irony was that JCP had been desperately trying to protect the brand. However, Jeremy was annoyed with JCP for what he'd said and continued to be on edge for fear of paps wherever we were. I felt terrible, as it felt as though the whole incident had occurred because of me, the mistress, being present. I hated the effect fame had on JC but most of all the upset for his children and wife. Fame can truly be a curse. The paparazzi can make you feel hunted.

What fuelled Jeremy's anger was that we had been followed the year before in Australia. I myself had been followed upon my arrival at the Versace Hotel in Brisbane. A conversation

I had with Chris was reported pretty much word for word in the tabloids as part of the story exposing Jeremy and I for having an affair. We had been followed all over Hamilton Island and beyond. It is definitely debatable whether it is fair to be photographed without your knowledge just because you are famous or associated with someone who is.

It was something that I didn't let get to me as I really don't care what people who don't know me think of me. However, in comparison to Jeremy, I had had very little intrusion. Jeremy was incensed by the infringement on his personal life.

The whole trip continued with a fragile and agitated Maharaja, and we all had to tiptoe around him. His irritation over paps continued, and he felt we were being followed everywhere, which to be fair we pretty much were. I tried to keep a low profile so as not to feed the paps with any photo opportunity.

However, this did not stop us having a good party on our favourite superyacht. Nothing could top our night on the beach with AC/DC, but we still had a pretty good go. This time James May got in the hot tub fully clothed and needed yet another new phone.

Our last day at the track felt like a bit of a relief. Everything had gone really well, the atmosphere was great, and the whole event was deemed a great success. The boys and all their celebrity guests had entertained over forty thousand people over the weekend. Chris decided to treat the boys to a serious present, one that they actually might like and have a use for. He sent me out on a mission to search for one. It was decided that a GoPro was the solution. With just a little hand-wringing and rubbing of his ears (something that Chris did when he was anxious or stressed), Chris splashed out on the new must-have gadgets.

The closing ceremony was refined down to just a comical but sincere thank you speech from Chris, and the boys were presented with their gifts, which they were really surprised about and very grateful for. It was a refreshing change to the usual ridiculous presentations. To add to this new-found, rather civilised behaviour, Chris had decided, on the back of the success of the weekend, to treat the whole Bubble, including lovely Michael who ran Brand Events in Australia, to a helicopter ride back to the house. Chris turned to me while we were watching the last few stunts and races and said, 'Get another chopper to add enough seats to get nine of us back to the villa.'

Previously, just the presenters, myself and Chris had been travelling by helicopter. The rest had had to allow more time and travel by road. No pressure, I just had to get hold of the pilot and ask him to get another helicopter to be ready to leave the venue alongside the other, within the hour. If he couldn't help, I would have to start frantically ringing around other companies. Thankfully, our current pilot came up trumps.

Another classic rock and roll moment played out as we left our trackside green room and bundled into Range Rovers that had to part the remaining crowds still enjoying the trade stands and exhibits at the festival. We had a short drive to the top of a hill at the edge of the race circuit which gave us a fantastic view of the festival and the last vintage car race. The moment was topped off by James asking, 'Is my wine chilled in the helicopter?' He laughed as he'd shocked himself with his diva moment.

What a treat. The helicopters took off minutes apart, both pilots enjoying showing off their skills flying alongside each other above and below, giving us all fantastic views of Sydney and beyond whilst we quaffed chilled beers and wine. We couldn't land in the usual spot but the pilots had identified a piece of common land close to our villa. Imagine the shock of the residents of the one house that was located on this remote peninsula as not one but two helicopters landed to disturb their quiet Sunday evening, and to then be surprised further by the very familiar faces that disembarked. The shocked, rather feral-looking family were blown away and the kids were so excited to get the autographs of their motoring heroes.

I was so excited as a beautiful kookaburra had landed seemingly at the same time as us and was perched on a post for us all to enjoy. He actually got more attention and photos taken than our celebs.

Luckily, our last-minute plans all worked out. One of our Range Rovers and a spare car had had to leave the showground as soon as I'd confirmed the second helicopter and race to find the new landing spot to collect us and deliver us all back to the villa for a BBQ, celebratory drinks and a compulsory watch of the latest *Top Gear* special that was due to air in England when we would be on the flight home.

Never off duty, Jeremy, without fail, watched every episode, as it was the first time he would see the final edit of what they had all produced. He always said Andy Wilman was the real genius who made the programmes the success they were, due to his masterly editing. He too was a workaholic known to disappear into an edit suite for days at a time perfecting the finished article.

Jeremy had instructed me to get hold of Andy during our stay and make sure he sent the DVD over to Sydney in time for JC to view before we left for home. My mission accomplished, JC would not settle and enjoy a party until he knew the TV was set up to view the latest masterpiece. We were all then instructed to sit and watch and be quiet. I had learnt that you did not speak during viewing, which I found tough as I wanted to ask questions, but my life wasn't worth living if I spoke over any of it. Unfortunately, the Bubble didn't know the seriousness of this screening.

Everyone was bellowed at for moving their chair, crunching snacks, slurping drinks or talking. You either watched in silence, except for laughing at the appropriate moment, or left the room. Michael from Brand Events and the festival director fell asleep. The Maharaja was not happy with that either. Thankfully, he was happy with the episode and our celebrations could continue, albeit a little more gently than usual.

The flight home brought a further upgrade for the boys. They were upgraded to cabin class, and Gem and I were lucky enough to be invited to dinner with them. It was actually quite an old plane. I never knew such a class existed. Both James and Jeremy had a cabin each like you would have on an old-fashioned train carriage, but without a roof, I guess so that cabin crew could keep an eye on each passenger.

The boys sent invites back to Gem and I via the cabin crew. As usual there were ridiculous in-flight rules that we had to persuade the crew to break. To be honest their argument, that it wasn't fair to intrude on other cabin-class passengers, didn't really hold up, because there were only a couple of other passengers in there, and as they were in their cabins we really weren't bothering them. In-flight rules – so ridiculous!

The boys slid open the sliding doors and invited us to sit down for a pre-dinner drink. It was like playing 'house'. A bit reminiscent of James trying to hold a party in a Wendy house but a lot more sophisticated. After a delightful dinner there were a few annoying interruptions from Chris, who was a little disgruntled that he wasn't upgraded, so just came to annoy the boys, something he was an expert at.

That reminds me of another long-haul flight when we were all in first class. Richard reported that his whole flight was disturbed by Chris, AKA the Piggy-Eyed Businessman, constantly raising his seat/bed to prepare himself for the next meal or snack. He didn't try to sleep for as long as you could, as most passengers did, because he did not want to miss out on any food. Richard's commentary on this was hilarious: 'Light on, table up, screen away, seat raised, table down, eat food, drink, table up, seat down, screen out, light off, light on, seat up' and so on. I myself was aware of his constant feeding, as I am a very light sleeper and noticed a light on the other side of the cabin when I got up to visit the loo. There he was, napkin over his portly self, like a child in a bib, tucking into something else. He was unbelievable but a great source of entertainment.

To get Chris back for disturbing him, Richard hid Chris's clothes so he had to disembark in his in-flight pyjamas. For those of you who have not had the privilege of flying first class, long haul, not only are you given eye masks and socks, you get pyjamas, too.

Police Escort

Back in London Town, the Bubble dispersed for a month or so off. The boys went about usual filming business and Brand Events put finishing touches to the next leg of the tour, Amsterdam and Belgium.

To keep things fresh, and to fulfil one of the boys' dreams of travelling by tour bus, tour buses were arranged between the two cities. For their amusement they requested they had three buses with each decaled with one word of *Top Gear Live* so if they were out of synch on the road they made no sense. Just another example of their schoolboy humour. Chris had also come up with the idea that in Holland the buses were decorated with orange balloons, etc. and were hosted by pretty Dutch girls who, at the border, were thrown off the buses and replaced with Belgian girls who decorated the buses with red decorations.

I heard there was the usual excess drinking and a lot of fun during this novel trip but I was literally not interested as I wasn't there. This was the start of a one-night-only strategy that was planned for further European cities, but next stop was Durban for another huge festival.

I flew out a day later for some reason. I can't remember why, probably childcare issues. Anyway, as I arrived at Durban airport I received a text from Jeremy saying Clinton would meet me to drive me to the venue, the majestic and huge Moses Mabhida Stadium (with a roof shaped like a lady's special bits, stated the boys).

The airport was quiet and it was easy to spot Clinton, who rushed to meet me and take my bag like a true gentleman. He guided me outside to meet the waiting Range Rover. I felt very 'VIP' but this was nothing. Jeremy had arranged for a surprise. Denzel, our faithful, armed South African driver/security, using his police connections, had organised a police motorbike escort to speed us through the traffic, of which there was very little, to get me to the stadium as quickly as possible. I was quite overwhelmed and a little embarrassed, but it was very cool and possibly the most romantic thing Jeremy had ever done for me. Not roses, dinner or jewellery but a police escort!

The police motorbike escort had become a bit of a treat in Durban. It wasn't quite like you get here in the UK. It was as if two policeman just got hold of a couple of fast bikes, not the big sturdy road bikes like they have in the UK, but a couple of scramblers or anything with two wheels would do. They appeared to have just rigged up a blue light and siren and fitted radios to them. They ducked and dived through the traffic, thoroughly enjoying themselves leapfrogging each other, one speeding ahead and holding traffic at lights or roundabouts so we could keep moving. This obviously wasn't really necessary for me but did come in useful when getting our celebs and the Bubble through our own event traffic, in and out of the venue.

I arrived late morning at the huge green room that would normally be a hospitality suite. It had its own bar and kitchenette and the Durban team had created our usual green room comfort area of sofa, bean bags, large TV, etc. One end had become an office area where scriptwriting was done and any other work by Gem, JCP and Chris, although if there were any big discussions to be had, they had to be taken elsewhere. Jeremy insisted he did not want to see or hear the inner workings of the Bubble, or as he would say, 'the swan's legs'.

Soon the boys were ready for a run-through. The dreaded fitting of the earpieces was carried out and they began the rather long walk to the specially created track and arena within the stadium. As soon as they were busy with rehearsing, Chris collared me to get involved with a surprise for the boys as he felt they were a bit low.

We had all three boys on board for Durban and they were unsurprisingly a little jaded as they hardly ever stopped working and travelling the world. This had been going on intensely for over ten years as the tour had expanded, and with the continuing success of the TV show, by this time in its twentieth series. Plus all their other individual projects. Burnout was close for them all.

You'd think Chris might have thought to book them in for a day in a spa for massage and general relaxation, but what he had actually come up with was a little gag of setting up three beds in the green room equipped with drips to rehydrate them. Myself and Nicole from the Durban team sourced beds, sheets and pillows from the hotel and asked the paramedics to supply the drips – luckily they had no real medical emergencies to attend to.

Nicole found a nurse's outfit for her and a stethoscope for Chris to act out his caring doctor's role. The emergency rest and recuperation ward was prepared and set up for when we arrived back in the green room the next morning.

It was hilarious. Chris and Nicole were ready to greet them. The makeshift beds were made up in a row of three with drips on stands beside them. The boys played along but were seriously quite grateful and happily lay down for the doctor and his nurse to come along and deliver their best bedside manner. One of the paramedics had lent Nicole his huge bag of medicine, which had about a hundred different glass bottles containing liquid drugs ready for shots, along with Jeremy's favourite, the B12 pick-me-up. James and Jeremy were fascinated and investigated all of them like a couple of drug pushers.

I have a fab picture of the three of them thoroughly enjoying their plumped-up pillows and comfy beds whilst all puffing on cigarettes (RH on his electric one). This scene was a sign of the times. Our Bubble big nights out were getting fewer, with normally just one big one per leg/city. Cosy dinners and early nights were becoming preferable.

The show itself in Durban was awesome set in such a great venue with very enthusiastic crowds. A new big stunt had been added: a Rage Buggy doing a 360 mid-air. It took a very fast and long drive from outside the arena, then sped up a short but near-vertical ramp, to land on another ramp as it came out of its breathtaking somersault. It was pretty impressive.

Our big night out was pretty big. We had hired a venue for our exclusive use at the end of a small pier. It was a stunning setting and even had a red carpet for our Range Rover convoy to pull up at. Everyone was on good form, and our Bubble was extended with Mika Häkkinen and a few friends of Jeremy's.

Our crew was big so we created a good party. Richard and I had made a pact to look after each other and stick to gin and tonic all night, and tell each other when to stop in order to avoid any excessively bad behaviour and/or huge hangovers. There were face painters and a small band and DJ.

It wasn't long before James and Richard had their faces decorated with flowers and stars. James had also adorned himself with bits of pink feather boas that were floating around as party props. Richard and I weren't doing too well at pacing ourselves and soon we were all up on the dance floor throwing ourselves around. Two girls and I, one a friend of Jeremy's, the other may have been Gem, I don't remember, became backing singers for the inevitable performance from Chris of 'Mustang Sally'.

The next thing I do remember was the three of us falling in what felt like slow motion. We were in perfect drunken synch with each other as our feet went from under us and we ended up lying flat out on the floor, microphones still in hand. It was comedy gold, rather like when Del Boy from *Only Fools and Horses* fell through the open bar.

After this, Jeremy took me to see the paramedics, not to check if I was OK after my fall but to see if they could help me sober up. I was forced to drink something and was injected with something – by the paramedic, I hasten to add.

I checked in with Rich, who I affectionately called Bro. (We had decided on one drunken evening that we were brother and sister who had been separated at birth. Another classic drinking night when we were having a heart to heart leaning on each other in the back of the Range Rover.) Richard was faring better than me but we decided to call it a night at the club and head back to the hotel.

The majority of the Bubble headed along the pier to meet the Range Rover convoy. It was around midnight so the hotel was quiet when we got back and we took over a lounge area and carried on drinking. Chris got on the piano and played some fairly civilised background music. Jeremy had decided to go and have a drink with his friends in their hotel next door. Richard had eased up his drinking and relaxed on one of the sofas. James, who was always a happy drunk, gave his seat up for one of the girls. He sat down next to me on what he thought was another sofa.

As he leant back, it became apparent very quickly that it was not a sofa but a large footstool. He did a very elegant backwards roll straight off the back and emerged quite calmly, hair all over the place but holding his glass of wine without a drop spilt. Another comedy gold moment.

I don't know what time we all dispersed but in the morning we were all a bit fragile, especially Jeremy who had put in an all-nighter. We gradually congregated for breakfast out on the terrace overlooking the beach and pool. A few of the Bubble, including myself, ventured to the beach to try to clear our heads, although my drinking strategy with the support of JC and RH had worked – I wasn't catastrophically ill for a change.

We had time to kill before our flight back to Johannesburg to catch our flight home, so we chilled and sunbathed around the pool. By lunchtime it was time to have a drink again. If you could handle it. Work was finished for this visit to Durban. The boys were chatting to Mika and everyone was enjoying the downtime.

Then along came Chris who was walking around the pool on his mobile. The boys had a moan at him for doing business in a place of leisure. He just bantered back at them and continued to pace around the pool, on the phone, gesticulating and complaining about how hot he was. Jeremy and Richard took that as a cue to cool him down and strategically walked around the pool to catch him unawares, remove his phone and throw him in the pool fully clothed. I guess that was our hat-trick of comedy gold moments.

Chris being Chris got out laughing and repeating 'You fu**ers' over and over as he squeezed the water out of his clothes whilst standing at the edge of the pool. He didn't get changed, just sat out to dry and then rallied us all for lunch and a low-key leaving ceremony.

By this time on our never-ending tour, we had two professionals from the world of motorsport helping coordinate our ever-growing crew, Becks and Emma. They had helped gathering silly gifts for the presenters amongst a lot of other much more important jobs. They were also great company and were becoming part of our Bubble family.

The gifts were so apt, thought of by Chris. The boys were each given a portable drip fitted on a lanyard, stethoscopes, blood pressure machines and other medical equipment (the latter being children's toys). Becks and Emma, being the more sober and sensible ones, reminded us of our schedule and chivvied the slightly slow and fragile original Bubble members to gather their bags and assemble at the foyer to depart.

We spent a lot of time hovering around hotel foyers with our Range Rover convoy. Gem and I would check everyone's luggage was on board, while the boys would be having last-minute fags, as long as there weren't too many people about to harass them. When I say the boys, I mean Jeremy and Richard as James was often the last to appear. Jeremy didn't hold back in informing us, always, that James would be having a poo.

Apparently, James, much to JC's annoyance, always held up departing for anything, film shoots, flights, train journeys, etc., because he needed a crap. And then he would appear in his Eeyore type way, head down, carrying his very cute, retro, hard leather suitcase. 'Come on James!' Jeremy would bellow. Once all aboard, we would set off.

This time it was to a small airport to board a private jet. En route the boys had described the incredible security they had when they arrived in Durban and disembarked. They effectively had a 'walking train' from the jet to the small, private, arrivals lounge. Jeremy described the security guys being built like man-mountains. They were all 6 ft 5 plus, making him feel small and Richard Hammond absolutely terrified. They were dressed in black, head to toe, and were very straight-faced, with the essential security guard's curly wire behind their ears. Jeremy likened them to one of the assassins in the Jack Reacher novels. Jeremy so often had his head in a Jack Reacher book (Richard and I got hooked on them too). The giants of safety had certainly made the boys feel secure, flanking our innocent little line of Bubble members, who were in fact a bit nervous, as they felt that if they had put a foot wrong, these guys would have just taken them out in seconds.

Unfortunately, our return flight, although on another luxury jet, was taking off from a small but public airport. Somewhere along the line there had been a miscommunication and we were left in a very public area with no security. Denzel and Clinton were long gone after dropping us off. A 'Chris Hughes' panic broke out as the boys became agitated by fans surrounding them. There were only a few and most were kids, but Jeremy, James and Richard, in their fragile, hungover state, were not feeling too sociable.

We were in a big open space of the airport, where there appeared to be no first-class check-in or luxury lounge for private jet passengers. It did become a little overwhelming as the small crowd of enthusiastic fans grew frantic for a photo or autograph. Chris had shot off on the phone, trying to find security and calling Becks and Emma to get them on the case. Gemma had run in another direction trying to source assistance. JCP and I tried to keep the crowd under control.

It became an awkwardly long wait. Unusually for JC, he didn't lose his temper but adopted another tactic. His really bad hangover was catching him up – to be honest I don't think he'd actually had time to sober up. In the absence of any seats he lay on the floor with his head on his man bag. James joined him with his head on his own man bag.

It did dupe the crowd as the two lay there seemingly asleep. At last a security man appeared followed by a rather sweaty, stressed-out Chris who was intent on finding out what had gone wrong and why his precious celebrities weren't being looked after. I meanwhile, chivvied the rather laid-back security man, to find a private room for the boys to wait.

The security man didn't speak English but kept ushering us along, saying, 'This way, I find.' He led us a very short distance to what was effectively a glass box, obviously a kids' play area. It was kitted out with very small tables and chairs and a few toys. Chris was going mad – you could almost see the steam coming out of his ears. I had started to laugh and encouraged the boys to go into the box while Gem, JCP and I formed a human wall to prevent fans from taking pictures. There was an illuminated sign above the glass wall in front of the boys, who were now perched on the very small, children's chairs, with their knees under their chins and man bags, like satchels, beside them. The sign read, 'Unaccompanied Minors & Assisted Passengers'. That was comedy gold.

Bigger than the Beatles?

It was time for another one-night-only gig, this time Poland. For a change we took a regular BA flight, with no VIP experience apart from taking over the front row in those slighter larger seats with one free seat in the middle and more leg room. For our famous VIPs this was actually a little ridiculous, because they then sat with the world and his wife walking past spotting them. However, it did enable a speedy exit, which meant poor Gem and I had to bun-fight our way out from further down the plane, from behind the infamous luxury curtain, to get ahead of the three amigos and ensure special services were meeting us, enabling a swift exit through customs, etc.

We were met by our usual fleet of Range Rovers to head to the venue, the National Stadium, Warsaw. Another huge stadium, but unlike Durban, where we used one end of it, this show and audience were going to fill it. The boys were, for the first time ever, really quite daunted at the prospect.

The event was in association with VERVA Street Racing, an annual event in Warsaw. Prior to the boys' big entrance, there were races and stunts performed around a circuit built in the stadium. It was quite an overwhelming setting. The stadium had only been finished in 2011 and was very shiny and new and incredibly state of the art, like the amazing Tottenham Hotspur Stadium. This too had a retractable roof and all sorts of different set-ups for different events. It was huge.

Along with large stadiums came large green rooms, and we were really getting the hang of getting everything we needed for our home on our whistle-stop tours. This leg of the tour was really feeling very rock and roll. The green room was in the bowels of the building amongst a maze of white tunnels and doors that all looked the same. Security had been arranged and now our passes had an upgrade to AAA – Access all Areas. Trouble was, you needed to know where all those areas were. We all got lost.

First things first: a little last-minute promotion was required, and we were all led around the maze to a room usually used for football pundits. It had an amazing bird's-eye view of the arena. It was breathtaking and once again the boys were actually quite overwhelmed and humbled by their own success. Had they actually become so popular that they could fill a stadium with a capacity of 58,000? Actually, no, but they near as damn it did. Very nearly beating the Beatles' largest ever audience of 55,000. Not bad for three middle-aged motoring journalists.

After the boys had completed their rather intense PR duties, with back-to-back interviews, tension was beginning to mount. It was back to the green room to go through the script with Rowly and make any changes necessary. They had a quick look at where they would arrive in the arena and the 'backstage' area, which wasn't backstage at all as they were effectively in the middle of a race track for the duration of the show.

A small hillock had been created as part of the circuit, i.e. at the edge of the track. It looked like a scene from *Teletubbies*. It was actually a portacabin that had a scaffold frame around it that was then draped in fake grass. There was a hidden doorway through which the boys could disappear out of the arena and sit having a fag and some light refreshment before their next act.

The day was beginning to feel long and our three amigos were irritable, so we headed back to our very agreeable boutique hotel in the old walled city of Warsaw. An early dinner was arranged and an early night by tour standards. Our heroes just had one rehearsal before their big moment the next night.

We were up and out after breakfast and back to the green room for a script read through and visualisation of the circuit and 'stage area'. The mood was tense. Chris had been told to 'Go away' on several occasions but he was stacking up little requests which he asked me to feed in to the boys as and when. On this tight schedule there was never a good time. I agreed with the boys that during a small window after the rehearsal, and before a rest prior to the show, they would meet and greet a few VIPs. I felt nervous for them. They were very together for this event, all in the same boat; even Jeremy was quite humbled. They actually didn't want too much free time. They just wanted to get on with it.

Eventually they did. Chris and I went backstage with them and acted out a Madonna style warm-up of a group hug and prayer – it wasn't a prayer. The boys actually didn't want to mess about. They were properly nervous like I had never seen them before and were actually speechless as they set off to the tunnel to make their entrance. Chris and I ran to get up to the Bubble's very own private box with bar and food. We were actually tearful with pride and overwhelming emotion as the boys made their fast and dramatic entrance on the V8 motorised stage. The crowd went mad.

The roof was on the stadium and the lighting and music were as good as any rock concert. It was amazing. It was huge, the atmosphere was incredible. I made a trip out to the Teletubby hillock to make sure they had all they needed. They were just their usual chain-smoking, laid-back selves waiting for their next cue.

The rest of the Bubble enjoyed the show, downing a few glasses of champagne. We had planned to 'bounce' as soon as they walked offstage, otherwise we would have got caught in our own traffic. As usual the Range Rovers were loaded with a bar, of rosé, gin and tonic, and Sauvignon blanc, engines running, bags packed.

The Bubble and the extended crew were on quite a high huddled together at the edge of the arena ready to greet our heroes, and we really felt they were superheroes that night. They looked like true rock stars, having waved to the roaring crowds amid the smoke from the exhaust fumes and in the glare of the lights, as they casually turned to walk through the tunnel removing their earpieces.

What a shock. The three of them were really quite deflated, in total contrast to the rest of us bouncing around congratulating them. I bundled into the lead Range Rover with them washing them with praise but they all said the same: they felt weirdly and unexplainably flat.

I never did really get to the bottom of why they felt so low and I don't think they did. I suspect it was a combination of exhaustion after an adrenalin high on top of fatigue from the last ten years, and maybe like all big stars say, the smaller more intimate gigs are the best.

Is That Brian May?

There was a short pause from touring, although filming and writing carried on for the boys as usual. Meanwhile, I was employed by Chris to project-manage our 10th Anniversary Party. Chris, Gem and I had a planning meeting in a pub in London somewhere, and Chris and I came up with silly ideas to amuse but at the same time please our three very precious celebrities and all the incredibly hard-working crew that had been involved over the years.

I found the perfect venue, Searcys in Knightsbridge. It was a beautiful Georgian house between Harrods and Sloane Square. It had a stunning entrance hall with huge fireplace and majestic stairway leading to a galleried hallway above. We had access to this, a living room/library and a small ballroom.

We went to town decorating it to make it ours. There was already a huge Christmas tree in the hallway and we decided to theme the place as if it were Clarkson's, Hammond's and May's home. We had an eighteenth-century style portrait made up of the three of them and the Stig, complete with authentic costumes, which was hung over the fireplace. This is where we had a champagne reception by the roaring fire and were entertained by an electric violin quartet known for playing rock and James Bond theme tunes. For some silly reason, we decided that all of us involved in setting up the party would dress up in period costume to befit the house and our tour characters. Gem and I were dressed as ladies of the manor, while Bas, AKA BasIcanfindanycar.com, dressed as a warrior from the Raj, complete with huge sword. JCP was a naval officer; Rowly was an army officer; and Chris Hughes, the Piggy-Eyed Businessman, was Henry VIII.

We had a corner full of props and more costumes for our guests to dress up in and have their photo taken in front of the fireplace under the watchful eye of our three amigos in their portrait (except for Richard Hammond, as his face kept getting blocked out – situation normal).

Around the whole venue we had placed framed pictures of our Bubble and tour family, along with the promotional posters from around the world. We had our favourite Rockaoke band booked and a great DJ who was part of Chris Evans's crew. The best scene of all was the one I had battled with the council over, to let us park, in a no-parking zone, the three yellow Reliant Robins with JC, RH and JM painted on them. JC's was in its familiar position on its side. To finish off our Dickensian Christmas look, we had a snow machine cover the street and Reliants in thick snow and created a light snow storm for the arrival of our guests. I even persuaded the doorman to wear a top hat.

Chris, Gem and I were beyond excited. The boys loved the Reliant entrance and the quartet, who played epic tracks from the show and then led us all, procession style, up the grand staircase for the party to get started. The guest list included all the guest presenters, such as Sasha, Shane-O, Tiff and Vicki Butler-Henderson, Jody Scheckter and all. Those who couldn't attend had made video messages, which we had projected in the ballroom.

A lot of the *Top Gear* TV crew had been invited as they had all been involved in the tour to some extent. They were blown away by such a brilliant and generous party thrown by Chris and Brand Events. They were used to dried-up sausage rolls, polystyrene cups and curled-up sandwiches in a dingy North London bar on Andy Wilman's BBC budget. Andy Wilman was not a fan of our excessive spending on the boys or the amount of time they were touring. He claimed it had an effect on their behaviour and I have no doubt it did, one because they were exhausted, and two because they were overindulged.

However, the party was a success and no one was going to dampen our spirits having toured so successfully for so long. The only real indulgence on this evening was for Jeremy. We had to make a special purchase of a crate of his favourite organic rosé, Léoube, and pay corkage on it. That and bottles of Baileys. It was actually a very civilised and tame evening in comparison to some of our big tour nights. There was a lot of emotion and appreciation between us all and a great deal of reminiscing. There was no extension on the bar and it was a strict kicking-out time along with the removal of Reliant Robins so we actually dispersed quite early, the right side of dawn.

And so it was Christmas, all back home for a little R & R and a detox before the tour kicked off again in January 2014. Closer to home this time in Glasgow. A simple affair and just the small luxury of a whole castle to stay in. The highlights of the visit were a party in the cellar with live music including a stroppy bagpipe player who did not appreciate JC talking over his performance and expressing his dislike for the instrument. He was a large man, and it threatened to get physical between our large man and him. Chris diffused the situation. The piper packed his bag and left. Awks.

We went on to have a jolly night. My only clear memory is of us Bubble members really getting into our own version of 'Hotel California' with James May dancing on the table. This song was named by Jeremy as James's anthem, as he likened 'Hotel California' to getting into an argument with James May – you could never leave.

The absolute best memory of this trip, though, was the wonderful hospitality of the local, fairly elderly staff who provided a fantastic breakfast in the very elegant dining room. We were very keen to thank them and they gave us a send-off fit for royalty as they formed a line-up in the hallway for our departure. Being one of the last to leave, I had the joy of overhearing one old girl say to another, 'Who are they? Are they from the Television?' 'Yes,' the other replied, 'it's Jeremy Vine, Richard Branson and Brian May.' Priceless.

Vodka and Caviar

Our next big adventure was back to Moscow followed by St Petersburg. It was touch and go whether we could do it, as the BBC were very nervous about the recent invasion of Ukraine by the Russians. We were notified just days before that we could travel. Jeremy was under added stress on this trip as his mum was terminally ill with cancer. He had deliberated over whether he should go away at all. He decided there was not a lot he could do if he stayed and he was only going to be away for a week.

Tragically, she died the first night we were there. After a sleepless night of upset and contacting his children and other family members, Chris had suggested he go home. He didn't spend too much time thinking about it, and after discussions with his sister it was decided there was little point in him going home as there really was nothing he could do now.

The show must go on, as they say. Obviously, the mood was fairly low but Jeremy was doing what he loved and apart from the obviously necessary phone calls to his distraught children and the rest of the family he carried on as usual, which to be honest was a bit of a worry. The rest of the Bubble were concerned about him and we had a little huddle and a few tears remembering Mrs Clarkson, who had visited the show regularly in London and Birmingham. Chris consulted me on what sort of an evening Jeremy would like and offered to do anything he could for him.

Jeremy just repeated his wish to carry on as normal, so we did. We had dinner planned in a famous steak house in Moscow and we were to be joined by the latest BBC watchman, whose name escapes me – I'll call him 'Norman'. We were never keen on these guys joining us, and on this occasion we decided to have a bit of a laugh at his expense and tell him, whilst Jeremy was in the loo, that no one ever starts eating or drinking before Jeremy has said Grace. 'Norman's' face was a picture.

As is often the case when you are a large party in a restaurant, the food tends to be served sporadically, so we all had to wait patiently with straight faces. Jeremy delivered Grace with great eloquence and welcomed our guest from the BBC. We all bowed our heads and listened in silence, not daring to look at one another. 'Norman' was totally taken in. We didn't reveal the truth until pudding, when 'Norman' could reveal his shock and relax a little, laughing with the rest of us.

However, there was some other trouble brewing within the BBC after Jeremy had used a racist term in the Burma special which had aired a couple of weeks before. Jeremy got a call just as we were laughing it out with 'Norman' over 'Grace'. It was someone senior from the BBC investigating Jeremy's latest controversy. He was totally riled and ended the call abruptly, asking to leave immediately and not wishing to spend any more time with anyone from the BBC.

'Norman' from the Beeb was asked to keep a very low profile and was not welcome in the green room. Things were pretty tense all round. The shows carried on as usual but even our leisure time felt stressful. We had extra security, partly due to the political situation and partly due to the ever-growing popularity of our stars. Gav (ex-SBS) had flown out with us to back up Olag, our familiar Russian ex-KGB man.

As a relaxing day out, someone, not me, had organised a trip to a shooting range. Just what you need when political tensions are high in a country known as one the world's superpowers famed for corruption and assassinations. To add to the tension, our Russian-speaking drivers didn't seem to know where they were going and we came to a dead end in what appeared to be Moscow's equivalent of a council estate. My imagination was running wild. I had thoughts of Olag turning on us, kidnapping us and holding us for ransom.

He didn't. We had actually arrived at the wrong side of a playground that separated us, across the way, from the shooting club, which looked quite innocently like a Scout hut. It wasn't so innocent inside. We were led through a series of huge heavy metal doors, past cabinets of lethal weapons and into a huge, soundproof, seemingly empty warehouse. It was actually the shooting range. Not, as I was thinking, the perfect place to keep us, a room with no windows and soundproofed so no one would have heard our cries for help. At one end it had targets, backed by a wall of sand, and there were a few what looked like high bar stools lined up but which were in fact what you stood behind to shoot.

The sinister-looking instructors went around talking the boys through a selection of weapons. Jeremy, Richard and JCP were like kids in a sweetshop. Chris not so much, and Gem and I were really quite terrified, choosing to stay at the back of the room.

However, eventually, my competitive streak got the better of me and I got stuck in under the expert guidance of Olag and the instructor. I very successfully fired an AK-47 and remained standing, and a Glock without injuring myself or anyone else. I got the ultimate compliment from both our ex-KGB and SBS guys who commented on my strength and accuracy. Gem had a go, too, and we all left on an adrenalin high which I found slightly disturbing. It was surprisingly fun and had certainly relieved the tension. JC and RH were very pumped as they relayed stories of their shoot-out.

Our other leisure time was mainly spent eating. One of Jeremy's favourite restaurants in the world is Café Pushkin, an extraordinary building with many original nineteenth-century features including a tiny open lift with metal concertina doors. It ran right through the middle of the restaurant, was very slow, and there was only room for two passengers. It was a great source of comedy especially with Jeremy and Richard on board, as their famous faces would literally appear alongside other diners on each floor as the lift travelled up between tables and they peered out through the metal lattice-framed box they were in. There was much laughter as we imagined what it was like to spot Jeremy's huge face appear, followed some time later by his crotch and later still by his feet.

Another very memorable meal was on our last night in Moscow, when we were advised by our Russian team to dine at the Bolshoi, an incredibly elegant restaurant next to the home of the famous Bolshoi Ballet. It was beautiful but totally soulless. The only other diners in there were a very showy couple and their guests. She looked like the classic Russian gold-digger, enhanced by much surgery, in a very revealing tight red dress. He looked very pleased with himself in his gold-embossed shoes and oversized watch to match.

The most entertainment came from the bodyguard stand-off outside the restaurant. Gav and Olag stood faithfully outside, ready to call our Range Rover convoy to action, but they had competition in the form of two huge, camouflage-clad and very obviously armed bodyguards, who were clearly employed by the couple in the restaurant. The two security teams respectfully kept their distance and in fact our team gave way when the camouflaged duo called to action their convoy of blacked-out, black-aerial-clad Hummers. They stalked about brandishing what looked to me like sub-machine guns. Who the hell were the people they were protecting? If I told you, I would have to kill you. Our party, keen to leave the disappointing, pompous restaurant, quite happily walked a few more paces to meet our humble Range Rovers, flanked by our humble security men. A few respectful nods were made and we left quietly. Moscow is scary.

Quite content to leave, we took a novel form of transport to St Petersburg, a train, albeit a first-class carriage that we had to ourselves. It was quite stressful herding our celebrities through a busy station with an enormous amount of luggage. However, once ensconced in our carriage, with our very special picnic of champagne and at least £1,000 worth of caviar, all was well. We all enjoyed the very scenic journey through miles and miles of empty Russia, past beautiful frozen lakes and snow-covered forests. In complete contrast to the wealth and ostentation of Moscow, the only signs of civilisation were clusters of the chicken-shed-like houses of poverty-stricken Russians.

St Petersburg is a stunning city designed by various European architects employed by the Tsars. It reminded me of Rome, Paris and Venice, all rolled into an extraordinary film set. The boys were particularly impressed by its incredibly wide roads and police hovercraft on the rivers and canals. Jeremy was so inspired, he created a *Top Gear* race with him at the wheel of a hovercraft, Richard on a bike, James in an electric car and the Stig on public transport. Another legendary episode.

I cannot remember the venue in St Petersburg at all, which is alarming. I shall blame it on the very strong vodka that we consumed plenty of. Not least on our trip to the Arctic Allied Convoys Club which had been arranged by the British ambassador. Embassy cars, complete with little flags fitted to their bonnets, came to escort our Range Rover convoy. I had imagined we would arrive at one of the numerous palace-like buildings and be met by men in suits or uniform for a silver-service reception and Ferrero Rocher (maybe not the Ferrero; however, we had all joked about it).

We arrived at what looked like a builder's yard that had seen better days. In a corner was an industrial-grey metal door with a small sign on with Russian writing underneath, which read, 'The Arctic Allied Convoys'. A large anchor resting against the wall was also a clue we were in the right place. We were met by a rather glamorous woman in her sixties with her hair swept up neatly, wearing a raincoat. She spoke perfect BBC standard Queen's English but was in fact 100% Russian. She was our interpreter for our visit.

We were welcomed into what was no more than a shed. Inside, there were a couple of threadbare rugs and a few wobbly tables and chairs that had been laid up with doilies, cups and saucers from our grandparents' era and plates of sandwiches and cake. The most senior of the group of about six men made himself known and invited us to sit. He sat at the head of the table and called us all to order by banging the table. He was short in stature but big in presence.

With the help of our charming interpreter, we were then told very emotive and extraordinary stories by these incredible men, one of whom had survived the Siege of Leningrad and told harrowing tales of death and survival 'n horrific circumstances. We were all tearful and extremely humbled and then extremely drunk.

Throughout all these incredible tales, we were served tea, coffee, sandwiches and cake by a dear lady who shuffled back and forth from a makeshift kitchen. Every so often, at least half a dozen times, 'Our Captain', the Chairman of the club, would bang the table and insist we downed a shot of St Petersburg's finest vodka. Our tears of sadness soon turned to the usual Bubble hysterics as we became very bonded with our new, wonderful veteran friends and were really quite pissed by midday. Especially Richard Hammond, who needed assistance back to the car.

I felt incredibly privileged to have met these amazing men and to have heard their stories first-hand. Apart from being a little tipsy, we were all very humbled and JC and RH loved our very special coffee morning. Jeremy, especially, having made his documentary on the Arctic convoys. We certainly didn't miss the Ferrero Rocher.

We were then treated to a private viewing of an icebreaker that had led the Arctic convoys in World War II. Originally built in 1916 in Britain, it had survived the war and been restored and preserved as a floating museum. It's quite hard to have a historical tour of a boat with a serious historian, an interpreter and a British diplomat when you're pissed. Richard had to be sidelined a couple of times to prevent any insult to our kind hosts, such as when he suggested that the huge collection of methodically laid-out spanners in the engine room were pure 'James May Porn'.

Despite not having any recollection of the venue or the shows in St Petersburg, I'm sure the shows were as successful as ever. Poor old 'Norman' was sent away with a large flea in his ear after Jeremy totally lost his rag with him during drinks at the hotel bar. 'Norman' had tried to suggest how Jeremy should conduct himself and that he should not be quite so controversial. For a new boy on the block that wasn't a wise move. He certainly had some balls and narrowly avoided getting a kick in them.

Our nights out were organised by our Russian hosts, whom I feel certain were receiving large backhanders from the restaurants and bars we went to. One evening we were taken to this bizarre restaurant/club that was set in a black, one-storey, warehouse type building at the edge of a port. It had been a full-on day and neither Gem nor I had the chance to give it the once-over as we normally would. It did not look glamorous at all and Chris was getting a bit twitchy about it. Gem and I were ready for action to make other plans.

However, upon entering you could not help but be amazed by the huge space that had been transformed into a luxury Chinese restaurant. We were sat in a reasonably discreet dark corner; mind you, everywhere was poorly lit by a red glow of Chinese lanterns. It was a little contrived. Nothing seemed too out of the ordinary, except for the sheer size of the place, but then during the first course of Chinese delights the men of the table were offered a head-and-shoulder massage by scantily clad 'Chinese' girls. The girls didn't get many takers, just our Tour Leader, Chris, who couldn't resist a massage. Both Jeremy and Richard did not feel comfortable, so after enjoying a few dishes of Chinese delights we were off. Apparently, it was the place to be in St Petersburg but not for us.

Gemma made sure she checked out our last night's venue and, after reporting to Chris and discussing options with the boys, it was agreed to go to the biggest club in town, where we would have VVIP treatment and a private dining room. VVIP it certainly was. We made the obvious queue-jumping entrance, flanked by more huge Russian bodyguards, and were led to a roped-off area for pre-dinner cocktails – vodka ones of course. It was early for the club so it was quiet and we had a chance to get our bearings in the extraordinary large venue.

In the centre of the ground-floor space was an enormous double staircase, more fitting for a palace, sweeping left and right above the main dance floor. It led to further bars in a galleried area that overlooked the whole club. After our cocktails, we were led up the stairs and through a series of doors to our private dining room.

Oh my God! It was like a scene from a James Bond movie. The largest table I have ever seen which sat about thirty of us. It was about 12 ft wide and was filled with ornate table decorations and candles. At one end of the table was a huge screen, I guess about 18 ft wide and at least 10 ft high. It screened the activity of the nightclub below. The whole room was windowless and decorated so the doors were hidden when closed. It so easily could have been a James Bond Baddie's lair.

Throughout a fantastic dinner, the strongest vodka shots I have ever experienced were constantly put in front of you, which obviously one couldn't refuse. Oh dear, this was going to be messy. And it was. I remember standing at the top of the enormous sweeping staircase feeling sure it was moving. I obviously looked like I needed help and dear Gav, our security guy, forever vigilant, helped me teeter down the stairs in my heels and minidress. We had been allocated another private area but were exposed to the rest of the clubbers. Of course, our boys drew a lot of attention. Thankfully, they were in good spirits (literally).

We'd never had a club night, so it was quite exciting, but once it got packed and was hard to move, Jeremy and Richard were imprisoned in our exclusive corner. There were a couple of crowd surges as people tried to join our VVIP area, and it became harder and harder to get a drink even with VVIP service. It was time to leave. I do remember leaning on Richard in the back of the Range Rover and having one of our drunken heart to hearts. JC always travelled up front and was very good at managing his drunkenness. He just laughed at us two babbling on.

As usual the night had to be finished with a nightcap in the hotel bar. The atmosphere was a lot lighter with the shows behind us and home in sight. Jeremy apologised to 'Norman' from the BBC and raised a glass with him. Better to be friends than enemies in Russia and the BBC. I wasn't really in a fit state to drink anymore or stand up. Jeremy got me safely back to the room and carried on without me, putting in an all-nighter with Chris, raising a glass or two to his mother. Meanwhile, I was having a few conversations with God on the big white telephone.

The rest of the Bubble only had about four hours' sleep before packing, breakfast, if you could stomach it, and boarding our Range Rover convoy back to the airport. Jeremy was not surprisingly a mess after a long, emotional night and so was I. I did not have breakfast. I don't know how we got through the flight but I do know I was very grateful to be travelling with my celebrity friends up front and getting well looked after by very knowing, sympathetic BA staff.

Back home Jeremy dealt with his mother's funeral and more controversy. Someone had leaked rushes (the film footage that isn't used in the final edit) from an old *Top Gear* programme, in which Jeremy had used the 'N' word reciting the old nursery rhyme of 'Eeny, Meeny, Miny, Moe'. He was using it to make a decision over a car. Although I know Jeremy loves to provoke trouble, this latest controversy was seemingly a bit of a witch-hunt. I never knew why it wasn't investigated by the BBC or others as to how the rushes got into the hands of *The Mirror* newspaper. The actual finished programme was clearly edited so as not to offend anyone. I can categorically confirm Jeremy is not racist. I also know that he was constantly agitated by the BBC's uber-PC views and regulation. He naturally would have thought of the rhyme as it is from his era, and he probably left it in the rushes to wind Andy Wilman up in the edit.

It was a storm in a teacup, but that teacup was constantly getting topped up and the eye of the storm did not need whipping up any more.

Obviously, racism is a very serious issue, and the media storm and the grief Jeremy was getting from the BBC caused him to stop me going to Barbados, the next leg of the tour. He said he'd been asked by Tony Hall, Director-General of the BBC, not to take me, so as not to attract more media attention. It also would have been a bit of a thorny issue with his wife and children as Barbados was where they had holidayed as a family for years. So I was forced to drop out of the trip just a couple of days before.

I was devastated at missing what was to be the Bubble's tour leg of a lifetime. Brand Events had landed an amazing deal to put on a festival like the one in Sydney, with the boys performing trackside. The Barbados partners in the deal were redeveloping Bushy Park Circuit with backing from the FIA. The *Top Gear Live* Festival was scheduled to launch the new, improved venue. It meant so much to Gem and me. We constantly joked, whilst checking our endless list of obscure demands, for each tour, 'And have you got the tickets for Barbados?'

I missed out on a very fun, star-studded festival which included a race between Lewis Hamilton in an F1 car and America's Ken Block, a professional rally and stunt driver, in his rally car. All played out in the tropical paradise of Barbados. It was a great success and there was no trouble for Jeremy.

The only stories I bothered to listen to from that trip (I was literally not interested as I wasn't there and was a little sore about it) were about the common drama of not having a decent printer, which Jeremy went mad about. Poor old Becks had to run around in the extreme heat begging, stealing and borrowing from hotels and offices around the island. The comedy story was that several Bubble members, including Jeremy and Richard, had left the Piggy-Eyed Businessman floundering out at sea on a jet ski after JC and RH had repeatedly tried to unseat him by speeding past him at close range. During this attack Chris lost his glasses and was left to find his own way back to the resort. He was missing for some time as he pootled along close to the shore, desperately trying to recognise the right luxury resort without full vision.

Not Interrailing

The tour schedule was really gathering pace now. Less than a month after Barbados, we were off to Durban again, with only a few days' break before setting off for our incredibly ambitious European Tour of Prague, Budapest, Zagreb and Turin.

As was the new normal, our social life in Durban was fairly low-key. Apart from the boys feeling a little jaded from their increasingly full-on schedules, the rest of the Bubble, including me, were full on preparing, constantly changing plans, for the European Tour.

Our big night out was not so big, at a pretty soulless restaurant with not terribly good food and dreadful service. A bit of a tour low. Our celebs were a little fractious, not least because of the poor venue, but as with family holidays, when the kids turn into teenagers who no longer wish to spend time with Mum and Dad and their siblings, our three amigos were struggling with each other and our dysfunctional tour family.

Jeremy was agitated as the restaurant didn't have a decent rosé wine. James was in one of his Eeyore moods, while Hammond was feeling generally anti-social and, as Jeremy always said, was rubbish at small talk so was just sinking himself into gin and tonics.

However, Chris would not allow for the mood to be low, and a leaving ceremony/birthday celebration for

Rowly, our dear, hard-working Moon-Faced Producer, continued. Clarkson, Hammond and May were presented with baseball caps which had been customised to have ridiculous foot-long peaks. The caps had been covered in tin foil and branded with each presenter's relevant rap star name. JC was MOTHER, and RH was MC HAMMOND, which was far too long a name for the front of the cap so stuck out either side. JM was BEYONCÉ – a new nickname owing to his increasing, surprising tour demands such as the right temperature Sauvignon blanc (very tongue in cheek as that was about the only demand – that and him asking very politely if we had bought him any beef Hula Hoops).

The baseball caps were accompanied by hugely oversized faux-gold chains which had each presenter's initial hung on them. The whole rap star image was reference to the Rap Star stunt driver part of the show which the boys hated. Their other gifts were stuffed toy monkeys on which our green room assistant Nicole had carefully stitched blue testicles. These cuddly gifts were inspired by a heated debate within the Bubble as to whether the local monkeys had blue testicles or not. They did but the cuddly toys were lacking that detail so clearly it had to be added.

Rowly was treated to a tin-foil-covered cap and gold chain of his own. We were all then entertained by a personalised rap from the Bubble's Ring Master, Chris. After a pitiful version of 'Happy Birthday' and a cake engulfed in excessive candle fire as a tribute to his girlfriend Naomi, the flame-throwing/eating stuntwoman, there was a fairly sharp exit for our celebs.

Although I have strong memories of quite a low and awkward evening, something must have kicked off back at the hotel as I have a picture of James May laid across Rowly and a couple of girls. He had launched himself upon them holding a glass of vino, which sadly he didn't save all of during his drunken stunt, leaving him with a wet patch right over his crotch. At least, I think that is what happened.

As I said, the tour schedule was really ramping up, and just three days after our return from Durban we were flying to Prague. Thankfully, the mood had lifted and the whole Bubble, presenters included, were excited to be embarking on what felt like a real rock star tour of four cities, in four different countries hundreds of miles apart, in just ten days.

Prague was a good start – such a beautiful city and we were staying at the Four Seasons right on the river. The people of Prague were good to us and the local crew was great – very welcoming and efficient, as were all the hotel staff. We enjoyed some lovely evenings that, unusually, were quite sophisticated. Most importantly, the one show that was performed went really well to a packed and responsive audience.

To make what was an ambitious tour as easy and efficient as possible, it was largely the same show in each city. The boys had become so familiar with the various scenes and stunts, and were so adept with their lines, that their job was actually relatively easy. Of course, the stunts, races and car football never played out the same, which kept them on their toes. Being the pros that they are, they always learnt a little of the local language to use in their intro. It started off with Jeremy, along the lines of, 'I asked the barman in the hotel last night to translate this for me, so here we go…' He would then deliver in fluent Czech or Bulgarian, seemingly unbeknown to him, something like 'My penis is very small but it's OK it's thin and is delighted to be in Prague.' This was then followed by similar comments from James and Richard. It worked every time as a great audience warm-up.

After a successful first show, we 'bounced' as we called it, that is, bags all packed and loaded into the Range Rover convoy along with rosé, Sauvignon blanc and gin and tonic. I loved those moments when the boys were usually quite high and desperate for a drink. There was an excited panic to get aboard our luxury convoy and get swept away for another delicious dinner. I was more often than not on board with the boys listening to them exchange stories of the near misses they had in races or the lines they messed up. They would usually be very upbeat and a joy and privilege to listen to as they took the piss out of themselves and each other, giggling like naughty schoolboys.

After a couple of drinks in the comfort of the Range Rover, another rock star drop-off was made at an exclusive restaurant, for a delicious dinner on a terrace overlooking the city.

Next stop, Budapest via private jet. A hell of a lot of planning and research had gone into the logistics of this tour, which were extremely complex. The crew had the toughest job. After the first show, they had to break down the set, pack their bags and travel overnight on incredibly long tour-bus journeys. Upon arrival at their cheap hotels, they had to hit the ground running to prepare for the next performance the following day.

Meanwhile, there had been many discussions about how our VVIP Bubble would travel and where we would reside in each country. I, having a direct line to the Maharaja, discussed with him directly what he would prefer; five-star hotels with commercial flights between each country, or private jets with private houses. The latter was his choice. He actually put forward the idea of hiring a villa somewhere central to all the shows' locations and flying in and out by private jet for each performance. Apparently, this was how Take That did it. I researched this extensively and found some beautiful villas on the coast of Croatia. Sadly, the regulations on night flights into small private airports did not favour our schedules.

I then set about reserving various high-end private houses and boutique hotels, and coordinating chefs, housekeeping, cars, luxury minibuses, private jets and commercial flights. Having run various options past Gem and Chris, we ended up with a combination of both. I had forewarned JC of the plan and he had reassured me that he was happy and not too bothered. I had particularly warned him that the house in Budapest was not of our usual standard but was the best of the best in Budapest. The city was divided into numbered districts, and we were in the best, District 1.

I had also warned him that there would be no Range Rovers to meet us from the airport as it was just impossible to obtain them in time. There was a shortage of them in Eastern Europe, and although Range Rover had offered to have some driven over from the UK, it was just not feasible. I did however arrange for a luxury Mercedes minibus, the type a rock and roll band would use. I felt sure this would suffice, as well as the promise of Range Rovers being delivered the next day.

Err, no. The Maharaja was in full swing. Having stepped off the private jet, the moaning began, started by Jeremy but then bolstered by James and Richard, who thought it must be a budget issue, and the jokes about the bank and Chris and JCP being on the phone, started. This was in some way situation normal and JCP, Gem and I just batted the verbal abuse away. (For some logistical reason, Chris wasn't with us for our first night in Budapest.) However, after just over an hour of driving, Jeremy was getting seriously agitated and declaring that we should never be more than forty minutes' drive from where we needed to be.

I was beginning to feel really anxious. Despite all my efforts to make sure we had new and good quality bed linen, plenty of comfy places to relax (the owner had actually purchased extra sun loungers and bean bags and provided extra beds for us all to fit in) and checking the house had enough to entertain us (it had an indoor/outdoor pool and I'd asked the owner to buy football nets, balls and other garden games), I was losing my confidence and was dreading having a disgruntled Maharaja in our presence. I felt wholly responsible for the happiness of the Bubble.

As we turned into an unmade road where our home for the next few days was situated, I really was worried. I had seen pictures of the house and although it wasn't to my taste it looked smart in a suburban way, unlike the houses that lined the dirt track we were on. My extensive research had taught me about the twenty-three districts. The house was in District 1, the Castle District – the best. We stopped outside an ugly solid metal gate (the electric gate as described on the website, not quite what I had in my mind). Next door was a derelict house and opposite were some aggressive dogs barking from behind a chain-link fence. God Help Me.

As you might imagine, the Maharaja was not impressed. I agreed with him that the house was not up to standard, but that as we discussed it gave us all privacy, and I pointed out the elevated veranda that had views of the valley below and was not overlooked. There was also the swimming pool and the fact that one of his favourite chefs, Julia, had been flown over from Australia to cook for us for the duration of our stay.

After pouring a glass of his favourite rosé that I had brought from the UK (as had Gem and Becks. We had each stashed a couple of bottles in our luggage and arranged for a case of it to come out with the crew), I made him, James and Richard comfy on the veranda. I thought I'd tamed the beast.

Unfortunately not, for along with the weather being a huge disappointment, very humid and grey, there was a bit of a pong of sewage in the air. The beast arose and turned the pongy air blue. He tore me off a strip or two and exclaimed, 'This is just not good enough,' slamming doors as he stropped out to the front of the house. He was swiftly followed by JCP who threw me a look to kill.

I went out to talk to James and Richard and see how they felt. They too were not too happy with the niff in the air but were quite happy with the house and carried on enjoying their drinks. JCP came out to join us and reported that the Maharaja was not happy at all and complained, to top it all, that he had the worst room in the house. I explained that although his room was smaller than the other doubles, it was the only one with its own bathroom. Richard and James were sharing a bathroom that connected to both their rooms.

The conversations that followed were frankly quite ridiculous. It was like the teenage older brother in the family was kicking off because 'it's just not fair.' James and Richard offered up their rooms and said they were happy to sleep anywhere. JCP rang the Four Seasons in town to check for availability and Chris Hughes to discuss contingency plans. I felt terrible but at the same time thought Jeremy was being a total arse. Chris rang me and expressed his concern. I thought I was going to get a bollocking from him, but in the unique situation that I was – being girlfriend to Clarkson and working for Chris – and after explaining that the Four Seasons would totally blow the budget, and therefore I felt the Maharaja should get over it, Chris agreed with me but wanted to come up with a solution to appease the big man.

After a perfectly civilised conversation with Chris, it was decided to offer JC a move to the Four Seasons. I was fuming. I really felt this overindulgence was going too far, and like spoiling a toddler we were just feeding the monster within. Just as Wilman had feared.

The monster calmed down and accepted that he could live with what we'd got. James, I think, decided to make a point of not being a diva and insisted on sleeping in the boiler/utility room on a camp bed, giving his room with a view to JCP.

Chris called me again to ask how the 'Pandas' were. He decided that our three amigos had become increasingly sensitive to their environment, requiring specialist and careful handling. As so often happened when discussing anything with Chris, I became hysterical with laughter. But I was on the verge of being truly hysterical.

Thank goodness our personal chef, whom I had discussed meal plans with at length, came up trumps with a delicious supper, and the mood in the camp was lifted, though it was still a little tense. We then settled down for an evening of World Cup football on TV, during which according to the Maharaja you shouldn't talk or fidget. The night was not good to us. There was a horrific storm of torrential rain, blinding lightning and thunderclaps as loud as Jeremy Clarkson. Once the storm died down, the angry dogs from across the road started a neighbourhood chat with all things barky. This did not help our already challenging accommodation issues.

I did not sleep a wink, partly worrying about the accommodation and how I might be able to make things better, and partly as I was so annoyed by Jeremy being a diva. Thank goodness we had a day off the next day. This tour schedule had been carefully planned at length so that after each travel day there was at least a day to let our celebrities rest and allow the crew time to catch us up and prepare for the next show the following evening. Part of the reason we had a house in Budapest instead of a hotel was because we had the longest layover time, and all the travel experts I'd spoken to had told me there was much more to enjoy in

Hungary than Zagreb, our next stop. All of which I had tried to explain to Jeremy. Jeremy doesn't like listening to reason. Jeremy doesn't like listening.

Remarkably, the Maharaja was calm apart from threatening to take a gun to the neighbours' dogs. Ironically, what with their barking and the incredible storm that disturbed the whole house, except for James who was safely tucked away in his windowless boiler room, the night's disruptions united the Bubble once more. (Except for two of us!)

The Maharaja had to grovel to me to borrow my laptop, as he'd forgotten his and needed to write and file his column for the *Sunday Times*. When he was ready, we set off in our Range Rover convoy (thank God they had arrived) for a day of sightseeing on another grey and humid day in Budapest.

Thank heavens also for the arrival of our jolly Piggy-Eyed Businessman, who got us all laughing again and also made the executive decision to leave Budapest a day early as it really wasn't pleasing any of us. It turns out the sewage smell is the scent of the city and the people of Hungary are not much fun. The audience was, by the boys' own account, ruder than Finland. They decided that at least the Finns gave some feedback, whereas the Hungarians barely showed any sign of life and disappointingly were mostly men.

The boys did enjoy spotting attractive females in their audience, especially ones attractive enough to put a fellow presenter off his lines, which provided their own private entertainment. It amazed me how dressed-up, or undressed, should I say, some women would be to sit in a grubby, exhaust-filled arena to watch three scruffy middle-aged men.

Having made the decision to head to Zagreb a day early, our crazy dysfunctional family relaxed into its slightly dysfunctional house and we had an epic game of three-a-side football. James sat it out as football is not his game. In fact I think sport in general is not for James. I suffered several injuries caused mainly by Hammond. After a good run down the wing (all of twenty yards), he made a rather overenthusiastic pass to me. Not to my feet. Chris immediately commentated, 'Right in the vag!' We all fell about laughing whilst Gem and I made another note for our sexual harassment file.

I was not laughing, however, when Rich missed the ball totally, kicking me hard in the shin. James was then forced to take my place to finish the game, and he really was useless. He had absolutely no coordination with anything, his body, the ball or any of his team. Full time was called when it looked as though Chris might actually lose his face while playing in goal; either that or Jeremy would have a coronary.

No hard feelings, only my shin. The sun shone, the Maharaja was happy again, and we all enjoyed a BBQ lunch before heading to another private airport and the most ridiculous security ever, before boarding another private jet to Zagreb.

The departure lounge was no more than a portacabin with the usual airport metal detector frame to walk through. There was no conveyor for our bags – they were just passed along a table to be hand-searched by one of the three-strong security team. Despite the simple and make-do facilities, there was an overzealous, slightly scary Hungarian woman in charge, to make up for anything lacking. Even though there were only eight of us getting on our own plane, she insisted on crowd control. We were all searched individually, belts and shoes removed, and individual paperwork was checked.

I was wearing strappy sandals with a paper-thin sole and bare feet. She insisted I took them off and actually scanned the soles of my feet. I found it very hard to disguise my disgust and annoyance, much to the rest of the Bubble's amusement. Security was not amused. Chris made it just that little bit harder for me to remain straight-faced as he went into one of his anti-security rants questioning why on earth you would want to blow up a small private plane that was filled with your own mates. Good question.

We were released to a rickety old bus to drive us, all of twenty yards, to the plane. The whole procedure was quite comedic. The process could have been carried out by one person, but as Jeremy pointed out it is how poor economies work – give everyone a job and pay them a pound a day but at least they are all employed.

Once we were safely aboard and had been briefed with a pleasantly brief safety briefing, we were up and away. And a wonderful piece of gossip came to light that Bruce Willis had been filming in Budapest and had stayed in a house just a few doors up from ours. He too had had a celebrity moment and insisted on leaving earlier than scheduled. I felt some relief, as if Bruce Willis's 'people' couldn't get it right, what chance did I have?

Zagreb was a welcome relief from our bad experience in Budapest. Luckily, the rather elegant hotel, The Esplanade, originally built for the passengers of the Orient Express, was able to put us all up for the extra night, and because it was Croatia it didn't make too much impact on the budget. All was calm again. We all enjoyed a lovely supper outside watching the World Cup on a big screen with a bar and terrace all to ourselves.

Within twenty-four hours, our crack team of troubleshooters (Gem, Becks, Emma and I) had rebooked flights, renegotiated accommodation, and hired three touring bikes to be delivered to the hotel for Hammond, May and JCP to explore Croatia. We had also researched activities, sightseeing and restaurants, with several bookings placed on hold. The only thing we couldn't find was Range Rovers for the extra day. Never ones to give up, Becks and Emma had found a friend of a friend who was prepared to lend their old Range Rover to Jeremy for exploring.

Slightly nervously, we informed the Maharaja that this was the only Range Rover available. He accepted graciously and rather enjoyed the retro mustard-coloured beast, which must have been about twenty years old. Funnily enough, brand new Range Rovers or any new cars were not terribly abundant in Croatia, a country not long rebuilt after a long war for independence. Even the Maharaja could recognise when to be a little humble and not all 'Bruce Willis'.

We all had an amazing day. Jeremy and I discovered the incredible, almost indescribable Plitvice Lakes, a World Heritage Site. Upon our arrival, Jeremy had a bit of a Panda/diva moment and refused to join the queues of people walking down the narrow path to the lakes. Thankfully, he had a change of heart. He was blown away. He had never seen anything like it and that means a lot coming from the man who has almost seen the entire world. He was so impressed he created a story around them in order to go back and film there. The biker boys were also blown away by the beautiful Croatian landscape – they had ventured up to the borders in the north. We all fell in love with Croatia.

We all enjoyed another touristy day, together, visiting a fascinating, humorous and moving boutique museum, the Museum of Broken Relationships. Exhibits included old routers that had never really 'connected' with their PC, and a pair of stilettos, stockings and suspenders, dropped by a prostitute, in contrast with heartbreaking letters from lovers and family members torn apart by the war. After one of our best lunches, in a charming courtyard garden of a tiny local restaurant, it was time to prepare for the show.

The people of Croatia won our hearts, too. They were a polite but expressive audience. After another successful show, it was time for a celebratory dinner, at a stunning, unexpectedly contemporary, Chinese restaurant on the edge of a forest. This was so fitting for our three amigos, now very aptly nicknamed 'Pandas'. I had let it slip that Chris had used this to refer to them while we were trying to solve the Budapest crisis.

The boys, finding it amusing, only encouraged Chris to embellish his theory, and suggested that perhaps treating them like pandas might be the way to go. Chris jumped at that idea. Just like pandas, the three boys were able to attract thousands, if not millions, of people keen to get even a quick glimpse of them. Equally, like pandas, the presenters were becoming tired of performing. So, if Chris were to find a venue where the most luxurious green room could be created, like the bespoke environment demanded by the pandas of Edinburgh Zoo, then perhaps thousands of fans would pay for the chance of seeing the presenters, who may or may not appear, just like the pandas who come out once in a blue moon to be observed eating. Our Pandas would obviously be smoking and drinking and would have to have typical Panda names. Chris and I came up with the following: F*ck F*ck, C**nt C**nt and Wa*k Wa*k. I'll leave you to work out who was who.

The Bubble was once more in hysterics including the now very relaxed Maharaja, who was in tears with laughter. Such a joy to see. To add to the hilarity, our table happened to be surrounded by huge bamboo plants which offered the perfect photo opportunity for FF, CC and WW to curl up at the bottom of the bamboo, like only a panda would, after a big meal. Add to that, the Piggy-Eyed Businessman believing that every dish that was served up was for him to tuck into, as if it was communal eating, like a Chinese takeaway, and you have another epic tour night out.

Sadly, trouble was brewing. Although ticket sales had been brilliant so far, selling out in each city, the ticket price had been set to reflect the local economies, and therefore the tour was only just breaking even. It was essential that the next stop, Turin, was a sell-out to get the tour into profit. So far, sales were down compared to the usual selling rate.

Chris had divulged the problem to the boys and asked if they would be prepared to pull off a PR stunt to help sell out. Jeremy was usually reluctant to do any PR, but in this case he was happy to help. After all, it would not look good for the brand if word got out that they couldn't fill the arena in Turin, the capital of the Italian automotive industry.

Jeremy, James and Richard actually began to get creative and helped Chris and the Brand Events team create the stunt. Within twenty-four hours it had been arranged that four Fiat 500 Abarths were ready for our three rock stars and the Stig to take part in an *Italian Job* style drive, up to a piazza where four old-fashioned ticket booths (i.e. tall slim sheds with hatches to serve customers) awaited for the fab four to promote tickets and sign autographs.

The Stig joined us on the private jet in order to get there on time. Press had been contacted; a coffee shop had been reserved for us to use as a green room prior to the stunt; and permission to close the road and take over the piazza was obtained. Security had also been booked as a large, frenzied crowd was expected.

Despite terrible weather, the crowd was even larger than expected. We all got soaked and we had to call time after about twenty minutes of our celebs being in the booths, for fear of a crush. The Stig was hilarious, basically standing in his booth, arms folded, ignoring everyone. The boys loved it at first but then began to panic as they became surrounded by crazy Italian fans. There was a hint of Beatlemania about it and it was very exciting to be part of, if a little unnerving.

Chris, JCP, Gem, the burly security guards and I managed to extract the Stig and the boys to the safety of our Range

Rover convoy, and we made an escape for lunch and to dry out. There is something special about an Italian crowd – they are so passionate and expressive. The Bubble was very happy and spirits were high for the final stretch of our whistle-stop tour.

There was another World Cup game scheduled for our first night in Italy, so we reserved a corner of a restaurant with our own large screen to watch the match. It was a big game for us, England vs Brazil. We settled ourselves in, beers at the ready. Disaster struck – the screen wouldn't connect to the right channel. JCP and Gem shot out to recce another restaurant which had a table available and could screen the game – a long shot but failure was not an option.

Success! We ended up with a private room at the back of a tiny Brazilian bar. It was really, really basic but absolutely perfect. It was run by a Brazilian couple and we had the most amazing steak sizzling on a hot stone with home-cooked chips and veg. The couple didn't speak English, only Portuguese or broken Italian. It was as if the Bubble had been teleported into a weird Italian-Brazilian bubble. They keenly watched the game with us. I can't remember who won, I just remember there was no hard feeling and we carried on drinking the night away enjoying free shots from our new-found Brazilian-Italian friends. A classic Bubble family night out.

The PR stunt had been a roaring success. The show sold out and the Italian audience did not disappoint, continuing to show their passion and enthusiasm for our famous trio. Our crew party was held in an Italian restaurant, with pizza all round and more football to be cheered on. The boys' end-of-tour presents were perhaps suitably humble. They each had a cuddly toy panda to take home, with a personalised name tag on: F**k F**k, C**t C**t and W**k W**k.

JC's schedule was forever pressing and he was flying on to Morocco early the next morning to film for *Top Gear*. At midnight on a drunken high, we changed my flight home so I could join him in Marrakesh and my adventure continued.

That Punch

Jeremy and Richard then returned to Italy to film for their Christmas DVD. I joined them a few days later. Jeremy was still getting grief from senior management at the BBC about his latest racial slurs and received bad news about their forthcoming trip to Argentina to film their annual *Top Gear* special. They couldn't get permission to film in a town that they had planned to use for the final scene. I spent an evening with Jeremy and Richard helping to come up with solutions whilst enjoying gin and tonics on the terrace of a former Italian monastery.

There was a plan afoot to book a well-known rock band to create an alternative finale to the special. Jeremy asked Andy Wilman to make it happen. In this particular instance plans changed but that was now the draw they had, and they could call just about anyone from any Hall of Fame and they would be willing to get involved. Jeremy once flew out to film with Bruce Willis on the set of his latest film for a short piece to camera for one *Top Gear* episode.

I have two favourite and surreal memories from being at the *Top Gear* filming, as the boys rose to dizzying heights of fame. My favourite was meeting Tom Cruise and Cameron Diaz trackside as they battled it out in a reasonably priced car under the tuition of the man in the white suit. What was really mind-blowing to hear was both Cameron and Tom said it was the best day out they'd had in a long time. Tom

Cruise! Cameron Diaz! Loving a day out with my mates' ridiculous motoring programme. I was so proud and felt so lucky to be involved having watched the pokey BBC2 motoring show evolve into the iconic series it became.

Coming close second was Will Smith, again a superstar who must have had so many incredible experiences, but he too loved his time in a shitty warehouse and flinging himself around a track in a crap car. He totally got *Top Gear* humour. He and Jeremy bantered away very naturally. Apart from them both being total pros, they genuinely got on. Just remembered: Will was accompanied by the gorgeous Margot Robbie, but I wasn't so interested in her. I do remember she played it very well performing alongside two huge egos.

After a long stint of filming and touring, Jeremy, James and Richard took their annual synchronised summer holidays, apart of course, although this summer, Jeremy and I did meet up with the Hammond family in the South of France. After a good break from each other and work, it was back to filming and the famous Argentinian incident that was genuinely terrifying for them and the crew.

For those of you who may have missed the news, Jeremy had chosen a Porsche 928 as his car for the special celebrating V8 engines. Unfortunately, it had a number plate, H982 FKL, that turned out to be rather provocative to certain disgruntled Argentinians. Who were provoked further by the joy of social media. The whole crew including the presenters ended up in a hotel under siege by an angry mob who were seriously offended by the supposed reference to the Falklands War.

The mob were ready to attack with missiles of bricks and stones. After diplomatic involvement from both countries, they were all forced to leave the country. The presenters were flown out, but the rest of the crew had to drive and were attacked, narrowly missing serious injury as bricks and stones were thrown, smashing car windows. They were forced to abandon cars and equipment, fearing for their lives and desperate to get out of the country.

The trouble and yet more controversy followed Jeremy for some months after, including the Argentinian ambassador to the UK making a formal complaint to the BBC after he wrote about the incident in his columns in *The Sun* and *The Sunday Times*. She complained of his 'provocative behaviour' and 'offensive remarks'. Unfortunately, Danny Cohen, the BBC's Director of Television, was cataloguing all of *Top Gear*'s and Jeremy's controversial incidents, so when the big one occurred, the punching of Oisin Tymon, a producer on the show, Danny had had enough. Despite Lord Tony Hall, the Director-General, being a huge fan of Jeremy, he could not defend him any longer.

The last straw was when Jeremy just had to push it a step too far, fuelled by alcohol and adoring fans at a charity dinner at the Roundhouse. Whilst auctioning a prize of a track day with him at Dunsfold, he gave his current opinion of Danny Cohen and the BBC using quite a few words that I can't be bothered to repeat here as there would be too many '**' filling in the blanks.

The whole outburst was recorded by a *Mirror* reporter who was there reporting on the event. After painful weeks of speculation, meetings and investigations, Jeremy was suspended and not re-contracted to continue with what was effectively his baby, a very precious one at that.

Jeremy and Andy had conceived the new-look *Top Gear* back in 2002 and they were both absolutely devastated. Jeremy had started his television career at the BBC and was very proud to be part of the iconic national and world-renowned institution that he had grown up with and genuinely respected.

Although Andy hadn't been asked to leave the BBC, he chose to resign. Even after he left, he used to go to the BBC and sit in his office. He was bereft and lost. A colleague told me what a tragic sight it was; he didn't know what to say to him or how to help him. I was close to Andy, having known him since I first worked for *Top Gear* back in the nineties. Andy and I were often in contact during any dramas with JC. We looked out for each other and for Jeremy. Andy was worried about Jeremy and his mental and physical state, so we had numerous chats through this challenging time.

Jeremy was under siege in his flat in Holland Park, by the press. For at least a week there were satellite vans parked outside permanently. Huge crowds of press, equipped with cameras with long lenses, waited outside for at least eighteen hours a day. Jeremy often felt he was trapped in a weird prison at the best of times, albeit a luxury one, but this was on another level. The next few months were not pleasant. I got caught up in it, too, and often felt as if we were being hunted. I had paps opening my boot, trying to get in my car, or leaning across the bonnet facing me with lenses and flashes as I tried to drive away. Although I don't approve of some of Jeremy's behaviour, I definitely don't approve of the behaviour of some of the press and the paps. They too are extremely provocative, literally forcing you to react and hoping it will be dramatic.

Despite an awful time enduring constant press intrusion, Jeremy has huge resilience and determination and I only remember him once collapsing into an exhausted mess. We had taken cover in Rebekah Brooks's house in the Cotswolds for the weekend – he slept through most of it.

However, Jeremy never seems to lose. The negativity of the Argentinian saga did not prevent him and the show coming out on top, but it did provide a dramatic end to an otherwise fantastic, funny and entertaining show which turned out to be the last special they would ever do for *Top Gear*.

As you well know, not too long after the devastating blow (excuse the pun), he and the others were offered their Amazon deal along with plenty of others. James and Richard had actually considered leading a quieter life and staying at the BBC, but the draw of the big man and big money pulled them all back together again.

However, the boys' great success leading up to this had nearly destroyed the lot. There is always a price to be paid. An increasingly demanding worldwide schedule of live shows and filming, with twenty-hour days, whether it was driving, filming, writing or drinking (or all four), with very little down time, was too much. Jeremy, James and Richard saw more of each other than their families. The stress and tiredness was definitely becoming more evident.

On the day of the fracas with poor Oisin, Jeremy had been working every day for at least three weeks after a year of working in at least eleven different countries. He was constantly writing, filming, attending photo shoots, doing voice-overs and fighting to clear his name in one controversy or another. On top of that, his mother had died and he was going through a separation from his wife and children. I think poor Osh (as he was nicknamed) was literally Jeremy's 'punchbag'.

In the weeks running up to 'THE END', the tour had been to Liverpool and Newcastle one weekend after another. There had been the usual tour antics. We had used private jets and continued to be creative with our nights out. In Liverpool we had hired a penthouse apartment for the night and had our own five-star, private dinner party. We had learnt that JC loved a magician so we hired one for the evening. Jeremy loved it.

Our tour was actually becoming more and more professional. In the UK, Brand Events had gone into partnership with Live Nation, who manage a huge number of arena events in the music and entertainment business. They provided fantastic catering and superb, true rock and roll green rooms. The boys felt they had really made it when they were given the entertainment system used by One Direction in their green room. I also evolved with my catering skills and provided what became known as the 'Shit Picnic'.

My Spam, egg mayonnaise or cheese and pickle sandwiches, wrapped in foil and bundled in a carrier bag, were actually very welcome and enjoyed by our superstars and the rest of the Bubble served up as a wonderful juxtaposition on a private jet, in true *Top Gear* style.

Liverpool came and went without too much drama apart from Jeremy being dissatisfied with his kippers for breakfast; to be fair, they were extremely undercooked. The other more comedic drama was when Richard lost his jeans through the hotel's laundry service. I was contacted immediately to solve the problem. I got onto housekeeping and they said they had been delivered. After a lot of discussion about room numbers and explaining the difference between Clarkson, Hammond and May, the jeans were discovered. They had been delivered to James, so I called James.

No, he hadn't got them. I got back to housekeeping, and next thing I know Jeremy is complaining as he has been delivered some jeans which definitely weren't his. I called housekeeping to pick up the jeans from Jeremy's room and deliver them to Richard. Problem solved.

Not quite. I met everyone at the breakfast table in our private dining and lounge area. Richard hadn't been delivered his jeans, but James had been made to get off the loo and answer the door to receive them in his room. This was in fact the second time he'd had his morning ablutions interrupted, as they had knocked just after I'd called him to check if he had them. How could housekeeping get it so wrong? The hotel was so quiet and all the staff were very aware of the three well-known presenters staying, except for, I can only assume, a *Fawlty Towers*, Manuel type character, in housekeeping.

On to Newcastle, where spirits were high as, despite the tiredness, the northern English audiences were loving the shows. It felt like after all these years everything was really coming together to create the most efficient and fun tour: travelling by private jet, with private dinners and entertainment, and professional, well-equipped green rooms. The boys could do the shows standing on their heads, as they knew each other and each scene so well. The crew were really slick and worked together brilliantly. They were as bonded as the Bubble was as a family and had a lot of laughs, happy without the superstar luxuries.

The mechanics and stunt team had created some brilliant acts, the latest being a drifting and doughnutting competition between the boys. They had each chosen their preferred cars. James, Captain Slow, was of course predicted to be useless. Jeremy and Richard tore around the circuit as you would expect, Jeremy ripping out most of the barriers and Richard narrowly missing his fellow presenters' cars on the start/finish line.

However, James set off in his Black BMW 5 series. He was remarkably swift and absolutely amazing at doughnutting and drifting, so good and competent that he leant out of the window, waving at the cheering crowd. He had completed the course without making a single mistake. He went into his winning celebrations but Jeremy noticed something odd about his car. He discovered the Stig sitting behind blacked-out windows in the back seat, with a steering wheel. James tried to defend himself claiming there were no rules about passengers, but the Stig gave away the engineering trickery as he drove off at speed leaving James standing.

Unfortunately, nothing is ever perfect, predictably so, with so many complex and adapted vehicles and people involved. Jeremy had a mechanical issue with one of his vehicles and it kept failing him at crucial moments. Having reported the problem to Rowly, who had spoken to the mechanics and reported back to JC that all was sorted, when the problem occurred again Jeremy went mad, first at Rowly and then demanding that the mechanics came up to the green room, where he laid into them verbally for what felt like an eternity whilst the rest of us cowered into sofas or corners. The air was blue; the mechanics left quietly, heads held low.

Jeremy was pushing himself to the absolute limit. Between performing the afternoon and evening shows he was writing and editing the TV show. His life was out of control. That night he laid into Rowly. It was the worst dressing-down yet and I thought totally out of order and unnecessary. We were having a night in, at the hotel, with a Chinese takeaway in a private room with our own bar and big screen for a quiet movie night. When Jeremy snapped, quiet it wasn't, apart from the eery silence from everyone else. Rowly was close to tears. And no one dared stop Jeremy or hold him to account, including myself. I did however talk to Rowly privately to make sure he was OK and make excuses for Jeremy's behaviour. Rowly was used to getting blasted by Jeremy but that episode was on another level. I believed we were witnessing a man unravelling.

I was shocked, scared and worried about Jeremy and his behaviour. I persuaded him to apologise to the mechanics and Rowly, and the air was cleared once again. We had a crazy night out in an Indian restaurant which we took over. After an arm-wrestling and shot-putting oranges competition, inspired by the presence of Louise Hazel, an Olympic heptathlon champion (Louise took James on in a race, car against athlete, in the show), we enjoyed the usual band-jacking of a small band that had been squeezed into the end of the room.

Another successful leg of the tour completed, but the mood in the Bubble was tense. Jeremy even lost it when we landed at Luton, because his chauffeur-driven car wasn't outside the plane waiting.

The boys were in the middle of a series of the TV show, which meant that after each of these northern trips, from which we arrived home late on a Sunday night, the Mondays and Tuesdays were spent preparing for the forthcoming recording at the studio and track at Dunsfold on the Wednesday.

On that fateful day, 4 March 2015, I had gone to the studio as I was hosting some competition winners who were there to be in the audience. Jeremy liked me being there as extra support. The crew and presenters started their day early. Jeremy, James and Richard would run through and amend scripts, and meet and spend time with the celebrity guest, including watching them perform around the track under the Stig's tuition. The day was pretty flat out also preparing and working on the next few shows. With the extra days filled with touring, the filming, editing and preparation for this series were behind schedule.

There would usually be at least two producers present on a studio day. Filming with the live audience, and meeting and interviewing the celebrity guest were both quite stressful. Andy Wilman, Jeremy's equal in the success and workload in all of this, was not there as he usually would be, because he was still editing sections of the show to be ready for the Sunday-night screening and the following shows. Andy was the secret genius behind the editing that created the final masterpieces. Jeremy would always be singing his praises apart from when he couldn't get hold of him as he'd gone 'underground' and untraceable in an edit suite.

That day, they were generally short of crew as Osh and another team were preparing for filming in Yorkshire the next day. By the end of the day, which was about 8.30 at night, Jeremy came out of the studio, voicing how tough it had been without Andy and the normal crew. As usual he had not really eaten all day. (None of them ate much at all before performing.) All three of them went straight to their dingy little green room at the back of the portacabin production office to pour a much-needed drink and tuck into the notoriously bad buffet.

A helicopter was waiting to fly them up to Yorkshire, and one of the crew was trying to encourage them to get going. Jeremy said, 'Give us a break, can't we at least have one drink in peace?' Or something similar. I was aware and concerned that Jeremy sank almost a whole bottle of wine in a very short space of time. I actually poured myself half a glass in order to slow him down. Later than planned, they set off with a box of alcohol for the journey.

You know the rest. Although what you won't know is that Richard Hammond was dying for a pee before they landed. As they did land, slightly the worse for wear, he had already unzipped his trousers and relieved himself on the lawn of the hotel as soon as he had untangled himself from the helicopter seat belts. What he hadn't realised was a member of staff from the hotel was there to greet them.

Time to Sober Up

With *Top Gear* no more, the tour was thrown into disarray and near disaster. Jeremy's dismissal from the BBC meant that the tour could no longer go on as it was, with its connection to the BBC. However, Chris and JCP worked extremely hard to pull a deal together with BBC Worldwide, which meant that the tour could go on but under a different name. Well that wasn't difficult: it became and was relaunched as *Clarkson Hammond and May Live*, because it was.

As soon as Chris and JCP had signed the deal, the Bubble was called to assemble at Jeremy's flat for a celebration. It was quite emotional and very stupid. I don't know how but a very large piece of street furniture – one of those illuminated boxes that sits in the middle of a pedestrian crossing – ended up in the flat.

Brand Events frantically set about rescheduling shows that had been postponed, and filming was set up to promote the rebranded events at enormous cost. I was part of the crew and gathered various props and essential creature comforts for the filming days in various locations. Unfortunately, there was a slight miscommunication between Jeremy and myself for the first one. We travelled from London to Hampshire in a Lamborghini. I was crushed in my seat with my overnight bag and all the bits and pieces for the day ahead. We argued all the way but a truce was declared when I made Jeremy laugh as I sent a comedy text to Chris who had been calling, desperate to know where we were. The text read: 'I can't hear you as I am jammed into a Fu**ing Bumby Lambogink!' Laughter is the key to happiness and ending all arguments.

The boys, Rowly and the rest of the team had come up with some brilliant ideas to create promotional videos to hit social media with. The main concept was that the presenters were loading a huge truck with everything they needed for the tour. This included a horse, which it was decided Richard should mount in order to get him loaded. This inevitably ended in disaster as he took off across a field with RH, supposedly never to be seen again.

Jeremy was put in charge of a huge crane in order to load James May's piano on board; this ended up with the piano being dropped on a classic car. I found it quite upsetting seeing an immaculately preserved car from my childhood totally destroyed. There was no room for feelings of nostalgia when filming with these guys. James was filmed with a clipboard ticking cars off from a huge convoy that stretched out as far as the eye could see. They were clearly not going to fit in the huge but not huge enough hauler. With camera trickery, it looked as though they did as they endlessly filed up the ramp into the *Clarkson, Hammond and May Live* 'Circus' truck. The cars included Reliant Robins, which Jeremy drove and of course rolled over – James just left him stranded, like a beetle on his back, as he continued with his clipboard ticking off all the cars.

The live show now could have nothing to do with *Top Gear*, so to make up for the loss of all the old *Top Gear* highlights that used to be shown as a pre-show warm-up and fillers throughout the show to give time for set changes, several films were made at breakneck speed. In one film, they created a spoof three-car challenge at Thruxton race track, which included looking for a racing driver to help – the Stig had decided to stay with the BBC. He didn't like change.

The film was telling the story of how they had to learn to become TV presenters, as if they had never done it before and certainly had nothing to do with *Top Gear*. Whilst 'learning' how to talk to the camera about supercars, they demonstrated their incompetence by getting tangled up in camera wires and walking too far away from the sound man (so all you could hear was the howling wind and flapping jackets whilst they over-gesticulated their story and facts about the cars).

It was a brilliant send-up of themselves. Their search for a racing driver ended when they found a driver who had been living rough among the pit garages. This driver claimed to have worked on TV before and was supposedly Daniel Craig. It was in fact Ben Collins, the former Stig. They found him lying in his own urine with a shopping trolley full of things including a Daniel Craig mask. (Ben is the stunt driver for Daniel in his Bond movies.) He was dressed in a very grubby, once-white racing suit, with holes in his racing boots and a cheap open-faced helmet.

Whilst he drove at high speed around the track, the boys were standing gossiping about him and deciding what to call him. Richard said, 'What shall we call him?' Jeremy said, 'Why don't we call him The Stog?' 'That's stupid,' replied Richard. James said, 'Why don't we call him The Ben Collins?' Jeremy asked, 'Why would we do that?' James said, 'Because that's his name.'

To create an opening film for the live show, they filmed 'The Interceptors', a montage of a spoof seventies detective show using Jensen Interceptors as their mode of transport. Jeremy's friend Sir Charles Dunstone was on the board of Jensen in a bid to resurrect the iconic brand. I believe he lent them the cars in return for the exposure the brand would get.

Our three amigos played three seventies private detectives, complete with flares and moustaches. Richard showed his fighting prowess by taking out a small child (Chris Hughes's son) with a karate chop. James May shot a dog (no dog was harmed in the making of this film). And Jeremy ended the film alongside Richard confronting a villain. Jeremy took the villain out with a punch, at which point the director, Rowly, shouted, 'Cut!' JC said, 'Why did you do that?' The director replied, 'You've crossed the line, you're sacked.' Richard asked, 'Now what do we do?' And that cued the start of the new live show. This did not go down well with BBC Worldwide, but it was used nevertheless. Neither the actions of Jeremy nor the bad press had had any negative impact on ticket sales, or as it transpired all their careers.

The tour set off again, first stop Belfast. The Bubble stayed in a beautiful stately home previously used by Northern Irish prime ministers and other dignitaries. It came with a butler and staff. Jeremy was on his best behaviour and in fact stopped drinking for a while. Chris was horrified and blamed me for being a typical girlfriend: having got my claws into him, I was trying to change him. Really, can you imagine anyone changing or trying to manage Clarkson – I don't think so. At breakfast one morning, as we were all sitting around in the wonderful family kitchen enjoying breakfast, Jeremy walked in wearing tracksuit bottoms and trainers. Chris exclaimed, 'Oh God! Now I feel like I'm on tour with Sporty Spice.' Jeremy was taking his health seriously and we were planning to make use of the tennis court. He really didn't like everyone's reaction of laughter and disbelief.

Jeremy is surprisingly very good at tennis, and what he lacks in fitness he makes up for with power. As a beginner, I was no match for him. He had no patience or ability to lower his game in order for us to have a knock-up, so a coach was employed to take him on. The Irish coach, to our amusement called Bjorn, was the son of a tennis coach who was around in the seventies.

Despite Jeremy's surprise sobriety, we had a good time at this wonderful house, albeit a bit sedate. James and Richard took on the girls and Chris at croquet on the front lawn, and we had a BBQ for our party night, inviting some of the rest of the crew up to our manor. The night ended in a human pyramid in the grand hallway. Jeremy, committed to his new regime, went to bed early.

The shows went down really well in the new format and actually benefitted from the rebrand. I think it was refreshing for the boys to have a change of tack and just make fun out of what had happened. As always slightly controversially.

James and Richard opened the shows on motorbikes and celebrated that now the bike-hating orangutan they used to work with had gone, they could enjoy filling the show with bike stunts, talk about them endlessly, and ride bikes. James went on to say, 'Unfortunately, we have some bad news.' Richard added, 'It turns out the orangutan isn't quite as gone as we'd hoped.' Jeremy then came out on a hovercraft to the sound of Abba's 'Dancing Queen', about which he protested, at first refusing to appear, but as Richard explained and encouraged, 'Come on, plenty of people have come out to "Dancing Queen".' And so the show went on.

Moving on to Sheffield, there had been much deliberation about where to stay, trying to accommodate the Maharaja's new clean and healthy life style, and not have too long a journey from the stadium. We took a risk on the weather conditions (some cloud and a few spots of rain can interfere with VIP travel) and arranged for a superior eight-seater helicopter to transport the core Bubble to and from another stately home, near Skipton. This was a risk because if the helicopter was grounded, the stadium in Sheffield was an hour and a half away by road, if traffic was kind, even in the comfort of a Range Rover. The house, Broughton Hall, was stunning and huge, equipped with tennis courts and a croquet lawn for our newly found recreation.

Our social life was then contained within our new manor and Chris went all out to surprise us with a unique dinner set-up in the spooky cellars of the house. The girls from Brand Events, Lou and Georgie, spent the day dressing the cellars' main room as a candlelit dining room. After cocktails in the drawing room, we were led down the steps to be met by our host, a ghost, AKA Chris Hughes in a sheet and wearing a mask in the style of Edvard Munch's *The Scream*.

We had an amazing dinner and the magician from Liverpool, Stephen Williams Jr., who had impressed us so much appeared, as if by magic, and wowed us all once again. He even made a goldfish appear in Lou's water glass and managed to make Jeremy Clarkson speechless. Now that's magic. From Sheffield the boys went back to Norway to conquer a new town, Stavanger, and then back down under to Sydney and Perth. They named their Australian tour, *The CR-ASHES*, and created some promo films to prove they had an understanding of Australian sport. Dressed in cricket whites, they mocked up their own interpretation of cricket, with Jeremy rubbing the ball on his crotch for far too long and Richard leaping for a catch that cut to him being trapped under a giant Aussie rules football. Those three in cricket whites was comedy enough.

They were now in talks with Amazon, and Jeremy was staying off the booze to have a clear head to be able to deal with all the complicated legal calls day and night. Along with Andy Wilman, the three of them decided to start a production company, for which, after much thought, they came up with the name of W. CHUMP and Sons Ltd. (W for Wilman, C for Clarkson, H for Hammond, U for und/ and, M for May and P for productions; they added the 'and Sons' for effect). They all had to grow up a little and face new responsibilities, company regulations, employment law and the like. However, the PR stunt for the launch of their new company still portrayed the child in them. They bought company cars, Reliant Robins that they had branded with their company name to drive about London Town in. They actually got a lot of attention because they caused traffic jams due to them breaking down regularly.

They had a temporary office in Charles Dunstone's TalkTalk HQ in Notting Hill. They were all quite excited about their future without the restraint of the PC BBC. The tour, however, was in jeopardy and was uncertain of its future. If Amazon were to take ownership of our three amigos, where would that leave Brand Events and the rest of the crew?

In the meantime, the Bubble set off again for a tour favourite, Johannesburg. Things weren't quite the same, not least because the Maharaja wasn't drinking, but Chris was feeling rather vulnerable. He and Hammond, along with Mindy Hammond, had a drunken, emotional, all-night chat about the future. It was a really strange atmosphere. We were in another luxurious setting of private villas set around our own pool; however, the Bubble was feeling a little deflated. It was becoming clear that this would be our last trip to South Africa, ironically, where it had all begun.

We had an incredible trip out to the Cradle of Humankind, courtesy of Jeremy's contact who owned the private reserve that was the location of one of our favourite tour restaurants, The Cradle. We had a private safari and an *Out of Africa* style breakfast, complete with elegant white tablecloths, in the middle of the bush. I am really quite emotional as I write this, as there was a sense that this was the end of the road and we were in a highly emotive setting. Our very special Bubble family was feeling it.

As a further distraction, we were treated to a private tour of one of the original sites where they found some of the oldest recorded human-like (hominid) remains suspected as being the missing link between ape and man. Our guide was one of the leading professors who was part of the team who had recently found what appeared to be a mass burial site of fossil skeletons. We were some of the first to know about the find, prior to an official announcement. A mind-blowing privilege which we all felt honoured to be part of. As so often happened when we met extraordinary people, they were equally if not more excited to meet Clarkson, Hammond and May.

I took the obligatory picture which had accidently occurred whilst the boys were intently listening to the professor and looking at bones that were right in front of their eyes, just breaking the surface of the ground. Unwittingly, they had taken on an evolution of man pose. Jeremy was standing tall facing the professor, while James was leant over and Richard had bent right forward in order to get a closer look at the remains. I'm not convinced that was a true depiction of man's evolution but it was a classic for the tour album.

The shows themselves, apart from having different films, were full of comments followed by 'We can't say that for legal reasons.' Clarkson, especially, was very facetious about his situation, even with the threat of legal action over the incident with Osh. All three were constantly denying anything they had ever done with *Top Gear* as a way to actually reference what they had done. For example, Richard would say he had never crashed a jet-powered car.

James had his race, car against athlete, but this time with the unfortunately named Werner Kok, Springbok rugby sevens star. The name Kok of course was perfect for some banter between the boys. Jeremy and Richard never failed to enjoy delivering their lines, such as 'Hammond, I like Kok,' with sufficient pause to let a small titter from the crowd evolve before he added, 'and I like the Nissan GTR but I don't like

James May.' Richard would agree and add, 'Yes I want the Kok to win,' followed by 'I want the Kok to come first.' The casting of this very tolerant and fast sportsman was perfect for our childish trio to share their infectious laughter over the poor man's name and the innuendos they could create. James had to get the Nissan started, deploy its launch control, then race to some cones that Mr Kok had to run around. James had no time or space to turn so had to reverse back to the start/finish line. The Kok won, prompting the ultimate line of 'James, you have always wanted to be beaten by a Kok, haven't you?'

Ken Block was brought in to fill the gap left by the Stig. He performed some high-speed, very noisy stunts in his Hoonigan Mustang, including racing the three boys in one of his 'Gymkhana' challenges. The boys had to cheat to win. Ken pushed his talent to the limit, narrowly missing the boys who were in their much-smaller Mazda MX-5s. There was one too many egos in this performance.

Egos and tensions were at an all-time high in Johannesburg. In between shows, the boys were taking calls about their deal with Amazon. Once again, they were pushing themselves to the limit trying to work out their future, having complex discussions with Andy Wilman and lawyers in between international travel and performing to audiences of thousands.

When it came to the finale of a game of car football, it was more like a battle. The players, including all three boys and the stunt driving team, let rip. Perhaps releasing tension but I think there were possibly a few hard feelings between the stunt drivers and the presenters. The game became aggressively competitive. Bits of car were flying off and there were definitely some red card moments. I had never seen the game played so hard and fast before. Great entertainment but not so good for the cars that had to get through two more cities. Rowly had been pleading into their earpieces to calm down.

The penultimate show was scheduled for the amazing National Stadium in Warsaw again. It was so ironic that the live shows had reached true perfection commanding huge audiences in iconic venues.

The show content had gone from Swampy, the broom-handle-controlled monster, to record-breaking stunts; cars driving fast around a girl juggling flaming torches to flaming Porsches leaving trails of flames with a troop of flame throwing and swallowing girls; Fiestas changing colour through a plastic tunnel to BMW M3s covered in ever-changing LED lights performing a futuristic choreographed visual feast; the Car Porn had gone from borrowing cars from people we knew to a line-up any Kuwaiti would envy; James had gone from racing across the arena in a shopping trolley to racing a supercar against Olympic champions; Jeremy went from dodgy referee to car football legend (he came up with the brilliant idea of recreating Maradona's 'Hand of God' goal to win the match, by reaching his hand out of the car window). Richard was still small but incredibly brave, continuing to risk life and limb in the salad shaker of doom with not three motorbikes whizzing right past his nose and feet but seven.

Seriously though, the show was incredible. I had sat in all the audiences across the world and laughed every time, feeling exceptionally proud of the three middle-aged motoring clowns I could call my friends. Chris Hughes, the funniest and most annoying man I know, had brilliantly and uniquely managed an incredibly eclectic crew of people through over twelve years of worldwide tours and laughed till the bitter end.

To Quote Wham!
(the greatest pop band in the world in my fourteen-year-old brain), 'THE FINAL'

We were all set for perhaps the biggest show of all, in our home town, London, at the now world-renowned O2. Range Rovers were booked, exclusive hire of a boat arranged, exclusive hire of Gaucho nightclub booked, Rockaoke booked, restaurants booked, extra restaurants on hold, hotel rooms booked, green room equipped to the highest standard, yet including a big enough stapler to staple scripts together. It had taken me twelve years to find this. Simon Aldridge had it all along! I had taken a lot of grief from the three amigos about my shit stapling.

The mood was upbeat and sad at the same time. Jeremy, James and Richard had secured their deal with Amazon and were due to start filming the day after their final show. Not great timing. Jeremy had not had a drink for over two months and had promised himself one after the final curtain.

After Range Rover collections from around West London, the Bubble boarded our very own river cruiser to head east, to the O2. The journey became a real highlight as it's such a brilliant way to view some of the iconic landmarks of London. The boys actually enjoyed the relaxed vibe of river cruising. Of course, they had the usual luxury catering on board, too.

As we landed near the O2, we were greeted in true rock star style by the Range Rovers that had sped through London to meet us and escort us to the 'stage door'. It all felt very special, especially when the giant screens on the outside of the huge 'tent' came into view, with our heroes and their false photo shoot smiles grinning down on us. Actually, the boys were really blown away to see their names and faces in lights adorning the now iconic rock and roll venue. They all had their photo taken standing in front of themselves for their own personal albums.

The whole operation was remarkably slick. The scripts and acts had been pretty much the same for the whole year apart from changes such as the different athletes appearing in James's 'athlete against car' race. James was so close to introducing guests like Werner Kok (huge rugby player) as Louise Hazel (petite athlete). I guess better that way round than the other. All of them had been known to jump ahead in the script and start to introduce the Clarkson, Hammond and May Stunt Driving Team when in fact the salad shaker of doom was due on with RH and the amazing French motorbike stunt men. Or worse still calling the stunt drivers the *Top Gear* Stunt Driving Team. That could have cost a lot in legal fees.

The shows went really well and the audience were enthusiastic and reactive, which was a welcome surprise and change from the old days of staid suits at Earls Court. The space in the O2, like all the other larger venues that the tour had graduated to, allowed for a much more spectacular show, stunning lighting, more pyros and ear-bending sound.

The crew party was a very emotional one as you might expect. Tears were shed all around. Even the big man found it overwhelming. He had to leave the party at one point, overwhelmed by a cocktail of emotions: guilt, pride and sadness, to name a few.

He gathered himself to deliver a thank you speech and take part in the final official band-jacking.

Show four of the five-show schedule came and went and there was little downtime, as the presenters had so many guests popping backstage to congratulate the trio. It was so strange that throughout the whole tour, Jeremy, James and Richard took each show in their stride, apart from the slight wobble for the biggest audience ever in Poland. They never realised how amazing and entertaining the show was, despite the unending enthusiasm, excitement and praise I threw at them (with a little bit of sarcasm just to keep them grounded). As they all said though, they had never seen the show so how would they know? In a bizarre way, they were so busy speeding through their huge success that they never realised just how good they were or took time to rest on their laurels, for even a short while.

Apart from the odd diva moment, they were quite humble at heart (Clarkson's humbleness was hidden a bit deeper). Watching them, bewildered at the huge screens displaying their faces on the O2, and overexcited when they saw the posters of superstars adorning the corridors backstage, was hugely endearing and quite a juxtaposition.

The boys had planned to give Chris, their favourite Piggy-Eyed Businessman, a big surprise and special treat to mark the end of his remarkable journey as tour manager to the most famous trio. Bas, JCP, Rowly, Gem and I, with the help of Mindy Hammond, who fitted into our bubble so well (Sarah, James's partner, is far too sophisticated to mix with us reprobates), arranged for our loyal and very tolerant Rockaoke band to be wheeled out on a makeshift stage for Chris to perform his very own version of what had become our tour party anthem, 'Mustang Sally'.

As the last show came to an end, Jeremy, James and Richard parked up their car football cars at the side of the arena and stepped out to thank the audience and explain to them that this was the end of years of touring with an incredible crew.

They invited the whole crew out onstage and called Chris up front with them to announce their surprise. The stage was then wheeled out, complete with drum kit for Jeremy, keyboard for James and bass guitar for Richard. For once, the funny little fat man was lost for words, that is, until the music started and off he went with Gem, Mindy and myself as backing singers, and we all performed live at the O2!

Whilst running around checking all was in place for Chris's surprise and making sure boat and Range Rovers were in position for our departure for the last supper, I had a phone call from the restaurant that had been specially selected for the occasion. It ticked all the boxes: it was a favourite of Jeremy's and mine; it served great home cooking of meat and veg that all three boys liked; it was just the right size for us to have exclusive use of; and it was easy to get to. Unfortunately, the phone call was to tell me there was a power cut affecting the whole of Kensington, and therefore they could currently only provide cold food, of which they could prepare a huge selection of starters upon our arrival. They hoped to have the power back on by then and could resume normal service.

I, along with the rest of the Bubble, was now heading into the audience to watch the very last car football match, so we didn't have much option at such short notice. The lovely restaurant manager, Tad, had agreed that we could have the option of ordering in a takeaway so we could enjoy the privacy of the restaurant and still have a good supper to satisfy the hungriest of presenters. Chris was happy and that was the plan.

After our emotional and ridiculous performance of 'Mustang Sally', which you can actually view on YouTube (I didn't see that coming), the entire Bubble – Bas (BasIcanfindanycar.com), Rowly (our Moon-Faced Producer), JCP (AKA Johnny Boden), Gemma, The Boy, me (AKA Horse), Minderella (Mindy Hammond) and of course

Clarkson, Hammond and May – gathered for our final closing ceremony. It was quite sensible. Chris delivered yet another speech, a sincere but as ever amusing one, and Gemma, Poppy (a friend of mine who was green room assistant) and I walked out with presents on cushions to deliver the final special gifts to our very special celebrity friends.

They were all given a framed montage of photos from around the world, of the shows and some of the classic moments on our incredible Chris Hughes Cashless Holidays. Each was also given a special piece of personal memorabilia, such us the cricket bails and some sand from Beach Cricket, framed. Ashamedly and disappointingly, I can't remember the rest. I think emotion plus alcohol got the better of me.

Jeremy had the last word, a genuinely heartfelt thanks, to all, even expressing how lucky he felt to have ended up with me after our crazy adventures around the world. He also celebrated his achievements by enjoying his first drink after months of sobriety. Another emotional moment before we set off for our boat ride towards Kensington.

Chris had yet another gift for the boys as we sailed down the Thames. In his wonderfully crazy mind he had come up with the idea of officially 'letting the boys go'. As had been one of our in-jokes on tour, if someone was failing or had done something wrong, he would say 'I'm going to have to let you go,' which then got abbreviated to just signing the message, by looking up, raising a clenched hand that then opened as if releasing a balloon into the sky above. To mark the end of this incredible journey together, Gem, Chris and I had produced helium balloons with the faces of Clarkson, Hammond and May stuck on them.

As we approached Tower Bridge, he summoned us all outside to the front of the boat to present each presenter with their own balloon to let themselves go. And off they went, drifting above the river, past Tower Bridge and beyond. We all had a laugh about where they might land and who might find a deflated, washed-up Clarkson, Hammond or May.

On to the last supper. In all the excitement and emotion I hadn't had time to tell the boys what had happened at the restaurant until we were walking in the door. All three of them had been there before, and they had even used it for filming at some point. They all greeted Tad, the manager, with a comfortable familiarity and headed to the beautifully laid out, large round table that had been especially set up for us, filling one end of the restaurant. The terribly efficient staff started bringing out a selection of starters and fresh bread. Half of the Bubble were already sat at the table. JC had just come in from a smoke, and I had just returned from the loo, rushing back to enjoy the last few hours with my special family. Jeremy stopped me in my tracks to query what was going on with the food. I explained that if the restaurant were unable to cook for us then we could order in a takeaway. Before I was able to finish and give him the options, he bellowed at me, 'No, darling, this is not good enough!' I shook in my own shoes. Everyone else fell silent. He ranted on whilst walking out of the restaurant.

He was at it again. I was close to tears in shock at his outburst and upset for so many reasons. The manager jumped in to apologise and was offering up suggestions. Richard and Mindy were comforting me and Chris was trying to placate the Maharaja. The monster was back. Becks and Em were on it, trying to find an available and suitable table close by.

Off we went to our new venue. I apologised to Tad, I was so embarrassed. I avoided JC. My Bubble had burst. Chris consoled me and expressed his concern with some sarcasm, that JC definitely had a problem with cold food and 'hanger', which made me laugh. We had as you can imagine a slightly subdued supper, not only due to the outburst we had all just experienced, but because it really was time for the Bubble to deflate and take on another form in various different directions.

The ending for me was our crazy performance at the O2. The Bubble was very much together there, albeit out of tune and out of time. My phone had died so my last photo was of a heap of scrap metal, pieces of a car football car, piled up at the back of an empty arena. My incredible journey had ended.

Clarkson, Hammond and May walked off into an Amazon sunrise to work happily ever after. Except they didn't – James fell over on the way home from the last supper and broke his arm, missing the start of filming, and the train that Clarkson and Hammond were travelling on to start filming was delayed by striking Frenchmen. Jeremy was convinced this was all a bad omen and that they were doomed. I think not.

I give heartfelt thanks to Jeremy, Andy Wilman, James and Richard for letting me share their amazing journey. I had the best time.

With also huge thanks to Chris, Gem, Bas, JCP and Rowly for letting me join their Brand Events brilliance.

What a ride. Tears in my eyes as I bid a very fond farewell to my favourite three clever, funny, and very stupid motoring journalists.

Thank you.

After the Bubble Burst

Jeremy Clarkson – continues his motoring madness with *The Grand Tour* on Amazon and contributes to his online petrol head community forum, *DriveTribe*. He has also taken a sharp left turn in to the world of farming and is filming a new series about life on his farm.

James May – continues alongside the big man with *The Grand Tour* on Amazon and is also a founder and contributor to *DriveTribe*. James 'Fanny' May 'Cradock' has also gone right 'off-piste' and has written a cookery book, *Oh Cook!*, which accompanies a new series on Amazon. He also continues to produce his own diverse series such as *Our Man in Japan*.

Richard Hammond – also continues with Amazon's *The Grand Tour* alongside the other two and has set up his own production company, Chimp Productions which has just produced *The Great Escapists* for Amazon. He created his own series, *Richard Hammond's Big!* I personally loved it and found it fascinating (the series that is). Richard is also a co-founder of *DriveTribe* and regularly contributes amusing motoring themed films, pictures, chat, etc.

Andy Wilman – is still being Andy Wilman making the 'three am-egos' look good on Amazon's *The Grand Tour*.

Chris Hughes – AKA The Piggy-Eyed Businessman – still runs Brand Events, which survived COVID-19, with Chris's ever creative self at the helm. He and his team put on drive-in events such as Picnic in the Park with Tom

Kerridge, hosting great acts such as Kaiser Chiefs, Top Loader, Rick Astley, and Jack Savoretti, etc. He continues to plan for Chris Evans' epic *CarFest*, making it Covid-proof for the future, amongst many other motoring and lifestyle events. He is no longer piggy in many senses of the word and has lost loads of weight. During the pandemic, to our amusement, he actually gave food away, providing thousands of meals for NHS workers with the help of new mate Tom Kerridge.

Gemma Courtenay (now Huddleston) – AKA The Boy – after continuing to play a pivotal role in many other huge productions, including *Fast and Furious Live* and Chris Evans's *CarFest*, she has moved on from Brand Events (though remains a huge supporter of their events – as do I). 2020 has seen her supporting the inspirational legend that was the late Captain Sir Tom Moore who, following his record-breaking charity walk, went on to set up The Captain Tom Foundation – its mission to inspire hope where it is needed most.

Bas Bungish – AKA BasIcanfindanycar.com – continues to work hard at Brand Events and leads the production of many motoring events including *CarFest* and *The London Classic Car Show*. He's given up sex toys for good and has been perfectly happy during the pandemic as he is totally over international travel.

Rowland French – AKA Rowly, AKA our Moon-Faced Producer – apart from landing the deal with Universal Studios to put on a motoring theatre version of the incredibly successful *Fast and Furious* films, he has created his greatest production to date and now has his very own moon-faced baby with another on the way. Produced with a lot of help from his wife Naomi – AKA The Girl with Petrol Pumps for Arms – who is still flame throwing when the government allows her and she's not holding the baby. He continues to use his creative genius in the motoring world, after a stint at Sky One he is now Creative Director of Roborace, the world's first fully autonomous racing series.

James Cooke-Priest – AKA JCP, AKA Johnny Boden – was also part of the Universal Studios deal and worked alongside Rowly on the *Fast and Furious Live* shows. He has since had to leave the country shouting 'Get in the fucking van.' I jest. He is however spending time in Saudi Arabia heading up an events company, Extreme Events.

Me – AKA Horse – once I got over the grief of no more touring with my dysfunctional family, I made a huge U-turn, turning to my other passion and a gentler type of horsepower. I have trained as an Equine Facilitated Coach, helping children and adults get over trauma, fears, and mental health issues to reach their full potential. Oh, and I wrote this book.

Thank Yous...

Mum and Dad for putting up with all my madness and ups and downs.

My brothers Jes and Dan, and their good wives Claire (part of the original *Top Gear* crew) and Katherine, for also putting up with my madness and ups and downs.

Alfie, my boy, for being very happy to have loads of extra screen time while I wrote this and for making me laugh every day.

Ted, Alfie's dad, for putting up with my madness and for supporting Alfie and I through all my ups and downs.

My dear, dear friends for always being there through thick and thin, and keeping the laughter going – Clara and Rob, Sara and Neil, SJ (who was actually a 'green room horse' once), Rob and Katherine, and Nat and Geraldine.

Sue (Short) – Medicine Woman – and Rob (Furry) – IT Man – for always being there in tears or laughter.

Caroline for wise words and shopping, and Paul for more IT support.

Corrina for her support with Alfie and incredible on-demand childcare services. With thanks too to her whole family, Poppie (another 'foal' backstage on tour), Eden, Austin, and Bob who all embraced Alfie when I was away touring.

My amazing coaches from Learning to Listen who re-built me and inspired me to be the person I am today – thank you

Joanne, Jo, Sarah and Becks along with those magical horses you too are all magical.

Miss Mandy Keegan for constant financial and emotional support, and fellow Key Events legends, Steve, and Kay.

Mr Leonard Stall – publisher extraordinaire and great advisor. Thanks for a much, much more sophisticated tour.

Gavin Esler, the nicest man in news, with whom I enjoyed a tour of a far more sophisticated kind. Thanks for your kindness, support and for encouraging me to do this. I owe you and Anna at least one G&T!

Gail, Richard, Max, and Katie (my original foal and protégé green room assistant) – my surrogate family. Thank you so much for all your love, food and wine, and your forever open door.

Jane for my hair, yoga and listening.

The Golden Triangle – Joanne, Jake, Teah, Mel, Matt, and Josh – for a magical champagne-fuelled lockdown.

Adam Waddell for giving me my first *Top Gear* job.

My legal team – Andrew Reid – thank you for your time, wisdom, and generosity (yes, I did use the word generosity in a sentence about lawyers!). And James Farha and Paul Abounader from Farha & Associates for all your generous support and time.

Everyone at AdLib, especially John Blake who continued to believe in me and Rob Nichols who understood whatever the hell I was going on about! And, of course, Big Jon (I shall call him that because he's in charge) for backing me.

Finally, to all the stars of this book and the entire tour, with huge, huge thanks and love to you all.